ENGAGING HIGHER EDUCATION

ENGAGING HIGHER EDUCATION

Purpose, Platforms, and Programs for Community Engagement

Marshall Welch

Foreword by John Saltmarsh

In association with

Campus Compact

1996-2016   20TH ANNIVERSARY

Sty/us

PUBLISHING, LLC.

STERLING, VIRGINIA

Published by Stylus Publishing, LLC.
22883 Quicksilver Drive
Sterling, Virginia 20166-2102

Library of Congress Cataloging-in-Publication Data
Names: Welch, Marshall, author.
Title: Engaging higher education : purpose, platforms and programs
for community engagement / Marshall Welch.
Description: Sterling, Virginia : Stylus Publishing, LLC, 2016. |
Includes bibliographical references and index.
Identifiers: LCCN 2015050223 (print) | LCCN 2016012605
(ebook) |
    ISBN 9781620363843 (pbk. : alk. paper) |
    ISBN 9781620363836 (cloth : alk. paper) |
    ISBN 9781620363850 (library networkable e-edition) |
    ISBN 9781620363867 (consumer e-edition) |
Subjects: LCSH: Community and college–United States. |
Service learning–United States. | Education, Higher–Aims and
objectives–United States.
Classification: LCC LC238 .W45 2016 (print) | LCC LC238
(ebook) | DDC 378.1/03–dc23
LC record available at http://lccn.loc.gov/2015050223

13-digit ISBN: 978-1-62036-383-6 (cloth)
13-digit ISBN: 978-1-62036-384-3 (paperback)
13-digit ISBN: 978-1-62036-385-0 (library networkable e-edition)
13-digit ISBN: 978-1-62036-386-7 (consumer e-edition)

Printed in the United States of America

All first editions printed on acid-free paper
that meets the American National Standards Institute
Z39-48 Standard.

Bulk Purchases

Quantity discounts are available for use in workshops and for
staff development.
Call 1-800-232-0223

First Edition, 2016

10   9   8   7   6   5   4   3   2   1

For Glen Dyke and Irene Fisher:
Both of you set me on this path.

CONTENTS

FOREWORD
The Continuing Evolution of Community Engagement Centers

When Edward Zlotkowski (1998) wrote *Successful Service Learning Programs*, it proved to be an invaluable resource for a new cadre of professionals who were implementing community engagement on campuses. It was also required reading for the campus administrators who saw community engagement as a way to change curricular and pedagogical practice to improve teaching and learning and more effectively operationalize the civic mission of the campus. Zlotkowski did not focus his book on centers per se, but the programs he referenced were in fact the emergent infrastructure designed to coordinate campus-wide efforts. Zlotkowski captured the evolution of the infrastructure that was emerging, then focused primarily on service-learning, and now more broadly on community engagement. Today, community engagement centers are widespread. Of the 361 campuses that have the Carnegie Classification for Community Engagement as of 2015, a center of some kind that serves as a coordinating infrastructure is ubiquitous. This book is the new version of Zlotkowski's work and is equally invaluable. Like its predecessor, *Engaging Higher Education* captures the evolving nature of the infrastructure supporting campus engagement.

Research that we did in 2013 on community engagement centers (Welch & Saltmarsh) revealed complex organizational structures that have deeply sophisticated programming and serve multiple constituencies. The survey data told us much about the architecture, operations, and programming of such centers, but they could not tell us what we needed to know about the importance of these centers and the work they do, how they function, and what programs look like in practice. *Engaging Higher Education* brings the data to life. This book has the kind of detailed richness that can only come through deeply grounded experience; this is the vast and deep practical knowledge that Welch brings to our understanding of the work of community engagement centers. As was true with Zlotkowski's book, this is an essential guide for community engagement professionals and for democratically engaged administrators who are tackling the challenges of educating for democracy and transforming their campuses.

As you, the reader—whether you are a community engagement professional or an engaged administrator—encounter the wisdom of this book, I would like you to consider a few aspects of community engagement centers that may need to be addressed as this work continues to evolve and deepen. Let me use the structure of the book to make a few observations.

Purpose

In recent years, in some ways marked by the great economic collapse of the late 2000s but also as part of a larger and more extensive trend, community engagement work, particularly for public higher education, has become increasingly attentive to economic development. The role of colleges and universities in economic development is admittedly important, but at the same time there is a growing emphasis on economic development and its related concept, social entrepreneurship, as being synonymous with the whole of campuses' engagement activity. Community engagement as described in this book is primarily focused on impacting the core academic and developmental aspects of students' educational experience and on changing the fundamental educational operations of the campus. Economic development efforts aimed at procurement, employment, and investments do not impact the student experience or transform the core academic operations of the campus but are instead focused on the core business operations. This, of course, is not an either/or dichotomy—it should be a both/and approach. The last decades of the twentieth century witnessed the rise of the neoliberal, market-driven, highly privatized university and the demand for universities to more effectively address critical social issues, many of which were impervious to market solutions.

My concern is that the push toward economic development as community engagement is little more than a reflection of colleges and universities adopted prevailing neoliberal principles. As Burawoy (2005) wrote, "all too often, market and state have collaborated against humanity in what has commonly come to be known as neoliberalism" (p. 7). "The logics of neoliberalism" include "relentless attachment to privatization and the destruction of an ethical and relational public" (Simpson, 2014, p. 192), undermining the public commitments that are at the core of the "why" of the centers in this book. As centers continue to evolve, perhaps we need more awareness of the degree to which their role is to reassert the public, democratic purposes of higher education and counter neoliberalism's effects on the university. As Jones and Shefner (2014) have observed, "for critics of the neoliberal model . . . universities became places of civic engagement," with the result that "one answer to the abuses of neoliberalism became the engaged university . . ."

(p. 11). If this is a role for centers, what will it mean for how they operate in the next stage of their growth and evolution?

Platforms

As this book makes clear, if community engagement—or any innovation—is going to impact the core academic work of the campus, it needs to be owned by the faculty. The discussion here on the role of centers in leading change for creating faculty incentives and a culture of faculty rewards that values community engagement across the faculty roles is critically important.

An essential role for centers moving forward will be to facilitate the ability of non-tenure-track (NTT) faculty to "own" community engagement. Simultaneous with a rise in community engagement as core academic work and concomitant with the rise of neoliberalism, higher education has experienced an increase in the number of NTT faculty. The majority of all college faculty now work on part-time or full-time temporary contracts, and many lack sufficient access to the institutional support necessary for quality education. While faculty contingency is increasing, and increasing at higher rates for part-time versus full-time NTT faculty, there has been little attention to the implications of increased contingency for service-learning and community engagement. How will community engagement continue to expand and deepen with contingent faculty? What will be the role of centers in facilitating contingent faculty engagement?

Just as centers are taking the lead in advancing faculty incentives in the promotion and tenure process, there will need to be advocacy and leadership for developing incentives in NTT faculty contracts to support community engagement. In contracts for NTT faculty, there should be specifically articulated criteria that create incentives for faculty to undertake community engagement as part of teaching and learning. There should be explicit criteria rewarding (a) the inclusion of high-impact education practices like service-learning, (b) the inclusion of civic learning outcomes met through integration of community engagement experiences into courses, and (c) the ability to build successful long-term relationships with community partners to enhance the curriculum and student learning. There also needs to be faculty professional development for NTT faculty in community engagement—which will need to be delivered differently than traditional faculty development—in order to build the capacity of faculty to implement high-quality community engagement in their courses.

Programs

What kind of coordinating infrastructure is needed for a new era of community engagement? As centers continue to evolve, what will be the next, emergent development of campus infrastructure supporting community engagement? There may be some evidence of campuses where the coordinating infrastructure is moving from an emphasis on implementation of programs to a distributed model where the infrastructure takes on a distinct facilitative and capacity-building role.

Where this distributive model seems to be emerging is on campuses that have made significant advancements in institutionalizing and sustaining community engagement and where there has been a strong coordinating infrastructure tied to academic affairs (e.g., Michigan State University, Portland State University, and the University of North Carolina at Greensboro). Characteristics of community engagement on these campuses are that it has become such an integral part of the culture of the campus that it is implemented broadly and deeply; is central to the core academic mission of the campus; and is one of the defining features of teaching, learning, research, and scholarship across departments and research centers. Additionally, as community engagement has been broadly and deeply institutionalized, the function of the coordinating infrastructure shifted from an emphasis on implementation (running programs) to an emphasis on facilitation and collaborative coordination (providing support to individuals and units across the campus in advancing community engagement in the context of the units).

Organizationally, this more distributed, emergent infrastructure approximates the establishment of an organizational unit that aligns with "collective impact theory" (Kania & Kramer, 2011). Collective impact theory suggests that the way to achieve the most impact is to have multiple stakeholders all working on a single problem simultaneously. For example, if the community issue is childhood obesity, then the greatest impact comes about when schools, universities, community-based non-profits, health care providers, and municipalities all work on the issue collaboratively. To make sure that everyone stays focused on the issue, a so-called backbone organization is created to drive the process. In the end, the result is defined as a *collective impact*.

Translating collective impact theory to community engagement in institutions of higher education, this new phase of infrastructure development suggests that the coordinating infrastructure assumes the role of a backbone support unit. This assumes that the supporting infrastructure can plan, manage, and support community engagement initiatives through ongoing facilitation, technology and communications support, data collection and reporting, and handling the myriad logistical and administrative details needed for the community engagement to function smoothly and have the greatest impact. The infrastructure is less involved with implementing any particular set of activities, but it is dedicated to supporting and driving the engagement of many units across the campus so that the campus as a whole is engaged and making a difference in the communities with which it works. As centers continue to develop, what will it mean to function as a backbone organization, focused not on running programs, but instead on facilitating engagement across the campus?"

Since centers for community engagement emerged on campuses in the late 1980s, they have been located in the nexus of larger tensions and challenges faced by higher education, as they are today. This book allows us to see their purpose and functions more clearly as we face new challenges and they continue to evolve. We need this book now to better navigate the institutional complexity of community engagement in order to create the campuses we want for a healthy and vibrant democracy.

John Saltmarsh
Professor of Higher Education
Director of the New England Resource
Center for Higher Education (NERCHE)
University of Massachusetts Boston

References

Burawoy, M. (2005). For public sociology. *American sociological review, 70*(1), 4–28.

Jones, E. J., & Shefner, J. (2014). Introduction: globalization and the university—a path to social justice. In J. Shefner, H. F. Dahms, R. E. Jones, & A. Jalata, (Eds.) *Social justice and the university: Globalization, human rights and the future of democracy* (pp. 11–17). Basingstoke, United Kingdom: Palgrave Macmillan.

Kania, J., & Kramer, M. (2011). Collective impact. *Stanford Social Innovation Review, 9*(1), 36–41.

Simpson, J. S. (2014). *Longing for justice: Higher education and democracy's agenda.* Toronto, Ontario: University of Toronto Press.

Welch, M., & Saltmarsh, J. (2013, December 17) Current practice and infrastructures for campus centers of community engagement. *Journal of Higher Education Outreach and Engagement.* Retrieved from http://openjournals.libs.uga.edu/index.php/jheoe/article/view/1090

Zlotkowski, E. (Ed.). (1998). *Successful service learning programs: New models of excellence in higher education.* Bolton, MA: Anker Publishing.

ACKNOWLEDGMENTS

Aproject such as this cannot be accomplished without the assistance and support of others. I would like to take this opportunity to acknowledge the many colleagues who assisted me throughout the preparation of this book. First and foremost is my appreciation to Provost Beth Dobkin and Vice Provost Richard Carp at Saint Mary's College of California, who provided the time and resources that allowed me to engage in this important work for this project and on our campus. Second, I wish to thank my friend and colleague John Saltmarsh from the New England Resource Center for Higher Education at the University of Massachusetts Boston for his collaboration, advice, and overall leadership in the field. Most important, many thanks to my wife, Julie, for listening to me think aloud, reading drafts, and letting me embark on this adventure. This book would not have been possible without the four of you.

I also wish to thank colleagues who gave their time to meet with me to respond to my many questions and provide a wealth of information. Many thanks to Peter Ingle, my former doctoral student, now dean of the School of Education at Westminster College, Salt Lake City. Many thanks as well to my friend and colleague Sarah Munro of the University Neighborhood Partnership with the University of Utah.

I appreciate the input and participation of Andrew Seligsohn of Campus Compact, Laurie Warroll of New York Campus Compact, and Elaine Ikeda of California Campus Compact on this and related projects. Megan Voorhees of Minnesota Campus Compact assisted me in arranging visits and conversations at Augsburg College and Macalester College. I wish to thank Elaine Eschenbacher, Steve Peacock, Harry Boyte, and Dennis Donovan at Augsburg College and Karin Trail-Johnson at Macalester College for our great conversations. Many thanks to my kindred spirit, Kent Koth of Seattle University, for his work and caregiving and to my coconspirator, Thomas Schnaubelt from the Haas Center for Public Engagement at Stanford University.

I also wish to acknowledge the collective wisdom provided by Molly Mead and Sarah Barr from Amherst College and John Reiff of the University of Massachusetts Amherst. Thanks to Erin Cannan and Paul Marienthal of Bard College for sharing.

President Richard Guarasci, Patrician Tooker, Lori Weintrob, Arlette Cepeda, Ellen Navarro, and Samantha Seigel at Wagner College enlightened and inspired me.

Ira Harkavy and Joann Weeks and many staff members of the Netter Center at the University of Pennsylvania were kind enough to give up their valuable time to meet with me. Likewise, Lynette Overton, Steven W. Peuquet, Sarah LaFave, and Susan Serra at the University of Delaware were very helpful, sharing their amazing facilities, programs, and vision with me.

Many others also contributed their expertise and assistance via phone, e-mail, and correspondence. I appreciate the assistance enthusiastically given by Lina Dostilio of Duquesne University; Andrew Furco at the University of Minnesota; Barbara Holland, Barbara Jacoby, and Emily Janke of University of North Carolina at Greensboro; Seth Pollack at California State University at Monterrey Bay; and Gail Robinson from the American Association of Community Colleges.

Finally, I wish to express my deep appreciation to the staff and student leaders of the Catholic Institute for Lasallian Social Action and the faculty, administration, and community partners of Saint Mary's College of California for their inspiration, assistance, and important work—all of whom have made a significant contribution to this project and my vocation.

INTRODUCTION

The first word in the title of this book is both a verb and an adjective. As a verb, *to engage* means to devote full attention, resources, and effort to someone or something to accomplish something. As an adjective, *engaging* can describe or characterize a place or person(s) actively involved or immersed in a task, as well as the ability to captivate others. This book invites postsecondary institutions and those who work with them to be fully involved and immersed in promoting the public purpose of higher education. *Engaging higher education* means "connecting the rich resources of the university to our most pressing social, civic, and ethical problems, to our children, to our schools, to our teachers, and to our cities" (Boyer, 1996, p. 95). To do this requires engaging students, faculty members, and community organizations to find ways to form partnerships that create new knowledge and empower our communities.

This book emerged from previous research conducted with my friend and colleague John Saltmarsh, from the New England Resource Center on Higher Education (NERCHE) at the University of Massachusetts Boston. We were pleased and taken aback by the interest in and response to a national study we conducted on the infrastructure of campus centers for engagement that had received the Carnegie Classification for Community Engagement. Almost immediately, center directors began contacting us to say they were using the research as leverage to advance their work on their campuses. Those discussions revealed that these directors needed additional information they could share with upper-level and midlevel administrators as they endeavored to institutionalize community engagement. This book is designed for that very purpose.

This book is organized around the purpose (the why), the platforms (the how), and the programs (the what) that drive and frame community engagement in higher education. The information presented is intended to help institutional leaders understand how to establish and maintain community engagement programs on their campuses. Likewise, these pages are designed to provide valuable information on trends of current practice based on the criteria for the Carnegie Classification for Community Engagement to help directors of campus centers for engagement incorporate these practices into their existing programs. Finally, this book is for graduate students aspiring to become the future professoriate as engaged scholars.

The triadic framework of purpose, platforms, and programs (Figure I.1) was adapted from my previous work with Saltmarsh. The information presented here is intended to help administrators of institutions and campus centers for community engagement learn more about infrastructure and current practice to sustain and expand their work. A combination of methods was used to gather this information. These include reporting results from the study mentioned previously as well as from national classification by the Carnegie Foundation for the Advancement of Teaching and surveys by Campus Compact, a review of the literature, telephone interviews with scholars and administrations, and site visits to centers. This book also draws on my own 15-year experience as a director of two campus centers for community engagement: one at a large, urban, public research institution and the other at a small, faith-based, liberal arts college.

Figure I.1 Purpose, platforms, and programs of community engagement in higher education.

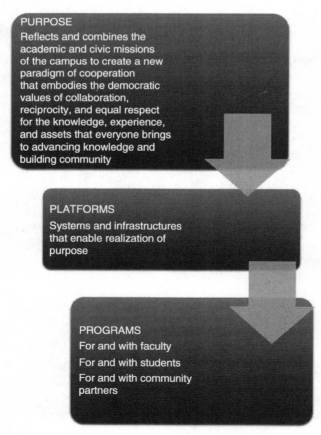

PURPOSE
Reflects and combines the academic and civic missions of the campus to create a new paradigm of cooperation that embodies the democratic values of collaboration, reciprocity, and equal respect for the knowledge, experience, and assets that everyone brings to advancing knowledge and building community

PLATFORMS
Systems and infrastructures that enable realization of purpose

PROGRAMS
For and with faculty
For and with students
For and with community partners

The three organizational frames (parts) of this book have been borrowed from computer science parlance and adapted to explore the pathways higher education has taken to meet its broad academic mission while it serves the community. *Purpose* reflects a macro perspective based on the tradition, mission, and culture of American higher education. *Platforms* represent a midstrata bridge from the macro perspective to the operational, micro level of *programs*.

Purpose

Webster's Dictionary defines *purpose* as "the reason why something is done or used, the aim or intention of something" (www.merriam-webster.com/dictionary/purpose). In this context the immediate purpose of this book is to empower administrators and educators with information that can be used to develop, implement, and assess community engagement programs in higher education. An underlying purpose of this book is to help readers understand the academic and civic purpose or mission of higher education that manifests itself through community engagement. By way of introduction, the purpose of community engagement in higher education reflects and combines the academic and civic missions of the campus to create a new paradigm of cooperation that embodies the democratic values of collaboration, reciprocity, and equal respect for the knowledge, experience, and assets that students, staff, faculty members, and community partners bring to advancing knowledge and building community (Welch & Saltmarsh, 2013a, 2013b). This purpose incorporates evidence from the cognitive sciences about how people learn, amplifying reflection, active and collaborative learning, and knowledge shaped by contexts; justifies infrastructure on campus that provides enabling connections between the campus and communities—what Walshok (1999) refers to as an "enabling mechanism" (p. 38); and builds legitimacy for community engagement as core academic work linked to teaching, learning, and research. It also requires accountability for outcomes and evidence of impact on students, communities, and institutions.

Chapter 1 explores the pathways of purpose by chronologically looking at how the mission of higher education has been shaped and influenced by the events, movements, and individuals that have brought us to now. Chapter 2 answers the question, what is engagement? and provides an introductory glimpse of various engagement formats and methods used by colleges and universities. These are examined in more detail in later chapters focused on programs for students, faculty members, and community partners.

Platforms

In computer science a *platform* is a computer's operating system; this system determines what programs the computer can run (techterms.com/definition/platform). This is a useful analogy for community engagement in higher education. Chapter 3 describes the institutionalization of community engagement by examining current and evolving infrastructure at the institutional level. Following the computer analogy, we will see how the infrastructure of the institution and campus community engagement center essentially serves as a platform from which programs for students, faculty members, and community partners can be operated. Embedded in the definition of a *platform* is the notion of a system, which is an equally useful concept, as we will incorporate systems theory into our understanding and application of community engagement. The implementation process is presented in chapter 4 using cases from exemplary colleges and universities.

Systems theory has long influenced many disciplines, including biology, business, education, and sociology. A *system* is defined as a cluster of interrelated activities, resources, and individuals interacting within an organization (Arbnor & Bjerke, 2009). Systems theory provides a way to address, use, and understand the whole while taking into account the interrelationship between the parts (Senge, 1990). Many models—each with their own strengths and weaknesses—exist. We have adapted a classic and user-friendly framework of five organizational domains in schools (Maher & Bennett, 1984) to examine systems within platforms.

Maher and Bennett's (1984) approach to systems in educational settings considers five domains of resources: human, physical, information, operational, and financial. Human resources are the people in the institution, center, and community, including administrators, staff, students, and community partners. Physical resources are geographical locations, settings, or buildings, including office space and neighborhoods. Information resources are broadly characterized as knowledge and ideas that influence activities, including mission statements, policies, rules, and regulations, as well as curricula or an understanding of skill sets or practice. Information can also be intangible, such as cultural values governing how things are done and why they are done this way. Sometimes this information is embedded in operational resources. These are tangible objects, or tools, used in an activity designed to meet specific goals and range from complicated computer programs to paper clips to data management programs. Operational resources can also include documents that convey information, such as risk assessment inventories and memos of understanding. Finally, financial resources are monetary funds that pay for activities, personnel, and equipment. This money may be part of the institutional budget or flow-through dollars from government, corporate, or private sources. These five domains effectively frame the infrastructural systems of institutions and campus centers for community engagement and will be used in chapter 3, examining the institution, and chapter 4, focusing on infrastructure and operation of the campus center.

Programs

Purpose and platforms fundamentally shape and support programming, which is the most visible activity of the institution, often coordinated by a center or a collaborative hub of centers. In computer science a *program* is an organized list of steps, commands, or instructions articulated in code that make the computer perform in certain ways to accomplish a specific task (Beal, 2015). For example, a word-processing program is used to help us articulate ideas in writing while a spreadsheet program provides a way to organize and depict quantitative information. In the context of community engagement in higher education, a program is the coordination of resources that allow administrators, faculty members, staff, students, and community partners to accomplish mutually beneficial tasks related to academic and civic goals. Programs use Maher and Bennett's (1984) five resource domains. In all areas of programming, there are elements of capacity building, leadership development, recognition and celebration, resource development and sharing, and strategic planning for making community engagement deeper, more pervasive, and better integrated with other institutional and community priorities. Much of this work is coordinated by a center or network of centers. A systems view of campus centers for community engagement is presented in chapter 5.

Student programs can be operationalized as curricular or cocurricular programs that may or may not include academic credit. While students are developing their own knowledge and civic skills through these programs, community agencies are the beneficiaries of the programs' work and resources. Professional development programs empower faculty members with new information and skills they can use to design, implement, and assess a variety of high-impact practices that meet instructional objectives for their students as well as the goals of community partners.

Chapter 6 provides an overview of various student programs and student leadership opportunities coordinated by centers. It differentiates and describes curricular and cocurricular programming provided by campus centers and includes a brief discussion of the pros and cons of offering an academic major in service-learning or community engagement. Examples of programs from various institutions are provided.

The main focus of programming for faculty, presented in chapter 7, is on professional development in constructing and delivering community engagement courses as well as community-based scholarship opportunities. The chapter also presents information on how centers provide faculty development and course development grants. Examples from faculty programming at various institutions are included. Finally, this chapter describes how faculty members can articulate their work during promotion and tenure review as well as how they can advance their engaged scholarship.

Chapter 8 addresses the complexities of and high aspirations for meaningful programs with and for the community. The narrative describes how centers identify, establish, and maintain community partners. Innovative and cutting-edge models of community partnerships are featured. Chapter 8 will include various partnerships ranging from simple one-time settings to more complex place-based programs and anchor approaches, which require campuses to have a physical presence in the community. Examples from several institutions are provided.

The book concludes with chapter 9, which explores the promise, peril, and projections of community engagement in higher education. The chapter presents a series of questions that remain to be answered and explored as well as recommendations for the future of the field.

PART ONE

PURPOSE

Purpose [pər-pəs] *noun*

: the reason why something is done or used: the aim or intention of
something
: the feeling of being determined to do or achieve something

—Merriam-Webster, 2016

PATHWAY OF PUBLIC PURPOSE

Getting to Now

The scholarship of engagement means connecting the rich resources of the university to our most pressing social, civic, and ethic problems. . . . Campuses should be viewed by both students and professors not as isolated islands, but as staging grounds for action.

—Ernest Boyer (1997, p. 92)

Higher education has always been comfortable with the *what*—the creation and dissemination of new knowledge. With this preoccupation, however, it is possible to lose track of the underlying *why*—the historical purpose of higher education. A prerequisite step to creating platforms and programs to promote engagement is to understand the path that led us to where we are today. The pathway of public purpose has taken many twists and turns over the past century. However, during the past 30 years, higher education has begun to navigate its way back to its original mission: serving the public. This chapter charts the course of this meandering pathway of purpose, which appears to have come full circle through five significant, related, and somewhat overlapping phases (see Figure 1.1).

The first phase of this journey is the public purpose of higher education to promote a democratic society. The missions of the first colonial colleges in this country—Columbia (Anglican), Harvard (Congregationalist), Princeton (Presbyterian), Brown (Baptist), and Rutgers (Dutch Reformed)—focused on preparing good citizens (primarily men at the time) through religiously based service (Harkavy, 2006). The Morrill Act of 1862 extended the value of secular service to the community at large. A progressive period emerged when educational visionaries such as John Dewey and William Rainey Harper began advocating institutions dedicated to creating and disseminating knowledge for the public good (Benson, Harkavy, & Puckett,

Figure 1.1. Higher education's public purpose pathway.

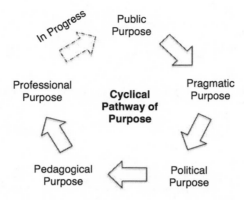

2011; Harkavy, 2004; Hartley, 2011). (Dewey's and Harper's work has been continued by contemporary scholars like John Gardner and Ernest Boyer.)

The second phase of this journey (pragmatic purpose) firmly took root immediately after World War II: the research university model exploded with the Cold War push toward big science (Benson et al., 2011). The seeds for this phase had been planted as early as 1876, when Johns Hopkins University adopted the German university model, which in turn created the American research university. Higher education during the Cold War era could be characterized as pragmatic. Postsecondary institutions shifted from focusing on grand, abstract intellectual idealism to focusing on producing academic commodities to be consumed by the government, corporations, and the general public, including students in search of a degree.

The third phase (political purpose), was a result of the political malaise that emerged in the 1980s. By that time much of the country was simply worn out from the turbulent 1960s and 1970s, and Americans shifted their attention to personal interest and gratification. College students of this period are often referred to as the "me generation," in part because they were essentially apolitical. Ironically, from this morass came the first inklings of a civic resurrection—on the part of students no less—supported by a handful of idealistic faculty members and university presidents. This third phase of the purpose pathway was political, albeit a pragmatic political movement rather than a partisan political movement. By the 1980s college campuses were scrambling to provide programmatic infrastructure that could support and sustain this new surge of student volunteerism.

College presidents and faculty members took note and began to combine service with learning, leading to the fourth phase (pedagogical purpose) of this movement, which was now beginning to arch back toward the original public purpose of higher education. By the late 1980s and early 1990s, educators and scholars had begun to establish professional associations and organizations as a scholarly scaffold to support this work. Research, publications, and conferences on the pedagogy of service emerged, creating the fifth phase: professional purpose. Today, we find higher education firmly grounded in this phase, which is primarily focused on programs for students, faculty members, and community partners. A list of important activities, events, scholars, and studies is provided in Table 1.1.

Therefore, civic and community engagement are really not new to higher education. At the same time the purpose and practice of engagement are not widely known or understood within the academy, even among administrators

TABLE 1.1
Chronology of Key Events and Publications

1978	National Society for Internships and Experiential Education is established.
1982	International Partnership for Service-Learning and Leadership is created.
1983	National Youth Leadership is formed.
1984	Campus Outreach Opportunity League (COOL) is organized.
1985	Campus Compact is formed.
1986	Brown University establishes the Swearer Center for Public Service.
1987	The University of Utah establishes the Lowell Bennion Community Service Center.
1989	Stanford University establishes the Haas Center for Public Service.
1990	President George H. W. Bush signs the National and Community Service Act, creating the Commission on National and Community Service.
	Ernest L. Boyer writes *Scholarship Reconsidered: Priorities of the Professoriate*.
	Bonners Scholars Program is created.
	The University of Colorado establishes the International and National Voluntary Service Training (INVST) Program.
	The University of Michigan establishes the Edward Ginsberg Center for Community Service and Learning.
	The University of Pennsylvania establishes the Barbara and Edward Netter Center for Community Partnerships.
	Portland State University establishes its Center for Public Service.

(Continues)

Table 1.1 *(Continued)*

1991	Breakaway is formed.
1993	President Bill Clinton signs the National Community Service Trust Act, creating Americorps and Learn and Serve.
	The Corporation for National and Community Service (CNCS) is established.
	The Pew Foundation publishes *University + Community Research Partnerships: A New Approach.*
	American Commitment initiative is launched by AAC&U.
1994	The Kettering Foundation publishes *Civic Declaration: A Call for New Citizenship.*
	Michigan Journal of Community Service Learning is launched.
1995	The *Chronicle of Higher Education* publishes "What Can Higher Education Do in the Cause of Citizenship?" by Alexander Astin.
	Campus Compact establishes the Invisible College.
1996	Community-Campus Partnerships for Health is established.
	Kellogg Commission is convened.
	Barbara Jacoby publishes *Service-Learning in Higher Education: Concepts and Practices.*
	Laurent A. Parks Daloz, Cheryl H. Keen, James P. Keen, and Sharon Daloz Parks publish *Common Fire: Leading Lives of Commitment in a Complex World.*
	Joanna Mareth, Melissa Smith, and Michael Kobrin publish *Service Matters: A Sourcebook for Community Service in Higher Education.*
1997	Robert Rhoads writes *Community Service and Higher Learning.*
	Barbara Holland writes *Analyzing Institutional Commitment to Service: A Model of Key Organizational Factors.*
1998	Edward Zlotkowski writes *Successful Service-Learning Programs: New Models of Excellence in Higher Education.*
	Wingspread Conference Series is first convened with the theme Strategies for Renewing the Civic Mission of the American Research University.
	Campus Compact publishes *Picturing the Engaged Campus* by Elizabeth Hollander.

	Larry Braskamp and Jon Wergin publish "Forming New Social Partnerships" in William G. Tierney's edited volume *The Responsive University*.
1999	Robert Bringle, Richard Games, and Edward A. Malloy publish *Colleges and Universities as Citizens*.
	Janet Eyler and Dwight E. Giles Jr. publish *Where's the Learning in Service-Learning?*
	Timothy K. Stanton, Dwight E. Giles Jr., and Nadinne Cruz publish *Service-Learning: A Movement's Pioneers Reflect on Its Origins, Practice and Future*.
	Campus Compact publishes the Wingspread Declaration on the Civic Responsibilities of Research Universities and the Presidents' Declaration on the Civic Responsibility of Higher Education.
	Imagining America is established.
2000	Thomas Ehrlich writes *Civic Responsibility and Higher Education*.
	The Kellogg Foundation publishes *Leadership Reconsidered: Engaging Higher Education in Social Change*.
	Campus Compact publishes *Establishing and Sustaining an Office of Community Service* and *Benchmarks for Campus/Community Partnerships*.
	American Association of Higher Education launches 18-volume set on service learning in the disciplines edited by Edward Zlotkowski.
	An entire issue of *Academe* is devoted to civic engagement in higher education.
	Project Colleague is launched by NERCHE.
	Project Pericles is initiated.
2001	The first annual K–H Service-Learning Research Conference is held in Berkeley, California.
	Barry Checkoway writes *Renewing the Civic Mission of the American Research University*.
	Sarah Long writes the Wingspread Statement on Student Civic Engagement.
	Sherril B. Gelmon, Barbara A. Holland, Amy Driscoll, Amy Spring, and Seanna Kerrigan write *Assessing Service-Learning and Civic Engagement*.
2002	An entire issue of the *Journal of Public Affairs* is devoted to civic engagement and higher education.
	Harry Boyte publishes *The Politics of Civic Engagement*.

(Continues)

Table 1.1 *(Continued)*

2003	Barbara Jacoby writes *Building Partnerships for Service-Learning.*
	Anne Colby, Thomas Ehrlich, Elizabeth Beaumont, and Jason Stephens write *Educating Citizens: Preparing America's Undergraduates for Lives of Moral and Civic Responsibility.*
	Campus Compact publishes *Introduction to Service-Learning Toolkit.*
	American Association of State Colleges and Universities publishes *American Democracy Project.*
	Eugene Rice writes *Re-thinking Scholarship and Engagement: The Struggle for New Meaning.*
	Pew Partnerships publishes *University and Community Research Partnerships: A New Approach.*
	Center for Information and Research on Civic Learning and Engagement (CIRCLE) and Casey Foundation copublish *The Civic Mission of Schools.*
	Andrew Furco writes *Self-Assessment Rubric for the Institutionalization of Service-Learning in Higher Education.*
2004	Tony Chambers and John Burkhardt write *Fulfilling the Promise of Civic Engagement.*
2005	Adrianna J. Kezar, Tony C. Chambers, John C. Burkhardt, and Associates write *Higher Education for the Public Good.*
2006	The Carnegie Foundation establishes the Elective Classification for Community Engagement.
	The President's Higher Education Community Service Honor Roll is established.
	Engaging Departments: Moving Faculty Culture From Private to Public, Individual to Collective Focus for the Common Good, edited by Kevin Kecskes, is published.
	Campus Compact and Tufts University copublish *New Times Demands New Scholarship: Research Universities and Civic Engagement.*
	Campus Compact publishes *Students as Colleagues*, edited by Edward Zlotkowski, Nicholas V. Longo, and James R. Williams.
	Campus Compact launches its Raise Your Voice Campaign.
	Higher Education Network for Community Engagement (HENCE) is established.
	Tulane University establishes the Center for Public Service in response to Hurricane Katrina.

2007	AAC&U publishes *College Learning for the New Global Century*.
	Lee Benson, John L. Puckett, and Ira Harkavy write *Dewey's Dream: Universities and Democracies in an Age of Education Reform, Civil Society, Public Schools, and Democratic Citizenship*.
2008	The Research University Civic Engagement Network (TRUCEN) is established.
2010	*Looking In/Reaching Out: A Reflective Guide for Community Service-Learning Professionals*, edited by Barbara Jacoby and Pamela Mutascio, is published.
	The Democracy Commitment is established.
2011	*To Serve a Larger Purpose: Engagement for Democracy and the Transformation of Higher Education*, edited by John Saltmarsh and Matthew Hartley, is published.
2012	National Task Force on Civic Learning and Democratic Engagement publishes *A Crucible Moment: College Learning and Democracy's Future*.
2013	*Deepening Community Engagement in Higher Education: Forging New Pathways*, edited by Ariane Hoy and Mathew Johnson, is published.
2014	As part of its Bringing Theory to Practice Project, AAC&U publishes *Civic Engagement, Civic Development, and Higher Education*, edited by Jill N. Reich.

and faculty members; paradoxically, engagement continues to evolve and expand in new ways. This evolution has had a significant impact on the academy as a whole and in particular on community centers for engagement, where more and more responsibility for this work has landed. This chapter provides a detailed chronology of the various pathways of purpose of community engagement, exploring events, individuals, and movements that were shaped by a variety of social, political, cultural, and educational contexts.

Public Purpose of American Higher Education

American higher education is grounded in a civic mission to prepare young adults to be meaningful and contributing members of a just and democratic society (Harkavy, 2004; Hartley, 2011). Early colonial colleges were religious institutions from various denominations with service to promote the common good at their core. Hartley (2011) suggested that colleges' commitment to civic leadership was a consequence of the American Revolution. Harkavy (2004) pointed out that land-grant universities established by the Morrill Act of 1862 were, by design, a form of outreach to rural communities to advance education, democracy, and agricultural science. But as a hint of things to come, the land-grant institutions created from this act were also intended to promote economic recovery and pay war debt; "education was the means; revenue was the end" (Roper & Hirth, 2005, p. 4). In 1903 the University of Wisconsin took a radical and progressive direction (known as the "Wisconsin idea"), making "the boundaries of the university . . . the boundaries of the state" by using academic resources to serve the lives of the state's citizens (Stark, 1995/1996, pp. 2–3). This approach was not limited to rural settings and institutions.

Urban universities also became more progressive in their civic mission. Daniel C. Gilman, president of Johns Hopkins University, articulated his desire for American universities to alleviate poverty, ignorance, bigotry, poor health, fraud, and political corruption during his inaugural address in 1876. Other urban universities, such as the University of Chicago, Columbia University, and the University of Pennsylvania, soon followed by creating innovative educational programs designed to reflect John Dewey's conceptual tenets to promote a democratic society (Harkavy, 2004; Harkavy & Hartley, 2012; Hartley, 2011).

Eby (2010) provided an exquisite reminder and detailed account of how civic engagement is also inherent in the purpose and mission of most faith-based institutions. He noted, however, that these institutions often incorporate different terms, such as *service* and *social justice*, that draw heavily on biblical traditions and language rather than using concepts such as democracy, common good, public good, or civic engagement. This difference depicts a semantic shift from the traditional, secular "public purpose" of higher education. Eby acknowledged stereotyped perceptions that faith-based institutions promote dogma and indoctrination but went on to point out that in fact most faith-based schools advocate a value-based liberal education to nurture students' critical thinking and to develop an engaged commitment to addressing social problems. He documented this by noting that many faith-based, liberal arts institutions have received the Carnegie Classification for Community Engagement and are included on the President's Honor Roll for Community Service.

Hartley (2011) noted the beginning of a shift from the civic mission in the late nineteenth century toward two models that would come to dominate the mission and structure of American higher education. The first model was commercial. Brown University in Providence, Rhode Island, for example, was established to attract business and increase property value around the campus (Cochran, 1972). The second model emphasized research and specialization by adopting the university model from Germany. This approach inadvertently promoted faculty loyalty to disciplines and professional organizations

(Roper & Hirth, 2005), and this loyalty generated a shift from the public purpose of higher education.

Meanwhile, a government report served as a blip in the historical time line and briefly returned focus to the civic mission of higher education after World War II. In 1947 the six-volume report titled *Higher Education for American Democracy* (President's Commission on Higher Education, 1947) served as a blueprint for recovery following the Great Depression and World War II. The report articulated specific goals for higher education, including education for a fuller realization of democracy in every phase of living, education directly and explicitly for international understanding and cooperation, and education for the application of creative imagination and trained intelligence to the solution of social problems and to the administration of public affairs.

Pragmatic Purpose

This lofty civic plan was soon sidetracked owing to cultural, political, and economic factors influenced by the end of World War II and the beginning of the Cold War. In 1944 President Franklin Roosevelt asked Vannevar Bush to draft a plan to help the country shift from a war-based economy to a peacetime economy. Bush's (1945) plan *Science, The Endless Frontier*, had a profound impact on American society and higher education; it advocated scientific research that would ensure military developments to compete with the Soviets and commercial growth (Harkavy, 2004). The National Science Foundation was created in 1950, and financial support for scientific research proliferated while the land-grant tradition of service began to decline (Roper & Hirth, 2005). This led to the commodification of higher education and what could be characterized as the entrepreneurial university (Benson et al., 2011). Higher education started to create "research parks" to develop products that would become intellectual property, leading to patents financially sustaining institutions. Extramural funding from government and commercial entities began to influence the research agenda at universities, directing studies toward subjects that would make significant contributions to the economy as a whole, while distracting scholars and researchers from other forms of civic scholarship. Thus, according to Harkavy (2004), American higher education at the time failed to meet its civic mission:

> The forces of Platonization, commodification, and disciplinary ethnocentricism, tribalism, and guildism continue to prevent American higher education, indeed American society, from translating its democratic mission into democratic process (p. 9)

In the late 1960s and 1970s, military buildup in the Vietnam War enraged Americans, and many college campuses—including the University of California, Berkeley; Columbia University; and Kent State University, where the National Guard killed four students in 1970—were engulfed in political turmoil. Consequently, the growing public perception was that higher education was part of the problem because it provided students a venue for protest (Roper & Hirth, 2005).

In the 1970s America also endured the Watergate scandal, which led to President Richard Nixon's resignation. By that time much of the country— its citizens and its college students—was emotionally and civically worn out. With this weariness came economic turmoil tied to inflation. Institutions of higher education were forced to compete with one another for limited funds, while at the same time many politicians and citizens turned to higher education for economic solutions (Holland, 1999; Roper & Hirth, 2005). The 1980s began with the passage of the Bayh-Dole Act, which allowed universities to patent research with federal dollars; the patents would generate royalties through the outsourcing of new technology and products to business (Roper & Hirth, 2005). This helped higher education cope with declining enrollment and rising costs and also fueled the transition from serving as intellectual bastions to serving as commodity producers.

Political Malaise and the Political Purpose

As American culture turned inward during the 1980s to insulate itself from the political turmoil of the previous two decades, many college students—the so-called me generation—eschewed any partisan political activities to focus on their own personal lives, educational pursuits, and careers. A study by Astin (1998; cited in Hartley, 2011) reported that in 1971, just as the Vietnam War was ending, nearly half of all college students reported they were attending college to make money; by 1991 nearly three fourths of college students reported going to college to "make more money." A consequence of this trend was a significant reduction in student interest and involvement in civic and political affairs. The Carnegie Foundation for the Advancement of Teaching published a report titled *Higher Education and the American Resurgence*, which stated,

> If there is a crisis in education in the United States today, it is less that test scores have declined than it is that we have failed to provide the education for citizenship that is still the most important responsibility of the nation's schools and colleges. (Newman, 1985, p. 31)

A special issue of *Liberal Education*, sponsored by the Kettering Foundation and the Association of American Colleges and Universities (AAC&U), in 1992 argued for making civic education a priority (Hartley, 2011). In 1998 the National Commission on Civic Renewal found that higher education was marked with a sense of civic *disengagement*. Another study conducted that same year by the National Assessment of Educational Progress revealed students were not knowledgeable about or interested in political and government institutions. Studies revealed that high school and college students had little interest in political affairs and little knowledge of or trust in the political system (Levine & Lopez, 2002; National Commission on Service Learning, 2002; Torney-Purta, 2002). Similarly, a national poll reported youth did not feel that they could influence government or that politics could solve community problems (Lake Snell Perry & Associates & the Tarrance Group Inc., 2002). However, Rimmerman (2006) argued that college students did, in fact, remain civically active, but in what he called a new form of citizenship rather than through conventional politics.

The sense of disengagement described in the report by the National Commission on Civic Renewal, coupled with a general sense of remorse and fatigue from the violence of those turbulent times, led many college students of the late 1980s and early 1990s to approach social change pragmatically by engaging in voluntary service. Many college students of the 1990s looked on the political actions of their peers a decade earlier and decided nothing had really been accomplished. Hands-on volunteerism surged as students realized that their direct service could provide immediate and tangible results. Surprisingly, the reaction against the trend of narcissism and political disenfranchisement sparked both students and scholars to launch a community engagement movement in higher education (Hartley, 2011).

Student Engagement

Educator-activist Wayne Meisel, who later became a Presbyterian pastor, did not necessarily share the popular view that students were apathetic. Instead, he perceived a difference between personal apathy and structural apathy. He characterized structural apathy as unawareness of meaningful opportunities to serve and of the programmatic resources available for service. Meisel walked from Maine to Washington, DC, visiting over 70 college campuses as part of his Walk for Action awareness campaign. In 1984 he and Bobby Hackett created the Campus Outreach Opportunity League (COOL) to promote community service and social action by college students. A major component of the organization was its national conference, hosted by a different college campus each year, with an attendance of nearly 1,500 students.

In 1999, retired entrepreneur Eugene M. Lang wrote an essay on the mission of liberal arts college for *Daedalus*, the journal of the American Academy of Arts and Sciences. Lang's essay explored the political malaise and civic disengagement of young people. Although Lang acknowledged the emergence of cocurricular efforts to address this problem, he wrote that these efforts were not enough and advocated creating and teaching explicit curricula on civic engagement. He believed higher education's civic mission and resources could be used to reclaim the legacy of the ancient Greek philosopher Pericles, who said the role of every citizen was to be actively engaged in a democratic society. Lang convened an organizing committee to create Project Pericles, initially consisting of 10 colleges, committed to educating students for civic and social responsibilities. Today, nearly 30 institutions are charter members of Project Pericles.

This group of liberal arts colleges and universities promotes civic engagement in higher education at all levels of the campus by working with college boards of trustees, presidents, provosts, administrators, faculty members, staff, students, alumni, and community members. The goal of Project Pericles is to transform institutions by integrating civic engagement and social responsibility across the college experience and curriculum through four key programs: Creating Cohesive Pathways to Civic Engagement, Civic Engagement Course, Debating for Democracy, and Faculty Leadership.

Campus Engagement

The presidents of Brown, Georgetown, and Stanford Universities took note of the public perception of the social and political malaise of college students around the country and met together in 1985 with the president of the Education Commission of the States to discuss ways of addressing the situation. These presidents had observed students on their own campuses becoming involved in loosely organized volunteer service activities. The goal of their meeting was to conceptualize, develop, and implement infrastructure that would support this type of service. From this meeting emerged Campus Compact, a national organization of university presidents committed to promoting civic engagement on their campuses. Four short years later, the group began to shift its focus from volunteer service to an academic approach that would become known as service-learning. The academic approach required providing support and resources to faculty members. This was accomplished by creating an infrastructure of offices or centers on campus. In partnership with the Ford Foundation, the Integrating Service with Academic Study initiative was launched; the initiative provided 120 faculty development grants and funds to create 130 campus centers to promote service-learning (Hartley, 2011). Soon, state chapters of Campus Compact began to emerge, offering similar support and resources locally. Thirty years later, Campus Compact has over 1,100 colleges and universities as members in 34 state and regional chapters.

The American Association of State Colleges and Universities (AASCU) launched the American Democracy Project (ADP) in 2003. The ADP is a consortium of 250 colleges and universities, each referred to as a Steward of Place, with the goal of preparing the next generation of informed, engaged citizens. From this project came the Civic Engagement Action Series, nine initiatives designed to help students become activists while learning about and addressing critical issues. The series also provided a lens to examine public policy and the roles and action of government agencies. The organization has sponsored a variety of projects and activities, ranging from voter education and registration campaigns to sponsorship of service and reflection on Martin Luther King Jr. Day. ADP has also hosted 12 national and 17 regional conferences.

Engaged Scholarship and Faculty

Ernest Boyer (1990) proposed expanding the concept and practice of scholarship into four categories in his landmark book *Scholarship Reconsidered: Priorities of the Professoriate.* The first category, *scholarship of discovery*, essentially reflected traditional research. The second, *scholarship of integration*, synthesized knowledge across a specific discipline or across several disciplines. The third and fourth categories laid the groundwork for what has generally become known as engaged scholarship: *scholarship of application* was defined as applying knowledge outside the institution and discipline to address real-world needs, and *scholarship of teaching and learning* was defined as democratizing education so that the content of what was taught was shared beyond the classroom, to be used and evaluated by others in the community. These last two forms of scholarship, combined with the growing student interest and energy around community service, prompted a series of scholarly books, reports, essays, and programs. In 1995 Boyer conceptualized engaged scholarship as

> connecting the rich resources of the university to our most pressing social, civic, and ethical problems, to our children, to our schools, to our teachers, and to our cities. . . . Campuses would be viewed by both students and professors not as isolated islands, but as staging grounds for action. At a deeper level I have this growing conviction that what is also needed is not just more programs, but a larger purpose, a larger sense of mission, a larger clarity of direction in the nation's life as we move toward century twenty-one. Increasingly, I'm convinced that ultimately the scholarship of

engagement also means creating a special climate in which the academic and civic cultures communicate more continuously and more creatively with each other. (p. 92)

Engaged Institutions

With the help of a grant from the Kellogg Foundation, the National Association of State Universities and Land-Grant Colleges (NASULGC) began a comprehensive study to promote a revised academic trilogy of learning, discovery, and engagement, creating an operational rubric for the engaged institution (Roper & Hirth, 2005). A series of Wingspread Conferences, titled Strategies for Renewing the Civic Mission of the American Research University, were convened in 1998 to explore and implement Boyer's reconceptualization of scholarship. From these discussions came a white paper titled "Wingspread Declaration on the Civic Responsibilities of Research Universities" (Boyte & Hollander, 1999). Shortly thereafter, Bringle, Games, and Malloy (1999) published *Colleges and Universities as Citizens*, giving examples of engaged scholarship and programs. Meanwhile, college presidents had clearly taken notice of these publications and in 1999 published their own document: *Presidents' Declaration on the Civic Responsibility of Higher Education*. As presented in Table 1.1, the new century began with a flurry of reports, articles, and books focused on civic engagement and the role of higher education in promoting it.

In addition to publications engaged scholarship continued to grow through the creation of events, organizations, and programs. The research and scholarship of engagement was further formalized by the convening of the first of several annual conferences on the research of service-learning in Berkeley, California, in 2001. In the next five years, the organizers of the conference not only continued to convene leading researchers, scholars, and practitioners in the field of service-learning and community engagement but also created the International Association for Research on Service-learning and Community Engagement (IARSLCE), which is described later in this chapter.

Two significant activities occurred in 2006 that marked the growing acceptance and institutionalization of engagement. First, the Carnegie Foundation established an elective classification for community engagement. To apply for this classification, campuses must provide evidence of campus practices, structures, and policies designed to deepen community engagement and make it more pervasive across the institution. The evidence is evaluated against a set of benchmarks established by the foundation to assist in designating institutions for this classification. Second, the Corporation for National and Community Service inaugurated the President's Higher Education Community Service Honor Roll, which annually recognizes colleges and universities that promote community service by involving students and faculty members in solving community problems using meaningful, measureable outcomes in the communities they serve. The awards provide objective recognition of institutions doing this work and give engaged scholarship legitimacy in parts of the academy that do not know about or particularly value it. They also provide a degree of prestige that offices of admissions and communication can take advantage of for recruiting students and faculty members as well as for promoting good public relations.

Meanwhile, a group of program directors and scholars from research universities gathered in 2006 for a conversation hosted by Tufts University and Campus Compact. From this group came *New Times Demands New Scholarship: Research Universities and Civic Engagement*, a report that ultimately led to the creation of The Research University Civic Engagement Network (TRUCEN; Curley & Stanton, 2012).

The activity of 2006 was not limited to scholars; students were also actively involved. Campus Compact initiated and sponsored the Raise Your Voice Campaign to promote student activism and published *Students as Colleagues*, edited by Edward Zlotkowski, Nicholas Longo, and James R. Williams, which featured the collaborative efforts of students and faculty in promoting community engagement. The Center for Information and Research on Civic Learning and Engagement (CIRCLE) was established in 2008 to conduct research that promoted civic engagement of youth.

In 2010 the National Task Force on Civic Learning and Democratic Engagement's report titled *A Crucible Moment: College Learning and Democracy's Future* challenged higher education to help students become engaged citizens. The report proposed that this work must be done by faculty members across disciplines, administrators in every school at every level, professionals in student affairs, and students themselves. It presented four key recommendations for higher education:

1. Foster a civic ethos across all parts of campus and educational culture.
2. Make civic literacy a core expectation for all students.
3. Practice civic inquiry across all fields of study.
4. Advance civic action through transformative partnerships at home and abroad. (National Task Force on Civic Learning and Democratic Engagement, 2012, p. 31)

This comprehensive report included a description of what a civic-minded campus would look like. Finally, it showcased how various institutions were implementing these recommendations and practices.

The Birth and Purpose of Campus Centers for Community Engagement

By the end of the 1980s and through the 1990s, many campuses created centers or offices associated with academic affairs to link community-based teaching, learning, and research to core faculty work. This was a new concept and practice in higher education; it thus lacked a historical and curricular foundation from which to grow and operate. Many of these offices had to make it up as they went because the empirical best practices and evidence on impact available in this emerging field were limited. To further support the growth of community service, President Clinton signed the National Community Service Trust Act, creating the AmeriCorps and Learn and Serve programs. The initiatives, reports, and practices enumerated previously helped shape the field and the administrative centers that advance and coordinate this form of engaged scholarship.

In 1986 Brown University president Howard Swearer created an on-campus center for community service, which was later named in his honor. The University of Utah created the Lowell Bennion Community Service Center in 1987, and two years later, the Haas Center for Public Service was established at Stanford University. By 1990 Portland State University had established its Center for Public Service, and the University of Pennsylvania had inaugurated The Center for Community Partnerships, which would later be named The Barbara and Edward Netter Center and generate an array of innovative community-based programs in Philadelphia. The purpose of these centers and others soon to follow was and continues to be providing and coordinating programs that promote community engagement, initially for students and gradually for faculty. Early on, many of these programs were cocurricular, non-credit-bearing volunteer experiences to promote students' civic role. Then President George H. W. Bush signed the National and Community Service Act in 1990, creating the Commission on National and Community Service. This began a pedagogical shift to integrate service with learning.

Pedagogical Purpose

As documented previously the national dialogue on engagement initially grew from the grassroots movement of students engaged with voluntary service. Over time, as the professional dialogue continued to push for civic engagement, efforts generally began to focus almost entirely on a pedagogy known as service-learning (Jacoby, 2009; Stanton, Giles, & Cruz, 1999). *Service-learning* emerged in the late 1960s, when Bill Ramsay and Robert

Sigmon attempted to find a term that captured the spirit and essence of their efforts to integrate experiential learning within traditional academics (Stanton et al., 1999). Ramsay recalls,

> I remember specifically deciding that we had to give this program a handle; we had to give it a name. These were not interns like medical interns, although there were some similarities. They were not practice teaching. We were trying to find a phrase that would describe the program, and tried all kinds of things: experiential learning, experience learning, work learning, action learning. We decided to call it *service-learning* because service implied a value consideration that none of the other words we came up with did. . . . We were looking for something with a value connotation that would link action with a value of reflection on that action—a disciplined reflection. . . . It has to be real service, not academics, not made up, not superficial, not tangential, but real and that's why it had to be agency based. (Stanton et al., 1999, p. 67)

The term *service-learning* is notable because of its hyphen, which, as is often the case in academia, is the source of much discussion and debate. The hyphen is purposeful in conveying reciprocity: through service one learns, and through learning one serves. Likewise, the roles of service provider and service recipient often blur, as do the roles of teacher and learner. The critical relationship of reciprocity depicted by the hyphen can be summarized in three broad principles articulated by Robert Sigmon (1979) that have stood the test of time: "those being served control the service(s) provided, those being served become better to serve and be served by their own actions, and those who serve also are learning and have significant control over what is expected to be learning" (p. 10).

Service-learning is defined as "a form of experiential education in which students engage in activities that address human and community needs together with structured opportunities intentionally designed to promote student learning and development. Reflection and reciprocity are key concepts of service learning" (Jacoby, 1996, p. 5). It quickly became a dominant form and catalyst for civic engagement. By the end of the 1990s, there was enough history and legacy of the movement for early advocates to publish a scholarly memoir, *Service-Learning: A Movement's Pioneers Reflect on Its Origins, Practice, and Future* (Stanton et al., 1999).

By the start of the new century, the field of service-learning had existed for nearly a generation, and it had experienced significant growth and evolution. Professional and disciplinary accreditation bodies were beginning to include service-learning in their benchmarks of best practice. The benchmarks created by Committee on Institutional Cooperation (CIC) were used to establish the Criterion 5: Engagement and Service accreditation standards of the North Central Association Higher Learning Commission (Roper & Hirth, 2005). The American Association of Higher Education published an 18-volume set on service-learning in the disciplines edited by Zlotkowski in 2000.

Over time programs began to expand from exclusively student-centered cocurricular and curricular service-learning experiences to scholarly activities for faculty members. This expansion included providing professional development to help faculty members effectively implement service-learning or pursue engaged scholarship and research. Eventually (as discussed later), the focus on engaged pedagogy expanded as faculty members began to conduct community-based research (CBR) that could be disseminated in a variety of disciplinary venues as it affected the community. This trend created a need for campus centers, which in turn required professional educators to serve faculty members.

Professional Purpose

Thus, a curious situation emerged: There was now a demand for professional educators to administer centers and provide support first for students and gradually for faculty members interested in this pedagogy known as service-learning. While community engagement had arrived pedagogically, there was no formal academic discipline guiding the field nor were there graduate-level professional preparation programs from which these educational professionals could emerge. As a result the trend had the characteristics of a movement rather than those of a professional, scholarly field.

Community engagement that combines epistemological, ontological, and pedagogical concepts and practice can be incorporated into a variety of disciplinary studies. It provides a new and hybrid form of integrating research, scholarship, teaching, and learning. Significant research is being conducted on the various forms engagement can take. A growing research base and cadre of researchers are systematically examining the process and impact of community engagement, and the number of scholars and practitioners who oversee and coordinate the practice is increasing at the same rate. This growth indicates a professionalization of the practice and field.

Formal professionalization of the field has been limited, however. That is, few degrees and certificates are awarded to professional practitioners who oversee and coordinate community engagement on college campuses. In some ways it may be more appropriate to characterize community engagement not as a field but as a unique pedagogical movement supported by a professional scaffold of organizations and associations. These professional collectives of scholars and practitioners provide a venue for dialogue and dissemination of new knowledge that can be applied in an array of engaged pedagogies and study.

Dostilio (in press) documented much of the gradual professionalization of community engagement by describing a handful of organizations and associations that have emerged over time. One of the earliest organizations that shaped and influenced this movement is the National Society for Experiential Education (NSEE). Established in 1971, NSEE fell under the broad umbrella of field experiences and internships that initially focused on professional preparation of students. Over time the organization began to view learning opportunities in authentic settings to "empower learners and promote the common good" (NSEE, 2014) as a shift toward the spirit of mutuality. Members of the organization became more interested in a distinct form of experiential education whereby students applied what they were learning through service to and in the community.

Another organization described by Dostilio (in press) is Campus Compact, introduced earlier in this chapter. Campus Compact works to educate students about civic and social responsibility by providing resources and support to campus centers for engagement. The organization also hosts regional and national conferences to provide professional development for student leaders, center administrators, faculty members, and community partners. Campus Compact collaborates with other professional organizations and associations.

Dostilio (in press) noted that in the mid-1990s the Pew Charitable Trusts and the Corporation for National Service provided financial support to establish the Health Professions School in Service to the Nation (HPSISN). Following the lead of NSEE, the program incorporated service-learning in the education of health professionals to provide a civic perspective and public purpose; this led to the establishment of the Community-Campus Partnerships for Health (CCPH). CCPH created and implemented an impressive set of operational principles and practice, as well as a growing curriculum of materials and resources.

By the turn of the century, service-learning had gained wide acceptance and practice despite little to no empirical research to document its efficacy as a pedagogy. Around that time the RMC Research Corporation received a grant from the W. K. Kellogg Foundation to host a series of conferences to provide a venue for dialogue about and dissemination of research on service-learning. The conference leaders compiled and published edited volumes of research from each gathering. Before the funding expired, key participants and leaders of the conference series had convened to establish IARSLCE in 2006 (Dostilio, in press). IARSLCE continues to host conferences and has formally established a mission of not only promoting and disseminating research but also nurturing the professional development of graduate students as the new engaged professoriate.

The New England Resource Center on Higher Education (NERCHE) was established in 1988 at the University of Massachusetts Boston as a center for inquiry, research, and policy to support administrators, faculty members, and staff as they promote social justice and democratic values in higher education. The center is unique in its approach of incorporating a grassroots perspective of practitioners and multiple stakeholders to create resources as well as guide policy and practice. A key project is the center's role in coordinating the Carnegie Classification for Community Engagement. NERCHE partners with the AASCU and Imagining America to implement the Next Generation Engagement Project to develop and implement programs designed to nurture the civic roles and scholarship of the next generation of students, faculty members, and scholars in higher education.

The Community College National Center for Community Engagement (CCNCCE) was established at Mesa Community College in 1990 to provide professional development, publish information about community engagement, and host an annual conference (Franco, 2010). It also publishes the *Journal for Civic Commitment*. The American Association of Community Colleges launched the Horizons Colleges Initiative in 1995 to promote community engagement at community colleges. Another initiative of that year was Campus Compact's Invisible College, 20 faculty members from across the country brought together to establish service-learning programs. Participants received minigrants to help fund service projects as well as a venue and opportunity to share ideas.

In 1999 the White House Millennium Council convened several meetings of scholars and administrators to "Honor the Past—Imagine the Future" of higher education. From these meetings Imagining America was created as a consortium of universities committed to public scholarship through the arts and humanities. The organization's mission is to address key social issues and to prepare young adults to be engaged citizens (Eatman & Peters, 2015). Thus, Imagining America has created a hybrid approach that could be characterized as community-engaged arts. Over 100 institutions of higher education and community partners are active members of the organization.

In 2005 the Council for the Advancement of Standards in Higher Education (CAS)—a group of professionals that since 1979 has set standards of best practice in student affairs and student development programs—developed standards and guidelines for implementing service-learning courses and programs; these standards were revised in 2015. The standards for service-learning include six student learning outcomes in six domains as well as guidelines for an organization overseeing service-learning programs at an institution. The organizational guidelines cover strategic planning; supervision; ethics; human resources; law, policy, and governance; diversity, equity, and access; finances; technology; and facilities (CAS, 2015).

A series of Wingspread discussions on engagement in higher education in 2006 led to the formation of a virtual network of scholars known as the Higher Education Network for Community Engagement (HENCE). HENCE was designed "to consolidate and advance research, practice, policy, and advocacy for engagement" (Sandmann, 2006, p. 41). In her detailed account of the network's history, Sandmann (2006) writes that HENCE was not designed to be another association or institutional organization. Instead, it was conceptualized as a network of leaders and scholars in the field of community engagement that could promote communication and collaboration across existing organizations.

Community colleges continued their commitment to community engagement by establishing The Democracy Commitment (TDC) project in 2010. Over 130 community colleges participate in TDC to engage in dialogue and exchange ways to incorporate community engagement in the mission and strategic planning of community colleges. TDC is a component of the ADP; both bodies recognize and appreciate that nearly half of the students from community colleges transfer to four-year public institutions (Murphy, 2014).

The AAC&U launched a comprehensive Civic Learning and Democratic Engagement (CLDE) initiative that provides a host of resources for scholars and students. The Task Force's (2012) landmark publication *Crucible Moment* was a product of this initiative, which had a steering committee comprising representatives from a comprehensive list of professional associations, initiatives, and organizations. The goal of CLDE was to confront complex challenges in the community using three place-based strategies: highlighting exemplary models of civic learning in specific geographical regions or cities; using a cohort of institutions to develop a collective action plan; and defining *civic learning* in different departments, programs, and disciplines. The *Crucible Moment* also played an important role in redirecting higher education to its original civic mission. This report acknowledged the pedagogical power of high-impact practice to facilitate teaching and learning and at the same time reemphasized a return to the civic and public work of the academy.

International Associations and Organizations

The growth of professional associations and organizations is not limited to the United States. Many groups dedicated to service-learning, engaged scholarship, and community engagement have been established around the world. In 2002 the *Centro Latinoamericano de Aprendizaje y Servicio Soli-dario* (*Latin American Center for Service-Learning*; CLAYSS) was founded in Buenos Aires, Argentina. The organization provides professional development to faculty members and representatives of community agencies to implement service-learning programs in schools and higher education.

Tufts University convened an international gathering of 29 university administrators from 23 countries in 2005 to explore ways of strengthening the civic roles and social responsibilities of higher education (Hollister et al., 2012). From this gathering came the *Talloires Declaration on the Civic Roles and Social Responsibilities of Higher Education*, which created the Talloires Network as an international consortium of colleges and universities committed to strengthening the civic roles and social responsibilities of higher education. Today the network has over 320 members in 72 countries with a combined enrollment of over 6 million students.

In 2011 the second gathering convened over 200 presidents and administrators in Madrid. A by-product of the Talloires Network was the collaborative creation of the Asia-Talloires Network of Industry and Community Engaged Universities (ATNEU). Like many other organizations, ATNEU convenes leaders from universities, industries, nongovernmental organizations, communities, and governments to establish partnerships to identify and address challenges in the community. Other related organizations, such as the ASEAN University Network Thematic Network on University Social Responsibility and Sustainability (AUN-USR&S) and the ASEAN Youth Volunteer Programme (AYVP), were also created. To help coordinate and maximize the efforts of each group, Asia Engage was created as an umbrella organization to promote and integrate the scholarly mission of higher education in industry and community agencies.

Engagement Australia (EA) is a professional group comprising 70% of Australian universities and private colleges. These colleges are committed to developing best practices for university-community engagement in Australia. EA provides an interactive network of university, business, government, and community organizations that advances knowledge, skills, and capacity to support community engagement. Similarly, Europe Engage was established to promote service-learning and community engagement throughout the continent. Some European countries have also created their own organizations, such as Campus Engage, hosted at the National University of Ireland in Galway.

The Ma'an Alliance for Arab Universities was established in 2008 as a regional affiliate of the Talloires Network. A total of 15 institutions from 9 Arab countries make up the alliance. Much like NERCHE in the United States, the alliance activities use a participatory consultative approach that allows various stakeholders, including students, faculty members, administrators, and public and civic partners, to work together to ensure that civically engaged youths graduate from colleges and universities.

The South African Higher Education Community Engagement Forum (SAHECE) was launched in 2009. This organization grew out of principles articulated in a 1997 white paper that led to the Higher Education Act of 1997. Community engagement, along with teaching and research, was included as a key responsibility of higher education in that document. The Higher Education Quality Committee (HEQC) was established to oversee program accreditation policy and procedures, including knowledge-based community service (Hall, 2010). Today SAHECE provides technical support to colleges and universities throughout South Africa to promote community engagement.

Summary

This chapter has presented a chronology of community engagement in higher education. Community engagement was initially a movement and has evolved into an international scholarly field. However, at the institutional level, as educators and scholars expand their view and practice of engagement, more and more support and infrastructure are required for this field. As they did in the early 1990s, when ad hoc offices in student affairs were tasked with coordinating cocurricular volunteer service and later service-learning, colleges and universities are once again turning to these centers to assume more and more roles and responsibilities (Welch & Saltmarsh, 2013b). More than a decade ago Checkoway (2001) predicted that civic renewal would likely require institutions to restructure, but he assumed there would not be a single infrastructure or model that all would follow. He speculated that likely approaches would entail either a centralized office or at least a combination of decentralized departments or new interdisciplinary units. No matter what format or structure, Checkoway emphasized, the restructuring would require first determining what the institution wanted to accomplish and then planning for how to accomplish it. This pragmatic vision nicely reflects the conceptual framework of purpose, platforms, and programs for community engagement centers presented in the introduction of this book (Welch & Saltmarsh, 2013a, 2013b).

The interest in and advancement of community engagement represent reciprocity, democratization of knowledge, and cooperation of the academy and the community—meaning that both entities should continue to operate independently of yet with and for each other. The purpose of the campus-community partnership transcends the independent objectives of both constituencies. The nexus of two organizational structures and cultures necessitates a platform through which they can cooperate. These new purposes and platforms will build on existing programs as well as create new programs that target specific types of mutually beneficial goals and products. This reflects an outside-the-box approach that is rich with potential as well as inherent challenges. At the heart of the academy is a deeply entrenched culture of disciplinary isolation that embodies a positivist perspective and practice made up of a set of expert attitudes, values, and roles. This expert paradigm of disciplinary silos will require a significant cultural shift. Using systems theory, as briefly described in the introduction of this book, institutions can create and implement platforms consisting of interrelated systems of human, financial, operational, information, and physical resources. System platforms, in turn, support programs for students, faculty members, and community partners that enable all stakeholders to engage in a variety of activities designed to realize Boyer's vision of engaged scholarship.

2

WHAT IS ENGAGEMENT?

All our work, our whole life is a matter of semantics, because words are the tools with which we work, the material out of which laws are made, out of which the Constitution was written. Everything depends on our understanding of them.

—Felix Frankfurter (Simpson, 1964/1998)

The civic engagement movement has something important to say about the way we teach and learn in higher education, because it seeks to redress patterns of narrow specialization and technocratic practices, especially in the humanities and social sciences, where their practices have resulted in a drift away from humanistic inquiry, understanding, and democratic engagement. The civic engagement movement has the potential to return higher education to its roots of preparing people to work with others to solve problems and build thriving communities in ways that enhance democratic capacity.

—Harry C. Boyte and Eric Fretz (2011, p. 83)

Engagement can mean many different things and manifest itself in a variety of ways. This variety has both benefits and drawbacks. An advantage is allowing institutions of higher education of various sizes and with different missions and resources multiple ways to approach this important work. This, in turn, can and often does create confusion as to what engagement is, how it looks, and how and where it is applied. Furthermore, our understanding and realization of engagement are influenced by a complex combination of philosophical, pedagogical, political, cultural, and systemic factors within higher education. Consequently, it is critical to have a common lexicon and understanding.

Saltmarsh, Giles, Ward, and Buglione (2009) noted the variety and frequency of terminology depicting engagement used in applications for the Carnegie Classification for Community Engagement. Their list comprised 14 terms, such as *service-learning, community engagement, civic engagement, engaged scholarship*, and *community-based research*. Other commonly used terms found in the literature are *civically engaged scholarship, public engagement, public scholarship, public professionals, civic learning*, and *engaged pedagogy*. Barker (2011) noted that the diverse terminology implies a fragmented movement and suggested that engagement as a field could make greater advancements through common articulation of terms and practice by all stakeholders.

There is even a degree of confusion as to the difference (if any) between community engagement and civic engagement. For some institutions, depending on their mission, there is a subtle yet important difference between the two. *Community engagement* may connote a pedagogical and sometimes even a moral relationship between the academy and neighborhoods, while civic engagement reflects a political character of citizenship. For some institutions, community engagement seems less political or, for some faith-based institutions, less secular. Saltmarsh (2005) captured the conundrum that may accompany the term *civic engagement*:

> Questions inevitably arise about what is meant by civic engagement and about how it related to civic education, service-learning, democratic education, political engagement, civics, education for citizenship or moral education. Moreover, the lack of clarity fuels a latent confusion about how to operationalize a civic engagement agenda on campus. (p. 2)

Similarly, the terms *scholarship of engagement* and *engaged scholarship* are often interchanged, even within a single publication. Some authors suggest these terms are synonyms whereas others argue there is a significant difference in their meaning, purpose, and format. This disagreement complicates not just the professional dialogue but also efforts to promote and institutionalize engagement. *Engagement* must be clearly defined and understood before platforms and programs are developed to support this work. This chapter characterizes the term *engagement* and then discusses civic and community engagement, engaged scholarship, and the scholarship of engagement.

Engagement

Ward and Moore (2010) traced the origin and application of *engagement*, noting that the term has different meanings in higher education. They suggest the term originates from Versey's (1965) concept of utility as working toward a common goal of practical application of knowledge to the world outside the academy. Versey viewed utility as consistent with the civic mission of higher education because it involved having academic utilitarians contribute to the dissemination of knowledge throughout society to promote democratic ideals.

Engagement means many different things in higher education (Ward & Moore, 2010). The Kellogg Commission (2001) played a key role in conceptualizing *engagement* by distinguishing it from other terms such as *public service*, *outreach*, and *extension*. This distinction intentionally moved *engagement* away from a sense of noblesse oblige or pity from the academic elite (Glass & Fitzgerald, 2010). The commission enumerated seven key components to characterize engagement: responsiveness to communities; respect for partners; academic neutrality; access to the academy; integration of the academic trilogy; coordination of efforts through a common agenda; and utilization of assets, resources, and partner groups in the community. The Committee on Institutional Cooperation (CIC) (2005) offered the following to characterize *engagement*:

1. Engagement is scholarly. A scholarship-based model of engagement involves both the act of engaging (bringing universities and communities together) and the product of engagement (the spread of discipline-generated, evidence-based practices in communities).
2. Engagement cuts across the mission of teaching, research, and service. It is not a separate activity, but a particular approach to campus-community collaboration.
3. Engagement is reciprocal and mutually beneficial. There is mutual planning, implementation, and assessment among engagement partners. (p. 4)

In essence, engagement is characterized as activities benefiting society that are integrated into academic purposes to generate new knowledge through research and to educate in programs of study (Colby, Beaumont, Ehrlich, & Corngold, 2008; Kuh, 2008; Ramaley, 2010). Bringle and Hatcher (2011) argued that the concept of engagement as a whole must reflect four characteristics: it must be scholarly; it must integrate teaching, research, and service; it must be reciprocal and mutually beneficial; and it must encompass and reflect civil democracy.

What makes engagement "scholarly"? Similarly, what constitutes excellence and rigor so it counts in promotion and tenure review? It may be useful and appropriate to begin by exploring what engagement is not. A faculty project in the community, with or without student involvement, is not necessarily scholarly work. The project may very well be of service to the community, but in and of itself, it would not be considered engaged scholarship. Scholarly work in the context of community engagement should include and incorporate some key components. First, it should be theoretically based. The work faculty members and their students engage in with community partners should be grounded in sound best practices based on ideas and procedures that have been empirically tested and validated. Second, the work should be driven by two sets of related objectives: a traditional academic or intellectual goal involving the generation of new knowledge for students' development or in a disciplinary field and an outcome that will benefit the partner. The academic goal represents intellectual inquiry and assimilation of new knowledge for students and in professional literature. In turn, the generation or culmination of the intellectual inquiry also serves a civic or public purpose. Third, the intellectual and academic product is disseminated or applied. From a traditional academic context, this includes publication or presentations in peer-reviewed venues. In this way scholars must write or present about their work. However, engaged scholarship includes mutual public benefit in which the new knowledge or product derived from the knowledge is adopted and applied by community partners. This could be considered a form of "authentic" dissemination as the new knowledge goes beyond distribution of written text housed on library shelves to distribution and assimilation by the community.

In some respects adoption of ideas, practices, and products created through engaged scholarship with community partners reflects an additional level of rigor through two types of scientific validation in the behavioral sciences. Kerlinger (1979) defined the first validation type, *concept validity*, as a process of making meaning of abstract properties of a concept, process, or phenomenon. Through engaged scholarship, students and community partners can see theory being applied, thus making it real rather than abstract. When faculty members and their students apply ideas, principles, or skill sets from a discipline through their engaged course activities or community-based research, they are essentially implementing concept validity.

The second validation type is *social validity*. This is a common construct in behavioral science, particularly in educational psychology and marketing, whereby clients or consumers are asked their opinion or the extent to which they would adopt or buy a specific method or product. Baer and Schwartz (1991) noted and challenged the traditional assumptions of scholarship and expertise by asking whether "we [scholars] are presumed more rational than 'they' [practitioners]" (p. 232). In this sense community partners validate the abstract and theoretical knowledge professed by professors.

Thus, it is not enough for marketing students to merely articulate or repeat memorized basic principles of marketing plans for a nonprofit organization on an exam. Instead, formulating, sharing, and adopting a marketing plan by an actual nonprofit organization validates students' mastery of concepts and skills, thus creating a more robust standard of authentic assessment.

Assessing Engaged Scholarship

In terms of assessing engaged scholarship, Glassick, Huber, and Maeroff (1997) used Boyer's reconceptualization of scholarship to develop six standards that could be applied to not merely to emerging engaged scholarship but to any form of scholarship (Box 2.1). Applying these standards to engaged teaching and learning helps bring scholarly credence to this work, elevating the activity far above a simple service project out in the community. An added challenge that is not evident in traditional, expert, positivist scholarship is following these standards in a collaborative and democratic fashion in which community partners have parity and a voice in the design and implementation of the scholarly activity. In this way faculty members are, indeed, bringing their scholarly expertise to the work, but in a respectful and mutually beneficial manner.

BOX 2.1
Standards of Scholarship

Clear Goals
Does the scholar state the basic purposes of the work clearly? Does the scholar propose objectives that are realistic and achievable? Does the scholar identify important questions in the field?

Adequate Preparation
Does the scholar show an understanding of existing scholarship in the field? Does the scholar bring the necessary skills to the work? Does the scholar bring together the resources necessary to move the project forward?

Appropriate Methods
Does the scholar use methods appropriate to the goals? Does the scholar effectively apply the methods selected? Does the scholar modify procedures in response to changing circumstances?

Significant Results
Does the scholar meet the goals? Does the scholar's work add to the field? Does the scholar's work open additional areas for further exploration?

Effective Presentation
Does the scholar use a suitable style and effective organization to present the work? Does the scholar use appropriate forums for communicating work to intended audiences? Does the scholar present his or her message with clarity and integrity?

Reflective Critique
Does the scholar critically evaluate his or her own work? Does the scholar bring an appropriate breadth of evidence to the critique? Does the scholar use evaluation to improve the quality of future work?

Under this broad umbrella of engagement is a common lexicon that includes the terms *community engagement, civic engagement, engaged scholarship, engaged pedagogy,* and *engaged campus.* All are related but take on slightly different meanings and iterations with various stakeholders. The terms' core meanings and purposes can be applied to what Boyer called a scholarship of engagement within any combination of four constituency domains: the students, the faculty, the institution, and the community. Likewise, the breadth and depth of engagement that can vary in what Morton (1995) characterizes as "thin" and "thick" engagement (p. 21). *Thin engagement* reflects minimal effort and resources committed, resulting in limited integration into the educational and public mission of the institution; *thick engagement* connotes meaningful and intentional work in process and outcomes.

Community Engagement

The Carnegie Foundation (2012) defined *community engagement* as "the collaboration between institutions of higher education and their larger communities (local, regional/state, national, global) for the mutually beneficial exchange of knowledge and resources in a context of partnership and reciprocity." Votruba (1996) characterized community engagement as activities related to an institution's academic mission of generating, disseminating, applying, and preserving knowledge that can directly benefit external groups. In this way the primary task and educational purpose of colleges and universities are to avail their intellectual resources to the community.

Youniss and Yates (1997) wrote *Community Service and Social Responsibility in Youth,* a landmark book documenting their empirical work with high school students involved with community engagement. Their guiding principles can be generalized to college students and community engagement in higher education. They enumerated the following 10 key points related to service in community engagement:

1. Meaningful activity: The emphasis should be on the quality rather than the quantity of community engagement experiences. A quality experience, rather than a "make work" situation, includes responsibility for decision making, reflection on values, an adult or educator working with students, new situations and settings, and credit for one's work.
2. Emphasis on helping others: The primary focus is on the service in order to promote caring attitudes and social justice, while the secondary focus is on the experience of the service providers.
3. Integrated part of articulated ideology: The service is explicitly part of the schools' mission statement.

4. Group rather than individual action: Collective action is promoted to create a sense of the "we" doing the action.
5. Reflective opportunities with peers: Reflection through discussion, written essays, and journals is an essential part of the experience.
6. Service organizers as models and integrators: Adults or educators who organize the service opportunities and work along with the students serve as engaged role models.
7. Site supervisors as models: Community partners can be models of moral commitment who offer their perspective on social issues and the dynamics of addressing them. They should be viewed as coeducators.
8. Acknowledging participants' diversity: The diversity of participants, site supervisors, service organizers, and service recipients in terms of race, class, and gender can be significant and can create discomfort or tension that should be acknowledged as part of the reflection experience.
9. Sense of being a part of history: The impact of the experience can create a sense of legacy on the part of all participants. Students become invested in community engagement when they believe that their actions are helping to make history rather than assume a disengaged role of observer when community engagement is treated as an isolated or decontextualized event.
10. Responsibility: Students recognize their civic responsibilities rather than focus on their individual rights and freedom.

Civic Engagement

Saltmarsh, Hartley, and Clayton (2009) noted that *civic engagement* is a commonly used term that is loosely defined and serves as an "umbrella term" (p. 5). They defined it as a campus-based activity related to an off-campus issue, problem, or organization. Lawry, Laurison, and Van Antwerpen (2006) noted the semantic confusion surrounding the term:

> The concept of civic engagement has been the subject to a profusion of sometimes overlapping, sometimes competing attempts at a greater definition. . . . Civic engagement has become the rubric under which faculty, administrators, and students think about, argue about and attempt to implement a variety of visions of higher education in service to society. . . . There is near consensus that an essential part of civic engagement is feeling responsible to part of something beyond individual interests. (pp. 12–13)

Adler and Goggin (2005) noted that civic engagement can take the form of behaviors, such as community service; collective action to influence larger civil society; and political involvement, or the form of a means to an end, such as social change in which active citizens participate in the life of the community. On the basis of these observations, they defined *civic engagement* broadly as "how an active citizen participates in the life of a community in order to improve conditions for others or to help shape the community's future" (p. 241). Ehrlich (2000) succinctly characterized civic engagement as "working to make a difference in the civic life of our communities and developing the combination of knowledge, skills, values, and motivation to make that difference" (p. vi). From an international perspective the Talloires Network viewed civic engagement as having two key purposes: educating responsible citizens and community leaders and contributing to social and community development (Tisch College of Citizenship and Public Service, 2005). The University of Minnesota defined it over a decade ago as

> an institutional commitment to public purposes and responsibilities intended to strengthen a democratic way of life in the rapidly changing information society of the 21st century. . . . In this light, civic is broadly construed as referring to all the important contributions that college and universities make to a flourishing democracy. These civic contributions include: access to learning, enhanced diversity, civic learning, public scholarship, trusted voice, public spaces, and community partnership. (Fogelman, 2002, pp. 104–105)

The Coalition for Civic Engagement and Leadership at the University of Maryland defined *civic engagement* as

> acting upon a heightened sense of responsibility to one's communities. This includes a wide range of activities, including developing civic sensitivity, participation in building civil society, and benefitting the common good. Civic engagement encompasses the notions of global citizenship and interdependence. Through civic engagement, individuals—as citizens of their communities, their nations, and the world—are empowered as agents of positive social change for a more democratic world. (Jacoby, 2009)

Civic engagement may involve one or more of the following:

- Learning from others, self, and environment to develop informed perspectives on social issues
- Valuing diversity and building bridges across difference
- Behaving and working through controversy with civility
- Taking an active role in the political process
- Participating actively in public life, public problem-solving, and community service
- Assuming leadership and membership roles in organizations

- Developing empathy, ethics, values, and a sense of social responsibility
- Promoting social justice locally and globally

In 2010 the AAC&U incorporated concepts from Ehrlich's (2000) edited volume to define *civic engagement* as

> working to make a difference in the civic life of our communities and developing the combination of knowledge, skills, values and motivation to make that difference. It means promoting the quality of life in a community, through both political and non-political processes. (p. vi)

From this operational definition, AAC&U acknowledged that civic learning can take many forms and therefore have a variety of outcomes. To make learning outcomes more explicit, the association created a values rubric as a heuristic assessment tool that could be used to create programs and activities designed to develop students' civic skills. The six dimensions assessed are attributes deemed to be essential for civic engagement: diversity of community and culture, analysis of knowledge, civic identity and commitment, civic communication, civic action and reflection, and civic contexts and structures. Each of these is assessed on a continuum ranging from an introductory or novice benchmark to a capstone level of mastery and application.

Democratic Engagement

Saltmarsh and Hartley (2011) distinguish democratic engagement from civic engagement. They view democratic engagement as a shift from the dominant institutional positivist paradigm of faculty expertise within the academy to a collaborative cocreation and application of knowledge *with* others, including students and community partners. This creates a new engaged epistemology in which faculty members and students work *with* the public—as opposed to *for* the public—to foster an engaged democracy. Ideally, this places the academy in a dynamic and collaborative "ecosystem of knowledge production" (p. 21), where faculty members, students, and community partners benefit from an ebb and flow of problem-solving and knowledge production. Reciprocity and mutuality are key components to this approach. Likewise, an engaged epistemology emerges when faculty members integrate research, teaching, and service that are catalytic not only for promotion and tenure but also for promoting social change as well as personal and professional fulfillment (Hoyt, 2011).

Public Engagement

Closely related to civic engagement is public engagement. The AASCU (2002) characterized a publicly engaged institution as being "fully committed to direct, two-way interaction with communities and other external constituencies through the development, exchange, and application of knowledge, information, and expertise for mutual benefit" (p. 9). The association continues by articulating four key components of public engagement. First, it is place-based. In other words the institution is linked to the community where it is located. Second, public engagement is interactive—the institution serves as a resource rather than "an answer" (p. 9). Third, public engagement is mutually beneficial to the mission of the institution and needs of the community. Fourth, it is fully integrated at all levels of the institution, including policies, structures, and priorities.

The University of Minnesota Office of Public Engagement (2012a) defined *public engagement* as

> the partnership of university knowledge and resources with those of the public and private sectors to enrich scholarship, research, and creative activity; enhance curriculum, teaching and learning; prepare educated, engaged citizens; strengthen democratic values and civic responsibility; address critical societal issues; and contribute to the public good.

Civic Learning

Civic learning is another term that emerged from this professional dialogue. Early on Newman (1985) argued,

> The most critical demand is to restore to higher education its original purpose of preparing graduates for a life of involved and committed citizenship. . . . The advancement of civic learning, therefore, must become higher education's most central goal. (p. xix)

In this way explicit instruction, learning experiences, and curriculum were deemed necessary to prepare students to become engaged citizens. Howard (2001) defined *civic learning* as any learning experience comprising knowledge, skills, and values that prepare students for active roles and activities in the community to promote a democratic society. Engaged pedagogy nurtures students' civic skills as citizens in a just and democratic society. Battistoni (2002) summarized eight specific civic skills students need to be engaged citizens; these skills can be applied to experiential learning and, especially, service-learning courses focused on social justice and change. The skills include political knowledge and critical thinking, communication, public problem-solving, civic judgment, civic imagination and creativity, collective action, community/coalition building, and organizational skills. In partnership with the AAC&U, McTighe Musil (2015) published a workbook designed to make civic learning a standard part of the curriculum in a variety of disciplines.

Civic Professionalism

Boyte and Fretz (2011) argued the fundamental purpose of the current movement of engagement in higher education is to prepare "civic professionals" (p. 84) who will realize the public purpose of higher education to empower community partners with a sense of agency. They insist this elevates creating new courses, programs, and publications on civic engagement to a practice of infusing civic skills, such as community organizing, in disciplinary professional preparation programs. The Public Achievement program in the Center for Democracy and Leadership at Augsburg College has been working with departments and programs around the country and the world to bring democratic purpose to classrooms, workplaces, and communities. For example, Public Achievement has collaborated with the Department of Special Education at Augsburg College to integrate public and civic engagement skills into its teacher preparation program (D. Donovan, personal communication, June 23, 2015).

Social Justice

Social justice is another term in this lexicon worthy of note as it is embedded in the mission of some institutions and vehemently avoided at others. Some consider the term to have religious or political advocacy connotations that should not be included in the mission of a public institution. Others view social justice as a form of liberal partisan politics. The Center for Economic and Social Justice (CESJ, 2015) defines *social justice* as

> the virtue which guides us in creating those organized human interactions we call institutions. In turn, social institutions, when justly organized, provide us with access to what is good for the person, both individually and in our associations with others. Social justice also imposes on each of us a personal responsibility to work with others to design and continually perfect our institutions as tools for personal and social development.

Social justice has been described as being simultaneously a goal, a process, and a stance (Grant & Agosto, 2008; Ness, George, Turner, & Bolgatz, 2010). As a goal it means pursuing equal opportunity and outcomes for everyone. Social justice is also a process of addressing injustice by confronting and dismantling oppressive structures and systems as well as respecting the identities of specific groups and their values. As a stance it means recognizing the need for and pursuing change. Pitzer College, an independent liberal arts college with no religious affiliation, includes social justice as an umbrella concept in its mission. Under this umbrella fall five core values that reflect a commitment to community engagement: social responsibility, intercultural understanding, interdisciplinary learning, student engagement, and environmental sustainability. Social justice is common in the missions of many faith-based institutions. Johnson and O'Grady (2006) describe in great detail how service-learning and social justice are linked at Gustavus Adolphus College, a Lutheran liberal arts college. Likewise, many historically Black colleges and universities (HBCUs) have a long history and tradition of including social justice as a concept in their community engagement mission. Some public institutions also incorporate social justice under the broader rubric of engagement.

Scholarship of Engagement

Scholarship is a purposeful and rigorous set of steps and procedures that incorporate sound and theoretically based standards in the pursuit and creation of knowledge (Cox, 2010; Diamond & Adam, 1993; Glassick et al., 1997). The term *scholarship of engagement* is widely attributed to Ernest Boyer. Interestingly, Boyer (1990) did not actually use that term in his landmark book *Scholarship Reconsidered: Priorities of the Professoriate*, in which he proposed and described four types of scholarship. Rather, Boyer appears to have introduced scholarship of engagement as an overarching umbrella for his four types of scholarship in 1997 during a keynote address at the American Academy of Arts and Sciences:

> The academy must become a more vigorous partner in the search for answers to our most pressing social, civic, economic, and moral problems, and must reaffirm its historic commitment to what I have chosen to call, this evening, the scholarship of engagement. (Boyer, 1997, pp. 81–82)

Boyer noted that the scholarship of discovery and the scholarship of integration reflected higher education's traditional notion of research. The scholarship of application, on the other hand, explores ways knowledge can be applied to problems, and the scholarship of teaching is an active, transformative educational experience for students rather than a passive means of receiving information. The scholarship of application is broadly framed as engaged scholarship, and the scholarship of teaching is presented as engaged pedagogy. Boyer noted that the scholarship of application is directly tied to a scholarly discipline, unlike simply doing "good work" or service in the community. Adding to the semantic confusion is the fact that Boyer's depiction of scholarship has been interpreted by many to more accurately characterize research rather than scholarship.

Engaged Scholarship

Engaged scholarship should not be confused with other active, participatory types of scholarly inquiry, such as anthropology or ethnography, as the latter embody a positivist, unilateral activity with a primary focus on making scholarly contributions to a disciplinary body of knowledge. Instead, in this context, engagement involves activities benefiting society that are integrated into academics in order to generate new knowledge and educate. This characterization reflects the democratic spirit of the engaged scholarship movement described by Saltmarsh (2010). Therefore, engaged scholarship may be thought of as teaching or research that incorporates the rich knowledge and resources of higher education to address social and community needs through Boyer's scholarship of application and scholarship of teaching. Furco (2005) argued that engaged scholarship is a form of research and teaching that integrates academic work in addressing community needs and challenges:

> Engaged scholarship research is done with, rather than for or on, a community—an important distinction. The research produces knowledge that is beneficial to the discipline as well as the community. Engagement creates a porous and interactive relationship between the academy and the community. The advantage to the community is that research draws upon community knowledge, reflects their concerns better, and ultimately yields a practical benefit. The benefit to the academy is that research agendas and methodologies are broadened to include critical questions that cannot be addressed without community engagement. (p. 10)

In this sense engaged scholarship is a democratic activity and principle that cocreates and applies knowledge in both the classroom and the community.

Similarly, Holland (2005b) defined *engaged scholarship* as

> faculty work that connects the intellectual assets of the institution to public issues such as community, social, cultural, human, and economic development. Through engaged forms of teaching and research, faculty apply their academic expertise to public purposes, as a way of contributing to the fulfillment of the core mission of the institution.

Likewise, Simon (2011) proposed that engaged scholarship

> continually pushes the boundaries of understanding; that is at the frontier of relevancy, innovation, and creativity; that is organized and openly communicated to build capacity for innovation and creativity; that creates

energy, synergy, and community independence to assess projects and processes, providing a reason and a capacity to gain new knowledge; and that is
accessible across the chasms of geographic boundaries and socio-economic
situations. (p. 115)

Community-based research (CBR) is a form of engaged scholarship. Heavily influenced by Lewin's (1946) action research model, CBR is
based on three principles: it is a collaborative scholarly endeavor conducted
by professors, students, and community members; it democratizes public
knowledge by validating multiple methods of discovery and dissemination
of knowledge; and it is aimed at social action and change to achieve and
promote social justice (Strand, Marullo, Cutforth, Stoecker, & Donohue,
2003). It is a legitimate form of research that incorporates questions derived
collaboratively by the researcher and community partner. The methodology
is codesigned and conducted in the partnership using theoretically based
and valid methods that can include traditional positivist methods as well as
critical methods. The beneficiaries of the results are both the researcher who
disseminates the new knowledge in scholarly venues and the community
as a whole through policy or program development (Paul, 2009). Beyond
a dyadic relationship of researcher and community partner, CBR can also
be used in a course with students as a form of engaged pedagogy through
service-learning, as described in a later chapter.

Scholarship on Engagement

Conversely, the scholarship *on* engagement is the scientific and disciplinary study of engaged pedagogy that makes a contribution to the field as a
whole. This is a burgeoning field in and of itself, as evidenced by the growing
body of literature in journals such as the *Michigan Journal of Community
Service Learning* and professional conferences such as the one sponsored by
IARSLCE. A growing number of researchers are studying the field of engagement and engaged pedagogy with a variety of sound scientific methods. These
researchers are not "doing" engagement research with community partners
to answer research questions per se nor are they designing and implementing
service-learning courses in community settings. Instead, they are researching
and contributing to the body of knowledge around this work conducted by
practitioners.

Engaged Pedagogy

Broadly speaking, pedagogy refers to student-centered methods of teaching
and learning. The term *engaged pedagogy* is used here to describe various

approaches of teaching and learning that reflect the basic tenets of engagement enumerated previously, typically, but not always, in community settings. In this context pedagogy is reframed as engaged teaching that integrates structured academic activities for students in community settings to avoid the instructor being the sole expert and to promote a reflective teaching that shifts the model of education from "banking" (p. 58) to "dialogue" (p. 75) to use Freire's terminology (Freire, 1970; Saltmarsh, 1996). In this way faculty members no longer make "academic deposits" of their expertise into the minds of their students as passive repositories of knowledge. Instead, educators and students exchange ideas through discourse and action in both the classroom and the community.

Common methods of engaged pedagogy include service-learning, CBR, and other high-impact practices described later. Engaged pedagogy is not, however, limited to credit-bearing courses. It can also occur in cocurricular experiences through volunteer service and a variety of established non-credit-bearing programs (Hoy & Meisel, 2008). Furco (1996) identified five engaged pedagogical approaches: volunteerism, community service, internships, fieldwork, and service-learning.

Cocurricular approaches to engagement are generally characterized as voluntary, non-credit-bearing experiences that are mutually beneficial to the student and to agencies and those they serve. Thus, cocurricular engagement programs are intentionally designed to promote students' civic growth. Although not directly tied to courses' formal learning objectives, these activities certainly afford learning opportunities. Unlike traditional extracurricular activities that tend to be recreational in nature, cocurricular programs often entail supervision and oversight by a professional staff person, often housed in campus centers of community engagement.

Engaged pedagogy can also occur through curricular programs, which are experiences and opportunities tied to formal learning objectives, typically associated with credit-bearing courses. These programs often involve the oversight and coordination of a faculty member, thus making them a form of engaged scholarship as described previously. Kuh (2008) has characterized most engaged curricular programming as a high-impact practice owing to the pedagogical significance each approach can have in students' civic learning experience. Many of these programs, including service-learning, community-based learning, undergraduate research, internships, first-year experiences, learning communities, diversity/global learning, and capstone courses (described in detail in chapter 6), lend themselves well to civic engagement. In sum engaged pedagogy entails a partnership working with the community that facilitates socially constructed and cocreated knowledge that is antithetical to the traditional epistemology of expert knowledge (Saltmarsh, 2010).

Partnerships

Beere (2009) noted while definitions of *partnership* can vary, the term typically denotes three key elements: the involvement of two or more individuals or groups, a relationship shaped by mutuality, and a commitment to a common purpose or goal. The Carnegie Foundation defined *partnerships* as "collaborative interactions with community and related scholarship for the mutually beneficial exchange, exploration, and application of knowledge, information, and resources" (Driscoll, 2009, p. 6)

Partnership Versus Placement

Pearson (2002) raised concerns over the true meaning of "community partners" as opposed to the predominant practice of "community placements." She suggested that if one looks at any form of partnership, business or personal, one observes a particular and unique set of behaviors and activities. This set might include ongoing face-to-face conversations, a shared plan, shared resources, and sustained communication. In the context of community engagement, the notion and practice of partnership are contrasted with higher education's traditional "placement" approach, in which students are placed at sites. Higher education has long recognized the value of learning experiences in authentic settings, where students are provided hands-on opportunities in the real world. These practices reflect experiential education. As pedagogically valuable as this approach might be for students, it can often be at the expense of community partners and agencies, sometimes with little to no benefit to them. Consequently, experiential education, such as student teaching, can be confused and coupled with engaged pedagogy; therefore, it is equally important to understand what is not community engagement.

Experiential Education

The purpose, philosophy, structure, and resources associated with the methods discussed in the previous sections are substantively different in spirit from the traditional approaches of experiential education. Furco (1996) acknowledged the similarities service-learning shares with other forms of experiential education but noted differences by placing these approaches on a continuum, with internships and practicums on one end, career development and volunteer service on the other end, and service-learning in the middle (see Table 2.1). Service-learning includes a focus on civic education that sets it apart from the other two ends of the continuum.

In some ways these formats require infrastructure, resources, and coordination similar to civic and community engagement, but these necessities are often provided by disciplinary programs rather than campus centers for

TABLE 2.1

Conceptualizing the Evolution of Engaged Pedagogy and Scholarship

Conceptual framework	Experiential education	Professional preparation	Community involvement	Civic/community engagement
Who	Working in . . . Undergraduate students	Working to . . . Preprofessionals (teachers, social workers, counselors, health care providers)	Working for . . . Students, faculty, and community partners	Working with . . . Citizen-students, citizen-scholars, and community partners
What	Student-centered learning	Student-centered assimilating and demonstrating mastery of specific skills	Working to address community issues while learning and teaching	Empowering community, educating students, and contributing new knowledge
Where	Labs and authentic settings	Clinical and authentic settings	Community settings and anchor institutions	Community settings and anchor institutions
When	Semester(s)	Semesters throughout academic year	Academic year or summer	Academic year or summer
Why	Earn a degree	Earn a license, certificate, or credential and a degree	Promote common good while meeting educational goals and earn a degree	Promote agency, develop citizen professionals, create, earn a degree, and disseminate new knowledge
How	Curriculum or objectives defined and outlined by expert faculty for students to experience	Supervised practicums/clinicals in authentic settings and internships for students to practice professional skills	Service-learning, CBR, immersion experiences, and internships through place-based education	Democratic cocreation of goals, content, process based on sound theory; community organizing; knowledge base

engagement. For example, rarely are campus community centers responsible for coordinating preprofessional fieldwork for students majoring in professional programs. Instead, this fieldwork is coordinated by staff in the disciplinary department program working with counterparts at training sites such as school districts or clinics. And although there is often indirect or direct but delayed benefit to the community, the focus of these experiential education formats is unilateral rather than reciprocal (i.e., students are the primary beneficiary of the experience).

While an effective and valuable form of experiential education, the placement model tends to be student-centric in that students are preprofessionals who are gaining practical experience and opportunities to apply and demonstrate mastery of specific information and skills associated with a career. Typically, professional accreditation bodies or state licensure agencies mandate possession of a particular skill set that must be mastered by students in an authentic setting monitored by faculty members or on-site supervisors. These approaches are commonly implemented in professional preparation programs in fields such as counseling, education, nursing, pharmacy, and social work. Thus, preprofessional placement typically does not embody the fundamental principle of using knowledge to address social issues through the reciprocity of partnerships found in community engagement.

Practicums, or field placements, are learning experiences in which students practice professional skills they will use in their careers. Practicums are common in teacher education programs in which students may spend time in classrooms practicing specific skills and that culminate in a capstone experience, such as student teaching. Similarly, *clinicals* are experiential education opportunities in that preprofessionals in health professions practice their newly assimilated skills in clinical settings with actual patients.

Internships are unique in that they could, in some ways, reflect the key components and principles of community engagement. O'Neill (2010) reported that a literature or Web search of the term *internship* returned more than 14 million results. However, for the most part internships, like practicums and clinicals, usually focus on career development rather than on the civic dimensions described previously. The National Association of Colleges and Employers (NACE, 2015) defines an *internship* as

> a form of experiential learning that integrates knowledge and theory learned in the classroom with practical application and skills development in a professional setting. Internships give students the opportunity to gain valuable applied experience and make connections in professional fields they are considering for career paths; and give employers the opportunity to guide and evaluate talent.

However, O'Neill (2010) goes on to suggest that internships can and do reflect high-impact practice related to community engagement. These internships must be intentionally designed to meet specific learning objectives and career goals. In addition, specific pedagogical practice, such as reflection, should be included, and benefits to the cooperating agency should be pursued. A robust internship experience incorporating tenets of community engagement should include (a) learning objectives; (b) ongoing and regular oversight by an educator or staff member from the campus center for engagement and someone with authority at the community agency; and (c) academic exercises, such as readings, reflective journals, papers, or seminars, coordinated by an educator at the institution.

Table 2.2 compares community and civic engagement with other traditional forms of experiential education designed for professional preparation.

The principle of partnership is in stark contrast to higher education's traditional expert approach of using venues in the community as "learning laboratories" or "placements" where students and faculty members are usually the sole beneficiaries of the experience. Saltmarsh (2010) compares and contrasts the expert-centered framework with the democratic-centered framework of engaged teaching and scholarship (see Table 2.3).

It is important to note that this paradigm shift does not dismiss or eschew expertise. Levine (2007) reminds us of the inherent value of scholarly expertise that has resulted in significant advances in health, economics, and engineering (to name a few) that have improved the overall quality of life. Saltmarsh and Hartley (2011) acknowledge that community agencies and those they serve invite and seek academic expertise through community-campus partnerships. They caution, however, that the process should be exercised democratically through parity and mutuality in cocreating knowledge that is mutually beneficial rather than solely for the professional advancement of scholars and students.

Engaged Epistemology

Epistemology is defined as a theory of knowledge leading to a way of knowing or justified belief (Steup, 2005). The dominant framework of epistemology in higher education (see Figure 2.1) can be characterized as a discipline-based expert model that creates technocratic specializations (Saltmarsh & Hartley, 2011).

An alternative paradigm of an engaged epistemology does not exclude or preclude scholarly knowledge but instead includes reciprocity in the generation of knowledge through an interplay and exchange of relationships that allow faculty members, researchers, students, and civic leaders to experiment,

TABLE 2.2

Community Engagement Versus Other Forms of Experiential Education

Community or civic engagement	Field placements/practicums/internships in professional preparation
Community engagement is "the collaboration between institutions of higher education and their larger communities (local, regional/state, national, global) for the mutually beneficial exchange of knowledge and resources in a context of partnership and reciprocity" (Carnegie Foundation for the Advancement of Teaching, 2012).	**American Psychological Association (APA)** "Internships are required to become a licensed psychologist and can give students an invaluable experience. Accredited internships provide high-quality training in clinical practice and specialties" (APA, 2016).
Civic engagement is an academically based activity that relates to an issue, problem, or organization off campus (Saltmarsh, Hartley, & Clayton, 2009). *Civic engagement* is "working to make a difference in the civic life of our communities and developing the combination of knowledge, skills, values, and motivation to make that difference" (Ehrlich, 2000, p. vi).	**National Council for Accreditation of Teacher Education (NCATE)** "**Clinical Practice.** Student teaching or internships that provide candidates with an intensive and extensive culminating activity. Candidates are immersed in the learning community and are provided opportunities to develop and demonstrate competence in the professional roles for which they are preparing. . . . **Field Experiences.** A variety of early and ongoing field-based opportunities in which candidates may observe, assist, tutor, instruct, and/or conduct research. Field experiences may occur in off-campus settings such as schools, community centers, or homeless shelters. . . . **Internship.** Generally, the post-licensure and/or graduate clinical practice under the supervision of clinical faculty; sometimes refers to the pre-service clinical experience. . . . **Student Teaching.** Pre-service clinical practice in P–12 schools for candidates preparing to teach" (NCATE, 2016; emphasis in original).
"Community engagement encompasses activities that are tied to the institution's mission to generate transmit, apply, and preserve knowledge and that are for the direct benefit of external audiences. . . . The primary responsibility and focus of colleges and universities is to make their intellectual resources available to communities in ways that are consistent with their education purpose" (Votruba, 1996, p. 31).	

Community or civic engagement	Field placements/practicums/internships in professional preparation
"Civic engagement has become the rubric under which faculty, administrators, and students think about, argue about and attempt to implement a variety of visions of higher education in service to society. . . . There is near consensus that an essential part of civic engagement is feeling responsible to part of something beyond individual interests" (Lawry, Laurison, & Van Antwepren, 2006, pp. 12–13). "Public engagement as a core value will yield benefits to all concerned. For community and regional entities, engagement with colleges and universities • Expands resources available to tackle local issues and problems; • Promotes local solutions to local challenges; • Offers the potential of 'neutral ground' for discussion and resolution of controversial issues; and • Provides an opportunity to address short- and long-term priorities and concerns with a key constituency" (AASCU, 2002, p. 9).	**Council on Social Work Education Commission on Educational Policy 2.2—Signature Pedagogy: Field Education** "Field education is the signature pedagogy for social work. The intent of field education is to integrate the theoretical and conceptual contribution of the classroom with the practical world of the practice setting. It is a basic precept of social work education that the two interrelated components of curriculum—classroom and field—are of equal importance within the curriculum, and each contributes to the development of the requisite competencies of professional practice. Field education is systematically designed, supervised, coordinated, and evaluated based on criteria by which students demonstrate the Social Work Competencies" (CSWE, 2016). **National Association of Colleges and Employers (NACE)** An internship is "a form of experiential learning that integrates knowledge and theory learned in the classroom with practical application and skills development in a professional setting. Internships give students the opportunity to gain valuable applied experience and make connections in professional fields they are considering for career paths; and give employers the opportunity to guide and evaluate talent" (NACE, 2015).

(Continues)

Table 2.2 (*Continued*)

Community or civic engagement	*Field placements/practicums/internships in professional preparation*
Civic engagement is "acting upon a heightened sense of responsibility to one's communities. This includes a wide range of activities, including developing civic sensitivity, participation in building civil society, and benefiting the common good. Civic engagement encompasses the notions of global citizenship and interdependence. Through civic engagement, individuals—as citizens of their communities, their nations, and the world— are empowered as agents of positive social change for a more democratic world" (Jacoby, 2009, p. 9)	**Commission on Collegiate Nursing Education** "III-E. The curriculum includes planned *clinical practice experiences* that: a) enable a student to integrate new knowledge and demonstrate attainment of program outcomes; and b) are evaluated by faculty. Elaboration: To prepare students for a practice profession, each track in each degree program and post-graduate APRN certificate program affords students the opportunity to develop professional competencies in practice settings aligned to the educational preparation. Clinical practice experiences are provided for students in all programs, including those with distance education offerings. Clinical practice experiences involve activities that are designed to ensure students are competent to enter nursing practice" (CCNE, 2013; emphasis in original).

TABLE 2.3
Expert-Centered Versus Democratic-Centered Engagement

Characteristic	*Expert-centered*	*Democratic-centered*
Community relationships	Partnership and mutuality	Reciprocity
	Deficit-based understanding of community	Asset-based understanding of community
	Academic work done *for* the public	Academic work done *with* the public
Knowledge production and research	Applied	Inclusive, collaborative, problem/goal-oriented
	Unidirectional flow of knowledge	Multidirectional flow of knowledge
Epistemology	Positivist/scientific and technocratic	Relational, localized, contextual
	Distinction between knowledge producers and knowledge consumers	Cocreation of knowledge
	Primacy of academic knowledge	Shared authority for knowledge creation
	University as the center for public problem-solving	University as part of an ecosystem of knowledge production for addressing public problems
Political dimension	Apolitical engagement	Facilitating an inclusive, collaborative, and deliberative democracy

Note. Adapted from "Changing Pedagogies," by J. Saltmarsh, 2010, in H. E. Fitzgerald, C. Burack, & S. D. Seifer (Eds.), *Handbook of Engaged Scholarship: Contemporary Landscapes, Future Directions* (pp. 331–352), East Lansing, MI: Michigan State University Press.

discover, and learn while developing and applying democratic principles and values (Hoyt, 2011). It also encourages faculty members to shift from a traditional perception and practice of separating research, teaching, and service to an integration of the three (see Figure 2.2).

Engaged Campus

Ramaley (2010) wrote that Russ Edgerton was one of the first scholars to use the term *engaged campus* when he made it the theme of the annual conference of the American Association of Higher Education in 1995. Four years

Figure 2.1 Dominant framework of epistemology in higher education.

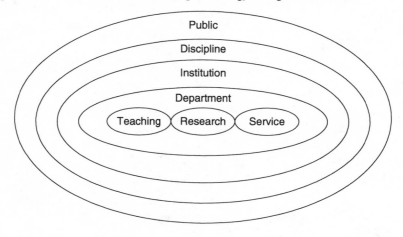

Figure 2.2 Alternative paradigm of engaged epistemology.

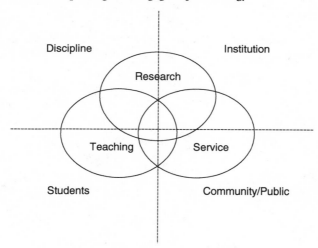

later, the Kellogg Commission (1999) published *Returning to Our Roots: The Engaged Institution*, which proposed that the engaged institution accomplish at least three things:

1. It must be organized to respond to the needs of today's students and tomorrow's, not yesterday's.
2. It must enrich students' experiences by bringing research and engagement into the curriculum and offering practical opportunities for students to prepare for the world they will enter.

3. It must put its critical resources (knowledge and expertise) to work on the problems the communities it serves face. (p. 10)

The report also presented the following seven guiding characteristics of an engaged institution:

1. Responsiveness to the communities, regions, and states the institution serves through communication and providing resources to address public issues.
2. Respect for skill and expertise of partners in collaborative efforts.
3. Academic neutrality in providing resources and expertise when public policy is at stake.
4. Accessibility of resources and expertise to all constituencies.
5. Integration of the service mission of an institution with teaching and research.
6. Coordination of service activities to ensure productivity.
7. Resource commitment to partners in pursuit of collaborative goals. (p. 12)

Ramaley (2000) differentiated the practices of an engaged campus from the traditional one-way approaches and practices of professional service and outreach that transfer knowledge only from the university to the community. She described an engaged campus as sharing goals, agendas, definitions of success, and to a degree, financial resources with the community in order to build capacity and competence for both stakeholders. Walshok (1999) argued that the view of the institution as citizen must be at the heart of our understanding of an engaged campus. She went on to suggest that to become an engaged campus an entire institution must become actively involved in economic, social, and civic issues by integrating research and teaching agendas with community agendas through dialogue and consensus building to enhance the lives of students, faculty members, and individuals in the community.

An engaged campus is an institution that intentionally uses its resources to meet the community needs (Ward & Moore, 2010). The AASCU (2002) characterized a community-engaged campus as "fully committed to direct, two-way interaction with communities and other external constituencies through the development, exchange, and application of knowledge, information, and expertise for mutual benefit" (p. 9). Stanton (2007) wrote that highly engaged institutions (a) believe in and practice improving life in the community as a pathway to excellence in the academic trilogy; (b) seek and nurture shared tasks of teaching, research, and service with the community; (c) work with community agencies to design partnerships; (d) encourage and reward CBR and engaged pedagogy; (e) provide an array of curricular and cocurricular opportunities to develop civic knowledge, skills, and habits; and (f) have leaders who articulate and integrate the civic and public missions throughout the institution through infrastructure and policies.

By examining the specific application components for the elective community engagement classification, one can surmise how the Carnegie Foundation conceptualizes an engaged campus. Applicants must demonstrate that their institution has implemented a variety of structures, polices, and programs. Welch and Saltmarsh (2013a, 2013b) sorted those components into five broad categories: institutional architecture and policy that support community engagement, campus center infrastructure to coordinate community engagement, campus center engagement programs for students, campus center engagement programs for faculty members, and campus center engagement programs for community partners. Institutional architecture includes formal and public statements of commitment to community engagement as well as budgets specifically allocated to programs for students, faculty members, and community partners. Official language and operational procedures that explicitly define principles and programs also make up institutional architecture. Becoming an engaged institution also involves cultural change within the institution. Financial resources must be made available. Physical space and adequate professional staff must be provided, typically in and through a campus center charged with campus-wide coordination of engagement activities or collaboration with other offices. These professionals develop and coordinate programs that support students, faculty members, and community partners.

The Engaged Cornell program provides an example of how these components are combined and incorporated. In cooperation with the Einhorn Family Charitable Trust, Cornell University established the program to integrate and create new community-teaching and research initiatives. As part of the program, the university established the Public Engagement Council, which includes one faculty member from each college on the Ithaca campus to oversee and coordinate efforts aligned with the institution's strategic goal of "excellence in public engagement" (www.cornell.edu/strategicplan/objectives.cfm). Other members of the committee include faculty already working with and interested in community-engaged scholarship and representatives from other units on campus, such as the Mario Einaudi Center for International Studies, Cornell Cooperative Extension, the Public Service Center, Engaged Learning + Research, and Entrepreneurship@Cornell. The council also reviews and discusses all Engaged Curriculum Grant proposals.

Summary

In examining the many definitions and methods of *engagement*, two key principles emerge. The first principle is related to Ernest Boyer's concept of the academy as citizen in which the academic experience includes yet transcends the traditional role of creating and disseminating new knowledge for a scholarly discipline to apply these intellectual and academic resources for the good of the community. Boyer served as the president of the Carnegie Foundation for the Advancement of Teaching and proposed that

> the scholarship of engagement means connecting the rich resources of the university to our most pressing social, civic, and ethic problems. . . . Campuses should be viewed by both students and professors not as isolated islands, but as staging grounds for action. (Boyer, 1996, p. 21)

Ward and Moore (2010) suggested the key element of engagement is the resources generated from teaching, research, and service that are used to address social issues outside the academy. They noted common threads of utility, democratization, access, and applied knowledge.

The second principle is the reciprocity of partnerships. Parity and respect are required to cocreate knowledge and resources for the mutual benefit of the academy and the community. Where, how, and among whom the engaged experiences occur vary as well, yet it appears more and more campus centers for community engagement continue to coordinate some aspects of these activities. This chapter provided an overview of definitions and descriptions of *community* and *civic engagement* as well as some of the many formats they can take for two main groups of stakeholders: faculty members and students.

PART TWO

PLATFORMS

Platform [plat-ˌform] *noun*

: a vehicle (as a satellite or aircraft) or structure used for a particular purpose or to carry a usually specified kind of equipment

: in computer science, the system in which a computer operates and which determines the programs that it can use

—Merriam-Webster, 2016

3

INSTITUTIONALIZING
COMMUNITY ENGAGEMENT

We owe it to the public to demonstrate that we are thinking through new ways of doing our work in partnership with each other and with other organizations. Colleges and universities are organized on outdated models. How do we imagine new ways of working together and creating more fluid boundaries, both within the campus and with other organizations outside the campus?

—Paul Pribbenow (2012, p. 28)

Boland (2012) wrote that institutionalizing and sustaining community engagement rely on several factors, such as philosophical and cultural commitment, institutional policies, and reward structures that reinforce meaningful efforts with community partners. However, results from a 2014 survey by Campus Compact suggest limited evidence of these factors in actual practice. Data gathered from 434 institutional members revealed that only 20% of institutions included community engagement in their mission statement and another 20% included curricular and cocurricular community engagement in strategic plans. Likewise, only 14% of the responding institutions reported faculty rewards for teaching service-learning and conducting community-based research (CBR) in the promotion and tenure review process. Finally, only 9% reported that searching and recruiting procedures for faculty members encourage community engagement. These data suggest that despite the rhetoric, most public and private institutions of higher education have yet to make philosophical or organizational commitments to support community engagement.

Institutionalization of community engagement is a complex four-way process involving cultural factors, systemic factors, support from institutional leadership, and support from all stakeholders, including community partners. Cultural factors include sociological factors, such as race, ethnicity, socioeconomic conditions, and gender, as well as institutional and organizational values, beliefs, roles, and responsibilities. Institutions of higher education and community organizations may have conflicting cultural elements, but to institutionalize community engagement, colleges and universities must make an effort to understand, respect, and work with the differing cultures of their community partners. Every institution of higher education and community organization also comprises structural systems that serve as platforms through which their missions are realized. Systems consist of human, financial, physical, operational, and information resources. Further, institutionalization requires a combination of top-down and bottom-up support. Formal leaders, such as presidents, and informal leaders, such as faculty champions on campus, must articulate the value of engagement as an integral part of the institution's mission and culture (Beere, Votruba, & Wells, 2011; Sandmann & Plater, 2009).

Etienne (2012) summarized three additional essentials for institutionalizing community engagement: long-term sustained leadership, substantial infrastructure, and widespread sense of self-interest. Curiously, his third essential may initially seem to contradict the underlying public purpose of higher education. Yet at a pragmatic level, he argued, self-interest is in the best interest of higher education's pursuit of knowledge, learning, and democracy building for a number of reasons. First, it helps facilitate the roles and responsibilities of the new engaged professoriate entering the academy who likely experienced some form of community engagement as students themselves. Second, it helps to be engaged in the overall well-being of the community as the academy is indeed part of the community and a beneficiary of the community's growth. Third, engagement advances not only the scholarship of engaged faculty members but also their research and the overall prestige of the institution as a committed partner.

Given the complexity of the process, there is no single way to institutionalize community engagement in higher education (Jacoby & Hollander, 2009; McRae, 2015). However, models for institutionalizing service-learning have emerged over the past two decades and appear to be applicable to the broader context of community engagement (Jacoby & Hollander, 2009). Institutionalization of engagement does not occur overnight, but a review of the literature suggests a general combination of steps occur.

All of the forces shown in Figure 3.1 can be considered institutionalization compass points that influence and guide the institutionalization process. Moving clockwise from the top of the figure, this chapter takes a closer look at each of the four compass points and their related functions and tools. While there is no particular starting point in the process, it is important that each aspect is addressed. The institutionalization process ultimately leads to

Figure 3.1 Institutionalization compass points.

TOP-DOWN INFLUENTIAL FACTORS
Mission Statements
Campus President Statements
State Government Mandates

Guiding Principles

Readiness Assessment
Strategic Plans

CULTURAL FACTORS

Shared Roles, Responsibilities, Expertise, & Knowledge

Institutionalization

SYSTEMIC FACTORS

Infrastructure
Hiring & Recruitment
Promotion & Tenure Policy

Collective Leadership
+
Intercultural Humility & Competency

Action Plans

BOTTOM-UP INFLUENTIAL FACTORS
Faculty Initiatives
Student Initiatives
Community Partner Initiatives
Trust Building

establishing organizational platforms to develop and coordinate programs, as described in later chapters.

Top-Down Influential Factors

Plater (2011) maintained that the power and influence of administrative leaders cannot be underestimated. Midlevel administrators and faculty members look to the president and the chief academic officer (CAO) to set the course of the institution. Once leadership has set an institutional course, whether for community engagement or any other initiative, few presidents actually work to establish the infrastructure to put those initiatives into place. Equally important, although not as visible, are the influence and support of external leaders, such as trustees and alumni, because they in turn can influence the institutional leadership (Plater, 2011). Beere and colleagues (2011) noted that support from leadership must include institutional governing boards of regents and trustees as well as midlevel administrators, such as deans. That said, leadership must not only talk the talk but also walk the walk by approving and allocating adequate organizational and systemic resources to create infrastructural platforms that will support and integrate community engagement into the fabric of the institution.

The application process for the Carnegie Classification requires documentation that community engagement is included in administrators' public messages—that is, that campus leaders essentially put their money where their mouth is. Research on administrators' written and oral statements articulating their institutional commitment to engagement reveals consistent themes and content, including (a) institutional accomplishments, (b) the public contract between the campus and community, (c) political and operational challenges within higher education, and (d) contribution to economic and community development (Ronning, Keeney, & Sanford, 2008; Sandmann & Plater, 2009). For example, in an essay articulating the public work of Augsburg College's institutional mission, President Paul Pribbenow (2012) argued,

> We owe it to the public to demonstrate that we are thinking through new ways of doing our work in partnership with each other and with other organizations. Colleges and universities are organized on outdated models. How do we imagine new ways of working together and creating more fluid boundaries, both within the campus and with other organizations outside the campus?—We fit experience into the students' coursework—internships, service learning, a whole variety of techniques—but it is all about learning. . . . That is why community engagement is among the most powerful learning experiences our students have. . . . The fundamental challenge is overcoming academic hubris; we have to get beyond our own arrogance. As we work to change our mindset, we begin to engage our neighbors differently because we engage them as fellow citizens and as potential members of our teaching and learning community. (pp. 27–28)

Mission Statements

As discussed in detail in chapter 2, community engagement must be a meaningful and intentional part of an institution's mission rather than a singular program operating in the margins. Every college and university articulates a mission based on the academic trilogy of research/scholarship, teaching, and service. Virtually all institutions include a statement pledging to create and disseminate new knowledge, teach students to become competent professionals and citizens, and provide disciplinary expertise to serve the community (Harkavy, 2004). Additionally, many faith-based institutions declare that their mission is to promote social justice and serve the marginalized.

A mission statement is more than a public relations sound bite. It reflects the institution's culture, guides its actions, and is a reference point for decision making and strategic planning. An authentic commitment to the public purpose of higher education through community engagement will appear in actions rather than in platitudes. The Carnegie Foundation (2008) enumerated some of these institutional actions as benchmarks in the application process to receive the community engagement classification. Among these actions is evidence of collaboration among and the inclusion of voices of faculty members, students, and community agencies. Collaboration is the manifestation of the cultural value of democratic inclusivity and requires bringing all stakeholders, including the constituents community organizations serve while planning and implementing community engagement programs, to the table for meaningful conversation.

Therefore, a prerequisite step to assessment and strategic planning is intentional review and consideration of the mission statement in the context of community engagement. This review can be accomplished through retreats or town hall meetings. Both involve campus leadership (CAOs), administrators (deans, center directors), staff, faculty leaders, students, and representatives of community organizations and their constituents.

Institutional Retreats

Institutional retreats are generally internal conversations for academics with administrators program directors, and key faculty or student leaders. Holding a retreat allows all the institutional stakeholders to set aside time from other important meetings to intentionally and critically review how the mission statement interfaces with community engagement. Equally important during this conversation is discussing what engagement means and looks like. As the previous chapter illustrated, engagement means different things to different people. To ascertain if an institutional mission statement reflects a commitment to *community engagement*, all stakeholders must have a shared understanding of the term. As the dialogue proceeds, midlevel administrators such as deans are likely to focus on and ask questions about logistics and infrastructure (Welch, Liese, Bergerson, & Stephenson, 2004). This is also an opportunity to introduce the public purpose of higher education, with which most academics grounded in their own discipline are unfamiliar.

Town Hall Meetings

There are two critically important factors to consider when hosting town hall meetings. The first is the physical location of the gathering. Ideally, the venue should be off-campus to demonstrate the institution's sincere intention to leave the proverbial ivory tower and physically be a part of the community. The second is copresence and meaningful participation of both institutional leadership and community leaders. Community members' presence not only is a gesture of commitment but also gives the community a voice.

During both retreats and town hall meetings, all participants are invited to ponder and articulate their understanding or expectations of the institutional mission. Distribute notecards and pens or poster board and markers so that participants can share their ideas in writing. Following this exercise, share the official mission statement with the participants so they can check their preconceived notions of the mission against the actual document.

The same procedure can be used to explore the meaning of community engagement. Again, the idea here is to activate prior knowledge, understanding, and preconceived ideas of what *engagement* is and then check it against the definitions and characterizations presented in chapter 2 of this book. This exercise can serve as a foundational step to collectively creating an institutional definition of community engagement that will be used throughout the institutionalization process.

State Government Mandates

Like the institutions themselves, some state governments are beginning to consider top-down mandates to promote community engagement. Seven states are currently working in partnership with the AAC&U to use the association's values rubric to move civic learning into the undergraduate education experience. In 2010 the Massachusetts Board of Higher Education created the Vision Project, with multiple goals designed to promote diversity and to better graduation rates, workforce preparation, retention, and students' civic skills. A study group created an implementation plan for all 29 public institutions of higher education in the state. The plan included student learning outcomes that reflect many of the key objectives suggested in *A Crucible Moment* (National Task Force on Civic Learning and Democratic Engagement, 2012), discussed in chapter 1. In 2014 a statewide plan for promoting civic learning in higher education was approved. The plan included four elements of civic learning: knowledge needed to be an active citizen in national and global contexts, intellectual skills, applied competencies and practical skills, and understanding of social and political values associated with democratic and civic institutions. The initiative also included a four-point action plan to reach its goals: attention to civic learning as a goal in campus strategic plans, facilitation and support for campus work in civic learning through conferences and meetings to share best practices and provision of funding for campus projects, development of new ways to measure and report students' civic learning outcomes, and collaboration with the Department of Elementary and Secondary Education to develop a cross-sector plan for civic learning from kindergarten through college. An evaluation matrix to assess implementation of the plan and student performance was also created (see Appendix A).

Readiness Assessment

Ward, Buglione, Giles, and Saltmarsh (2013) argued that the institution-alization process involves more than top-down and bottom-up support. It typically includes assessment of current programs and structures that promote community engagement. The assessment process usually includes or leads to institutional initiatives that formalize engagement by creating and implementing necessary infrastructural models. Initiatives are typically philosophical, cultural, and political proposals based on institutional mission and culture, designed to provide a rationale for institutionalization, often through pilot programs. This in turn leads to creating a strategic plan that articulates using and allocating formal systemic infrastructural platforms provided by the institution to support long-term and sustained programs for students, faculty members, and community partners.

Sponsler and Hartley (2013) enumerated five key questions that should be answered as a prerequisite step to readiness assessment in strategic planning:

1. How does the institutional mission statement express the civic mission of the institution? What institutional history can be used to shape the civic mission?
2. How do we define *community engagement*? What skills and values do we hope to provide students and graduates? How will our work strengthen the community?
3. Is the campus ethos for community engagement partial or pervasive? Who are key partners on campus and in the community to promote community engagement?
4. What programs already exist that we could build on? What areas could be enhanced through community engagement?
5. How do we measure student community engagement, and how do we measure impact on the community?

The collaborative framing of these questions is revealing as it invites both the institution and the community to constructively articulate their goals and aspirations, rather than employ a deficit-based framework focusing on issues or needs.

McRae (2015) wrote that many of the readiness assessment matrices and models developed two decades ago to institutionalize service-learning can be adapted and applied to institutionalize community engagement today. In addition to these models, the standards and benchmarks embedded in the Carnegie Classification for Community Engagement can also be used to guide campuses as they plan and develop community engagement programs (Welch & Saltmarsh, 2013b). Holland (1997) developed a matrix designed to help institutions plan, implement, and assess engagement initiatives using seven factors. Later, in pondering whether the Carnegie Classification will endure, Holland (2009) presented some useful benchmarks to assess the impact of the classification that could also be used to intentionally sustain institutionalization efforts. Furco (1999) developed a similar rubric, later revised in 2002, designed to identify, incorporate, and assess five components associated with service-learning through a developmental process from building a critical mass to sustaining institutionalization. Campus Compact identified and enumerated 12 characteristics of an engaged campus (Hollander, Saltmarsh, & Zlotkowski, 2001). Pigza and Troppe (2003) also generated a comprehensive list of nine indicators and mechanisms for enabling engagement. Driscoll (2009) described the Carnegie Foundation's process of creating the voluntary community engagement classification. She explained that the foundation's broad definition of *community engagement* was intended to provide great flexibility in conceptualizing and operationalizing community engagement. The Carnegie Foundation generated five indicators to guide the documentation and assessment process for awarding the designation. The components of each of these assessment matrices are summarized in Table 3.1. Any combination of these indicators could be used by institutions to consider, design, and provide the necessary components to establish and maintain community engagement on their campuses.

Systemic Factors

Infrastructure Platforms

A systems approach provides an infrastructural platform to consider existing and necessary resources for implementation and involves identification, attainment, and implementation of resources from each of the five domains.

1. Human: Administrators, adequate staff, advisory committees, executive directors of community organizations, and students
2. Information: Institutional mission statements, results from readiness assessment rubrics, technical skill training through professional development, policy
3. Financial: Institutional funds, grants, and donations that provide financial resources for salaries, benefits, and equipment managed through operational budgets

TABLE 3.1

Readiness Assessment Matrices and Rubrics

Holland (1997)	Furco (1999)	Hollander, Saltmarsh, & Zlotkowski (2001)	Pizza & Troppe (2003)	Driscoll (2009)
1. Mission	1. Philosophy and mission	1. Mission and purpose	1. Institutional mission	1. Engagement as an institutional priority
2. Promotion, tenure, and hiring	2. Faculty support and involvement	2. Administrative leadership	2. Internal and external points of access to institutional units	2. Administrative leadership and support
3. Organizational structure	3. Student support and involvement	3. External resource allocation	3. Cocurricular opportunities	3. Infrastructure
4. Student involvement	4. Community participation	4. Engaged disciplines, departments, and interdisciplinary work in the core of the institution	4. Curriculum infusion	4. Fiscal resources
5. Faculty involvement	5. Institutional support	5. Faculty roles and rewards of engaged scholarship in promotion and tenure review	5. Authentic community partnerships	5. Support for faculty conducting engaged pedagogy or research
6. Community involvement		6. Internal fiscal resources to establish and support programs	6. Faculty teaching, research, and service in balance	
7. Campus publications		7. Community voice in conceptualizing and implementing engagement	7. Identifying, collaborating, and capitalizing on engagement	
		8. Visible and easy access to offices and programs	8. Assessment and generation of knowledge related to engagement	
		9. Professional development for faculty	9. Administration and resource allocation	
		10. Cocurricular and curricular activities		
		11. Venues for public dialogue involving multiple stakeholders		
		12. Engaged pedagogy, scholarship, and epistemology that use community-based problem-solving in teaching and learning		

4. Operational: Asset maps and assessment rubrics; strategic plans; memos of understanding (MOUs); instructional technology such as phones, computers, and data management programs
5. Physical: Space on and off campus

A template for systems-based readiness assessment is provided in Appendix B.

Additionally, some basic components to institutionalization that reflect most of the system domains are included as benchmarks in the Carnegie Foundation's criteria for community engagement (Welch & Saltmarsh, 2013a, 2013b). These include central coordinating offices, reporting lines, administrators or directors, inclusion of community engagement in institutional strategic plans, official definitions of community engagement, and procedures for designating community engagement courses and activities.

Recruiting and Hiring Faculty Members

Institutional commitment is also demonstrated through the recruitment and hiring of faculty members. Announcements for faculty positions should clearly articulate the institution's commitment to community engagement and describe the expectations for faculty involvement in this type of engaged scholarship. Review and consideration of recruiting and hiring practices should reveal if the institution is looking forward to ensure a committed professoriate. The institution also communicates its engaged scholarship through its press releases, newsletters, alumni magazines, and website. Evidence of mission-driven efforts includes operationally defining *engagement* and the many formats engaged scholarship and pedagogy can take. This includes establishing benchmarks and criteria for designating courses and programs as specific methods and forms of community engagement to ensure consistent quality. Finally, the institution must establish and implement ways to assess and evaluate the impact of community engagement.

Promotion and Tenure Policy

Perhaps the single most important and often missing component necessary to advance community engagement is language to support this work in various institutional policies and procedures. Most paramount is the language of the promotion and tenure criteria in the institution's faculty reward structure. Research has consistently shown the most significant challenge to meaningful institutionalization of community engagement is the lack of reward structures (O'Meara, 2010). Conversely, recognizing and valuing faculty work in this area can be a catalyst for advancing community engagement. Values show themselves in policy and procedure documents. If this community engagement work is not valued, it is unlikely to be included in important policies and procedures, such as promotion and tenure review. Admittedly, this is a matter of shared governance on the part of faculty members. Formal and informal campus leaders must explore advocating for discussion and revisiting existing promotion and tenure criteria in ways that acknowledge this form of scholarship and teaching (O'Meara, 2010; Sturm, Eatman, Saltmarsh, & Bush, 2011).

Strategic Plans

A strategic plan guides action to meet specific goals and objectives. Unfortunately, strategic planning often becomes a tedious intellectual exercise that lacks well-conceived objectives and clarity in steps. Further, participants and stakeholders creating the document are sometimes lulled into thinking that creating the strategic plan is a goal in and of itself. In reality the creation of a strategic plan is merely the first step in an ongoing process that typically takes several years. As a result, the document is at risk of gathering dust on a shelf or becoming a doorstop. A strategic plan is a blueprint that must be used on a regular basis to guide the institution.

The University of Minnesota created its Office for Public Engagement in 2006. The office started work on its 10-point plan for advancing and institutionalizing public engagement in 2008 and finalized and updated this plan in 2012. The plan enumerates six overarching institutional goals: conducting research that addresses social issues; ensuring high-quality teaching; advancing curriculum to develop students as scholars, leaders, and engaged citizens; promoting interdisciplinary research and teaching; expanding the internationalization of the university through research, teaching, and service across the globe; and creating opportunities for students and faculty members to work in diverse, multicultural settings. Subsumed under this list is a comprehensive plan consisting of 10 broad objectives and steps for achieving these objectives (see Table 3.2). The entire plan can be seen in detail on the office's website (engagement.umn.edu). In addition to the 10-point plan, the office established the Public Engagement Council to serve in a consultative capacity as well as an executive body and steering committee to shape the university's agenda for public engagement and monitor the process of implementing the plan.

Suggested Templates for Strategic Plans

There is no specific format for strategic plans. However, most strategic plans incorporate the following basic components:

TABLE 3.2
10-Point Plan for Advancing and Institutionalizing Public Engagement at the University of Minnesota

1. Scholarly Value of Engagement

Develop, support, and implement strategic initiatives that raise the status and legitimacy of engaged scholarship in ways that advance the University of Minnesota as a top research university.

2. Accounting and Assessment

Establish a set of systems for accounting and assessing the broad range of engagement activities, programs, and initiatives across the university.

3. Student Experiences and Development

Institute strategies that promote a robust range of community engagement experiences that are academically integrated and incorporate high-quality practices.

4. Community Connections

Secure mutually beneficial partnerships between the university and businesses/industries, nonprofits, educational institutions, and governmental agencies at the local, regional, state, national, and global levels.

5. Cultivating and Supporting Campus Leaders

Institute initiatives that strengthen engagement leaders' capacities to further the institutionalization of engagement across the University of Minnesota.

6. Visibility and Value

Deepen system-wide understanding of the role engagement plays in advancing the university's research and teaching missions.

7. Program Alignment and Integration

Ensure the full integration of public engagement activities into the university's key institutional policies, priorities, and programs.

8. Internal Networking

Provide and support opportunities that bring together individuals and units from across the university to share expertise, cultivate new collaborations, and build alliances that enhance their individual and collective engagement work.

9. National and International Networking

Strengthen the university's participation as a key player in the leading national and international engagement networks.

10. Leverage Extramural Funds

Garner extramural funds that further the University of Minnesota's development as an engaged university.

Note. Adapted from *A Ten Point Plan for Advancing and Institutionalizing Public Engagement at the University of Minnesota*, by University of Minnesota Office of Public Engagement, 2012, Minneapolis, MN: Author. Retrieved from http://engagement.umn.edu/sites/default/files/10points_web.pdf

Mission Statement Preamble

A statement that articulates the institution's mission and reflects the institution's culture often serves as a foundation for the strategic planning process. In this way explicit and intentional language frames community engagement as an integral part of the institution, affording it relevance and credence. Planning committees and task forces are encouraged to adapt and include language from official documents to serve as a preamble to a strategic plan. Institutional missions are important but not enough. The strategic plan for engagement must include explicit statements that indicate the mission of engagement involves empowering the community.

Definition of Engagement

As noted earlier, it is helpful to have an institutional definition of *engagement*. At this point the planning team should wordsmith an institutional definition that reflects the campus culture and the professional literature.

Goals

Goals are desired outcomes, and they drive the strategic planning process. They serve as a target for engaged activities. Goal statements are generally broad but must be specific enough that it is clear when the goals have been met. That is, goals must be observable and measurable rather than philosophical. Strategic plans typically include multiple goals, each requiring its own action plan.

Action Plan

An action plan essentially stipulates who does what, when, and where (Sturm et al., 2011). It incorporates the five system domains that have been described throughout this chapter (see Appendix C). When working with others on a project, many professionals have heard or used the expression "being on the same page." An action plan is quite literally the manifestation of that euphemism. That is, an action plan consists of a series of steps and activities designed to meet a specific goal. Action plans include a time line, which is critical because colleges and universities typically operate on quarter or semester calendars that do not always sync with community partner calendars. Conflicting calendars create limited windows of time for the operation of projects and programs. Action plans must be reviewed and monitored on a regular basis.

Benchmarks and Indicators of Success

Finally, the strategic plan must include benchmarks as indicators of success. Benchmarks allow stakeholders to assess to what extent the plan met the goals and often include quantitative measures that indicate an increase or decrease of specific factors, products, or behaviors. Some benchmarks may evaluate the production of a specific product.

Westminster College and South Salt Lake City, Utah, embarked on an ambitious data-based partnership, known as Promise South Salt Lake, under the shared vision of the college president and the city mayor in cooperation with the local United Way program (South Salt Lake City, 2015; Westminster College, 2015). Representatives of the college, the city, and community agencies collectively created a concise strategic plan consisting of a mission statement, goals, an action plan, a resource list, community interactions, and indicators of success. Unlike most traditional strategic plans, which can often be complex and lengthy, this partnership between the community and college incorporated a succinct, user-friendly visual format for a summary document (see Figure 3.2). The program is driven by three broad "promises" to the community: that every child has the opportunity to attend and graduate from college; that every resident has a safe, clean home and neighborhood; and that every resident has the opportunity to be healthy and to prosper. Each goal involves its own more detailed action plan (see Table 3.3). The program uses 10 existing sites in the community, including community centers and schools, to deliver a variety of curricular and cocurricular programs co-coordinated by city employees, college faculty members, and their students.

Bottom-Up Influential Factors

There has to be buy-in from stakeholders and individuals who are expected to implement community engagement. Faculty members must see and understand the role of engagement in the context of their research, teaching, and service, and they must know it will be valued and rewarded within the promotion and tenure system. In fact, Hollister (2014) suggested avoiding the "third mission trap" (p. 52) of viewing community engagement as the public mission of higher education. He argued it is much more strategic to reframe efforts for institutionalizing community engagement as a pathway to a higher quality of teaching, learning, and scholarship. One way to do this is to concentrate on promoting faculty leadership by implementing faculty fellowships to pursue community-based teaching and research.

Students must come to recognize engagement as both an effective pedagogy that will enhance their learning and a way to develop a meaningful personal, civic, and professional life to learn "how the world works and the confidence to put that knowledge into practice throughout their lives" (Purce, 2014, p. 14). Students must rely on adequate and professional resources to ensure quality educational experiences based on sound theoretical principles and practice. If community engagement is haphazardly implemented, students will quickly perceive it as a perfunctory requirement on the

Figure 3.2 Summary document.

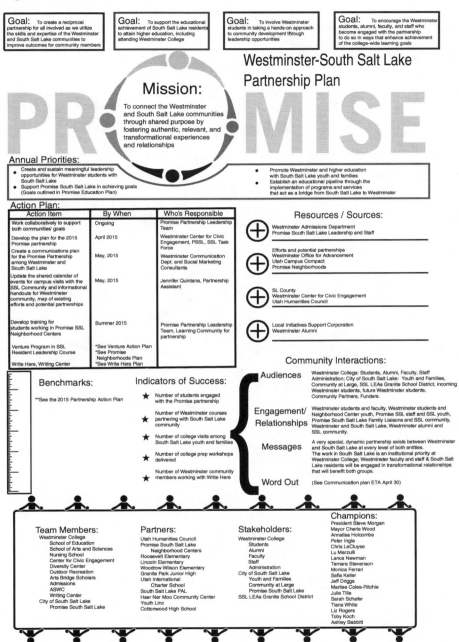

Goal: To create a reciprocal partnership for all involved as we utilize the skills and expertise of the Westminster and South Salt Lake communities to improve outcomes for community members

Goal: To support the educational achievement of South Salt Lake residents to attain higher education, including attending Westminster College

Goal: To involve Westminster students in taking a hands-on approach to community development through leadership opportunities

Goal: To encourage the Westminster students, alumni, faculty, and staff who become engaged with the partnership to do so in ways that enhance achievement of the college-wide learning goals

Westminster-South Salt Lake Partnership Plan

Mission: To connect the Westminster and South Salt Lake communities through shared purpose by fostering authentic, relevant, and transformational experiences and relationships

Annual Priorities:
- Create and sustain meaningful leadership opportunities for Westminster students with South Salt Lake
- Support Promise South Salt Lake in achieving goals (Goals outlined in Promise Education Plan)
- Promote Westminster and higher education with South Salt Lake youth and families
- Establish an educational pipeline through the implementation of programs and services that act as a bridge from South Salt Lake to Westminster

Action Plan:

Action Item	By When	Who's Responsible
Work collaboratively to support both communities' goals	Ongoing	Promise Partnership Leadership Team
Develop the plan for the 2015 Promise partnership	April 2015	Westminster Center for Civic Engagement, PSSL, SSL Task Force
Create a communications plan for the Promise Partnership among Westminster and South Salt Lake	May, 2015	Westminster Communication Dept. and Social Marketing Consultants
Update the shared calendar of events for campus visits with the SSL Community and informational handouts for Westminster community, map of existing efforts and potential partnerships	May, 2015	Jennifer Quintana, Partnership Assistant
Develop training for students working in Promise SSL Neighborhood Centers	Summer 2015	Promise Partnership Leadership Team, Learning Community for partnership
Venture Program in SSL Resident Leadership Course	*See Venture Action Plan *See Promise Neighborhoods Plan	
Write Here, Writing Center	*See Write Here Plan	

Resources / Sources:

⊕ Westminster Admissions Department
Promise South Salt Lake Leadership and Staff

⊕ Efforts and potential partnerships
Westminster Office for Advancement
Utah Campus Compact
Promise Neighborhoods

⊕ SL County
Westminster Center for Civic Engagement
Utah Humanities Council

⊕ Local Initiatives Support Corporation
Westminster Alumni

Benchmarks:

**See the 2015 Partnership Action Plan

Indicators of Success:
★ Number of students engaged with the Promise partnership
★ Number of Westminster courses partnering with South Salt Lake community
★ Number of college visits among South Salt Lake youth and families
★ Number of college prep workshops delivered
★ Number of Westminster community members working with Write Here

Community Interactions:

Audiences — Westminster College: Students, Alumni, Faculty, Staff Administration; City of South Salt Lake: Youth and Families, Community at Large, SSL LEAs Granite School District, incoming Westminster students, future Westminster students, Community Partners, Funders.

Engagement/ Relationships — Westminster students and faculty, Westminster students and Neighborhood Center youth, Promise SSL staff and SSL youth, Promise South Salt Lake Family Liaisons and SSL community, Westminster and South Salt Lake, Westminster alumni and SSL community.

Messages — A very special, dynamic partnership exists between Westminster and South Salt Lake at every level of both entities. The work in South Salt Lake is an institutional priority at Westminster College; Westminster faculty and staff & South Salt Lake residents will be engaged in transformational relationships that will benefit both groups.

Word Out — (See Communication plan ETA April 30)

Team Members:
Westminster College
School of Education
School of Arts and Sciences
Nursing School
Center for Civic Engagement
Diversity Center
Outdoor Recreation
Arts Bridge Scholars
Admissions
ASWC
Writing Center
City of South Salt Lake
Promise South Salt Lake

Partners:
Utah Humanities Council
Promise South Salt Lake
Neighborhood Centers
Roosevelt Elementary
Lincoln Elementary
Woodrow Wilson Elementary
Granite Park Junior High
Utah International
Charter School
South Salt Lake PAL
Hser Ner Moo Community Center
Youth Linc
Cottonwood High School

Stakeholders:
Westminster College
Students
Alumni
Faculty
Staff
Administration
City of South Salt Lake
Youth and Families
Community at Large
Promise South Salt Lake
SSL LEAs Granite School District

Champions:
President Steve Morgan
Mayor Cherie Wood
Annalisa Holoombe
Peter Ingle
Chris LeCluyse
Lu Marzulli
Lance Newman
Tamara Stevenson
Monica Ferrari
Safia Keller
Jeff Driggs
Marilee Coles-Ritchie
Julie Tille
Sarah Schafer
Tiana White
Liz Rogers
Toby Koch
Ashley Babbitt

Note. Reprinted with permission from South Salt Lake City and Westminster College.

TABLE 3.3
Action plan

Goal: Institutionalize the partnership between Westminster College and South Salt Lake through deepening the impact

Objective/Action Item	Measure/Indicator (How we know if we are successful)	Data Source(s) Baseline (Where we started)	By When	Who's Responsible	The Big Outcome
Develop our system for data/results to inform program improvement; facilitate data collection and analysis showing effectiveness of our collaboration	Number of projects, student involved, service hours, and SSL community members reached (use new database). Pre & post surveys of SSL residents worked with. Surveys of Center Managers. Survey of Westminster student learning	2013-2014 numbers of involvement compared with 2015. Surveys beginning in Spring of 2015	End of academic year	Dumke Center for Civic Engagement (DCCE), Promise SSL	Identify interest, impact of student learning of SSL youth and Westminster students, increase high impact practices/projects, better able to address community needs
Connect families (not just the youth) of South Salt Lake with the Westminster College Promise South Salt Lake Partnership	Families particpate in Welcome to Westminster programming. Invite to more open houses and have specific sessions. Have educational programming for parents in Promise SSL Centers. Write Here & Venture Programming	Spring Welcome to Westminster. 2015-2016 academic year Welcome to Westminster programming and open houses	Spring 2015; and each academic year	DCCE Admissions Promise SSL	More SSL community members engaged and parents buying into Welcome to Westminster. More awareness of higher education, specifically Westmisnter. More SSL residents attending Westminster

Create a set of guidelines/curriculum for Westminster students to follow when working with Promise South Salt Lake	Trainings to create curriculum for students working in SSL: diversity, working with youth, mentoring, college access, working with people, developing language skills; identify programs where appropriate to make mandatory and/or support	Fall 2014—Diversity Training for Take Action and America Reads	Fall 2015	DCCE w/ Diversity Center, Department of Education, Promise SSL	Better prepared students, better learning, better community collaborations.

Goal: Create pathways for South Salt Lake residents to attend Westminster College

Take a close look at the culture of Westminster and how accessible it might feel to South Salt Lake families	Input from students who participate in campus visits "Could you see yourself at Westminster?" Similar input from families who visit Welcome to Westminster students. More visits for SSL, exclusive visits. Info sessions at SSL Neighborhood centers	Baseline data gathered during Spring 2015 Welcome to Westminster and previous campus visits	Summer 2016	Lu Marzulli Diversity Center DCCE Promise SSL	Campus will be a more accessible place for SSL through addressing diversity issues

(Continues)

Table 3.3 (Continued)

Goal: Create pathways for South Salt Lake residents to attend Westminster College					
Objective/Action Item	Measure/Indicator (How we know if we are successful)	Data Source(s) Baseline (Where we started)	By When	Who's Responsible	The Big Outcome
Expand the School of Education involvement with the partnership, including graduate programs	1–2 Freshman LC in SSL (Marilee and Peter). Create Montessori school in SSL, send students for internships. Continue existing involvement MAT606 SSL as a local option	4 MAT summer methods partnered with center(s) Marilee's course with GPJH Peter's SL course	Summer 2016	Peter Ingle Kari Cutler Nancy Lindeman Marilee Coles-Ritchie	Support for creation of Montessori School Opportunities for students to practice social change model, work with diverse learners, & understand social issues affecting education and SSL students
Develop mentorship opportunites with Westminster students and South Salt Lake youth, with an emphasis on high school youth	Program for Humanities students (Lance Newman) Welcome to Westminster Program Examine best practices and models	Take Action projects (HNM, GPJH, STEM) Westminster students employed by Promise SSL	Summer 2016	DCCE Promise SSL	All students involved report learning More SSL youth attending college or other post secondary education More SSL youth at Westminster

Goal: Big ideas for Westminster South Salt Lake partnership success

Use our partnership to inform and shift how people access the natural environment	Increasing interest and number of youth; Interested families based on youth's interest; Repeat participation; Kids spending more time outside; Additional programming by environmental studies; capstone course; Potentially support community gardens	Tracking participant names, numbers, and family members/guests Baseline would be participants from 2014	End of summer 2015 and then ongoing	Westminster Outdoor Leadership Program	Inspire the desire to connect with the natural environment; address the perception that only those of privilege address the outdoors through recreation; change perception of barriers to spend time in nature
Establish clear communication channels with clean, simple, and visionary messaging delivered	Message to SSL families; 1 page visual of the partnership; "Short cut" of video Web page conference presentation. Welcome to Westminster materials	Materials that need consistent updates and attention	Fall 2015	DCCE Lucy Daynes Promise SSL Ashley Babbitt	Sharing our stories, opportunities, and visions
Create math support in South Salt Lake, through programming assistance, curriculum, summer camps, and tutor/mentoring	Conversations with math department faculty; conversation with Write Here team to better understand the ways to integrate with Write Here; potential support from education students; Integration of financial literacy	Lack of math support	Fall 2015	DCCE	Understanding if there is sufficient support across campus for creating increased math support

Note. Reprinted with permission from South Salt Lake City and Westminster College.

margins of their college experience. Representatives of community organizations must take on the role of coeducators and partners rather than serve only as a resource to be tapped for the benefit of faculty members and students. Similarly, community partners must understand that colleges and universities are educational centers and not social service agencies.

Building Understanding, Relationships, and Trust

As discussed in chapter 2, Pearson (2002) noted that all partnerships, business or personal, require ongoing face-to-face conversation, a shared plan, shared resources, and sustained communication. Thus, it is paramount that institutions of higher education approach the institutionalization process by building understanding, relationships, and trust with members of the community. This can occur only by talking to and getting to know community members. Votruba (2004) argued that community partners

> want us [academics in higher education] to treat them as partners, not supplicants. They want us to seek first to understand and then be understood. They want us to recognize that they have the capacity to teach us as well as learn from us. And they want us to appreciate that our future, as well as theirs, is dependent upon our work together. (p. 5)

Effectively building understanding entails a subtle but critical reframing of the traditional perspective and use of a deficit model to embody an asset-based perspective and approach to community engagement. In this way there is a shift away from experts' sweeping in from academic settings to impose their ideas for solving problems, meeting needs, or addressing issues toward exploring the community's assets and goals that can be used in mutually beneficial ways.

As discussed in chapter 8, the University of Utah began to establish its physical presence in a specific neighborhood of Salt Lake City for a place-based community engagement program. Over the course of nearly two years, an appointed special assistant to the president served as liaison to the community and conducted nearly 100 one-on-one conversations with community leaders and members. Additionally, a series of town hall meetings were convened at various locations in the community so that residents and participants could share stories that illustrated the culture, mission, assets, and priorities of both the community and the university. Community leaders and midlevel administrators and faculty members from the university participated in these gatherings, which ultimately produced the name of the program as well as guiding principles and goals that would later be incorporated into a strategic plan (University Neighborhood Partnership, 2015).

Similarly, and also described in chapter 8, Seattle University in 2007 embarked on a place-based partnership with surrounding neighborhoods to create an initiative focusing on building capacity to support local youth and their families. The relationship- and trust-building process included walking tours of the areas and a series of focus group conversations between representatives of community organizations, schools, and housing programs and university officials. This afforded an opportunity for the university to hear the community's goals and priorities rather than proposing its own. As a result an informal "kitchen cabinet" consisting of a university trustee and key campus and community leaders was formed to guide initial planning. This group evolved into a formal advisory board in 2012 (Yamamura, 2015).

Stakeholder Initiatives

Efforts to launch community engagement partnerships can also spring from various stakeholder groups, such as the community itself, students, or faculty members. For example, community members in West St. Paul, Minnesota, identified creating a culture of learning as a key aspiration, leading to the development of neighborhood learning communities. In partnership with the city and local school district, the Sabo Center for Democracy and Leadership at Augsburg College created a robust after-school and summer youth development and parent education program known as Sprockets.

Sometimes the work of an individual or a critical mass of faculty members can evolve into sustained, institutionalized programs that meet both the scholarly goals and needs of the community. An interdisciplinary cluster of researchers in engineering, physical therapy, and nursing in the College of Health Science at the University of Delaware conducted their individual projects in small, cramped quarters of older buildings on campus until the institution obtained and developed a former manufacturing plant from Chrysler Corporation. The university realized that a physical consolidation of the students' independent work could serve as a catalyst in proposing and creating the state-of-the-art Science, Technology Advanced Research (STAR) Campus Facility, which combines teaching, research, and patient care in the community.

Students can also be a catalyst for community engagement initiatives. Vogel, Fichtenberg, and Levin (2010) described how a group of students at Johns Hopkins University promoted public health with local school partners. The group, known as Students for a Positive Academic Partnership with the East Baltimore Community (SPARC), worked with faculty and administration to implement policy and curricular changes to "foster an organizational culture of civic responsibilities to the local community" (p. 373). However, it was the students' initial grassroots organizing via student surveys that ulti-mately led to a student assembly resolution, passed unanimously, that, with support from administration and the faculty, became a working mission and vision statement for academic entrepreneurship that affected both the insti-tution and the local community.

Collective Leadership

Plater (2011) proposed that collective leadership appears in the offices and recurring activities from which community engagement is realized. He wrote,

> Actions that are repeated year after year, offices that have budgets to do things, and people who have titles are the formal elements of infrastructure and thus the custodians of culture. But people with ideas, commitments, and a will to act are, above all else, the basis of leadership. (p. 112)

These people include faculty members, staff, midlevel administra-tors, and students who are recognized as champions with a legitimate role and definitive voice to act on behalf of the institution to advance commu-nity engagement. In this role collective leadership must successfully move through four developmental stages: interpreting the institutional mission to reflect engagement with a variety of audiences and constituencies, defining and proposing specific objectives and goals to realize that mission, cocreating and articulating the steps to achieve those goals, and demonstrating commit-ment through personal interactions (Sandmann & Plater, 2009).

Cultural Factors

Cultural factors come in a variety of forms. One form is the social, economic, racial, and political dynamics and contexts of a given geographical area, as described previously. Cultural factors can also exert their influence in a given organization, such as an institution of higher education or a nonprofit organ-ization in the community.

Intercultural Humility and Cultural Competency

Community engagement often places both students and faculty members in settings that offer different contexts of race, class, culture, gender, sexual orientation, and educational levels (Dunlap & Webster, 2009; Ross, 2010). While potentially transformative, these experiences require an intentional awareness of the inherent power and privilege associated with higher edu-cation, through self-reflection and self-critique referred to as *intercultural humility*, in order to recognize unintentional and intentional racism and classism (Ross, 2010; Savicki, 2008). In addition to allowing one to assimilate facts about cultural differences and practices, cultural humility promotes an understanding of the social, political, cultural, and economic dynamics that affect beliefs and behaviors of members in a particular community. Administrators, faculty members, and students must enter into community partnerships, especially those located in diverse and underresourced geographical locations, with an appreciation of and respect for those who have invited them as guests into their communities (Mattar, 2011, 2014). In this way faculty members and students begin to explore and gain insight into subconscious or conscious assumptions and stereotypes that may influence their behavior. The emphasis on humility promotes a democratic, nonauthoritarian trust and a collaborative relationship, described in chapter 2 as critical components of engaged scholarship and pedagogy. Further, members of the community come to know, understand, and ultimately trust students and faculty members as public scholars focused on mutual benefit rather than traditional exploitation. While academics often rely on curricula, materials, and workshops, a critical component of intercultural humility is building trust through face-to-face interactions and conversations (Savicki, 2008). Finally, there is the potential for a "town-and-gown" culture clash between faculty members and students of higher education and the community at large. Both groups operate with different sets of values, calendars, lexicons, roles, responsibilities, and purposes.

Academic Culture

That said, the fundamental culture in institutions of higher education need not be radically altered owing to the current proliferation of civic engagement occurring on campuses (Saltmarsh & Hartley, 2011). Instead, the continued institutionalization of community engagement reflects second-order changes, as characterized by Cuban (1988), that simply introduce new or altered ways of doing things. This form of second-order change is especially true if the academy shifts from its traditional view of the academic trilogy as three separate activities conducted in disciplinary isolation to an engaged epistemology. As described in chapter 2, this shift entails integrating research, teaching, and service for scholarly dissemination coupled with real-world application to address social issues. Such a shift can be difficult without both top-down and bottom-up champions. At the same time a gradual cultural shift is occurring and is evident in changes in institutional policies, procedures, and practices, all of which reflect cultural values.

Saltmarsh and colleagues (2015) gave examples of creating an academic culture that supports community engagement. These included revising promotion and tenure guidelines to reward and recognize civically engaged scholarship, creating awards that recognize faculty members doing quality work in engaged teaching and scholarship, and providing funds for public service grants. Given the dynamics of shared governance in faculty culture, these types of initiatives must emanate from the bottom up via faculty champions and faculty senates.

Understanding Roles and Purpose

It is important for administrators and program directors in higher education to understand and remember that community organizations have their own roles, purposes, missions, and goals, which revolve around the constituents they serve. Thus, it is not reasonable to expect or assume they will set their priorities aside to accommodate the instructional or research priorities of faculty members and students at colleges and universities. At the same time community organizations generally recognize the value of expertise and resources higher education can provide. That said, it is also important that members of the community understand that colleges and universities are not social service agencies whose sole mission is to solve society's problems. Instead, institutions of higher education can use their resources in partnership with the community in ways that are consistent with the mission of higher education (Votruba, 1996). It is incumbent on community agencies to understand the role of the academy and the academic trilogy of teaching, research, and service.

An important early step in the process is simply for the community organization and the institution to share information with each other. This includes providing a history, a mission, an overview of organizational structure, programs, stakeholders and constituencies, challenges, and goals. The exchange of information can be done through brief presentations or written materials. This allows both community partners and institutions of higher education an opportunity to tell their stories as they prepare to create a partnership for community engagement.

Participants in these discussions can begin to frame their introductory understanding of each other's roles in the context of community engagement by adapting a rubric of public service pathways developed by Stanford University's Haas Center for Public Service (2015). This rubric can be used as a template consisting of pathways of purpose and can be integrated with the academic trilogy. In this way both community partners and academics can see that the work of community engagement is not just charity or volunteer service nor merely the loaning of laboratories for teaching and research. Providing examples can be useful so that both community partners and academics can begin to see and understand their potential roles and the forms community engagement could take.

The first pathway of purpose for community organizations is providing a direct service to clients or constituents, a role most are familiar with. Second, many agencies advocate for those they serve. Third, they build community capacity in ways that empower the community at large in order to minimize dependency on support services. This can be achieved through the creation of anchor institutions, a complex approach described in chapter 8. The fourth pathway of purpose for agencies and organizations is developing policy based on best practices that influences government regulations and programming. Fifth, community organizations need to raise fiscal resources to support their programming. Finally, virtually every community agency needs to evaluate and assess the impact of their programs. Colleges and universities can often participate in all of these pathways of purpose through various applications and forms of research, teaching, and service that are mutually beneficial (see Figure 3.3).

Both parties must consider where and how their respective roles intersect in ways that are mutually beneficial. Intentional articulation of roles and responsibilities can be accomplished through developing and incorporating MOUs and project agreements, as described in chapter 4.

Figure 3.3 Roles of community organizations and institutions of higher education in engaged teaching and scholarship.

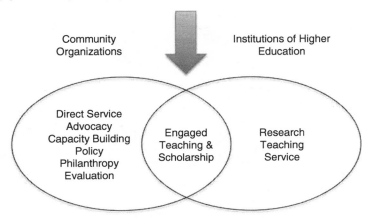

Guiding Principles

Collaboratively creating principles to guide the partnership is critical as these principles serve as benchmarks throughout a community engagement project. Strong partnerships are often built on an understanding of the purposes, processes, and goals of the endeavor. Guiding principles, such as those established by the University of Minnesota discussed earlier in this chapter, must be developed in collaboration with key stakeholders during early conversations, retreats, and town hall meetings. Participants should be invited to articulate values, beliefs, and assumptions on notecards or poster paper and to collectively review, edit, and ratify them.

Summary

Institutionalization in higher education is a complex process. It is influenced by an array of cultural and systemic factors. Institutionalizing community engagement is even more complex as it involves factors found in community organizations that may or may not easily mesh with the structures in colleges and universities. The process requires trust building and open communication, both of which are traditionally missing in town-and-gown interactions. Institutionalizing community engagement requires careful assessment and allocation of systemic resources articulated in a clear plan of action with dedicated commitment to ongoing communication and monitoring.

4

IMPLEMENTING
COMMUNITY ENGAGEMENT

Unfortunately, too many institutions are marked by a helter-skelter approach to civic engagement. Rather than a cohesive approach . . . happenstance and impulse more typically govern . . . all too often civic engagement is not rooted in the heart of the academy.

—Caryn McTighe Musil (2003, p. 4)

Profiles of Engagement

Two brief campus profiles are presented here to illustrate the influential factors in the institutionalization compass described in chapter 3. These are brushstroke examples of top-down, bottom-up, systemic, and cultural factors that influence the institutionalization of community engagement. These profiles serve as a bridge from the previous chapter, depicting how the institutionalization process is implemented.

The first profile is Wagner College, a private liberal arts college that embarked on its engagement pathway in 1998 as part of its ambitious cross-curricular program known as the Wagner Plan, which evolved over time into anchor-based community engagement. The second profile illustrates how the University of Delaware, a large public research university, used the application process for the Carnegie Classification for Community Engagement as a catalyst to guide the institution in its quest to enhance its involvement with the community. Each institution is different from the other, yet they share some common challenges and approaches. Both are on their own implementation time line and have varying histories. This chapter continues by exploring and describing organization structures for the implementation of community engagement.

Top-Down Factors

In 1998 Wagner College conceptualized and inaugurated its Wagner Plan to integrate a traditional liberal arts approach to higher education with the public purpose of engagement. Learning communities coupled with field experiences that included critical reflection were at the heart of the program. President Richard Guarasci began meeting with his administrators and faculty leaders to explore ways of enhancing the program to reflect and embrace community engagement through various initiatives (Guarasci, 2006). "At Wagner College, we believe that true leadership has less to do with power, rank, or authority, and more to do with the ability to bring together diverse groups in common purpose and inspire a shared vision of a better world" (Wagner College, 2014a). Guarasci and Cornwell's (1997) *Democratic Education in an Age of Difference: Redefining Citizenship in Higher Education*, coupled with a Learn and Serve seed grant, offered guiding principles for the plan while the college began to shift its efforts one department at a time to what became an anchor-based partnership in 2009.

Two hours away and 14 years later, the University of Delaware expanded its tradition and mission as a land-grant and sea-grant institution. The university included "becoming an engaged institution" as one of six goals in its institutional strategic plan. President Patrick T. Harker stated "We have the opportunity to work closely with public and nonprofit organizations in Delaware, the region and across the globe, applying research and human talent to address pressing social and civic issues while preparing our students as educated, engaged citizens" (University of Delaware, 2014).

The university created the Community Engagement Commission (www .udel.edu/engage/commission.html) as a task force and used the application for the Carnegie Classification for Community Engagement as a readiness assessment. Upon receiving the classification, the commission created an action plan targeting four specific areas: assessment, reciprocal relationships, faculty rewards, and integration and alignment with other institutional initiatives.

Bottom-Up Factors

In some respects the institutionalization process at the University of Delaware was built on the existing foundation of many faculty members already doing engaged research. Thus, a critical mass of faculty members helped push the initiative. For example, the Center for Community Research and Service in the School of Public Policy and Administration had already been in existence for nearly 30 years, conducting CBR with community agencies on issues related to homelessness, housing, and health. Similarly, pockets of faculty members were teaching service-learning courses and doing unique and robust CBR. These scholars were committed champions for engaged pedagogy and scholarship who helped drive the new agenda. Similarly, the nonprofit organizations that worked with these scholars were instrumental in seeking university resources to help realize their goals and address their issues. At the same time a handful of students were moving engagement forward by creating their own cocurricular programs that later interfaced with community-based courses for credit. One example is Lori's Hands, a program established by a nursing student whose mother had died from cancer. The program provides experiential learning by serving chronically ill patients.

Wagner College also had a number of committed faculty members who were ready to embrace the new agenda and move it forward. Trusting relationships had been established with organizations in the Port Richmond neighborhood near the campus (U.S. Department of Housing and Urban Development, 2013b). Port Richmond, on the northern shore of Staten Island, once served as the borough's commercial center. Adding to long-standing economic and commercial challenges is a resurgence of immigration that has affected health care, education, housing, and employment in the neighborhood. After a series of conversations between community and college leaders, a partnership between Wagner College and Port Richmond was officially established with the signing of a memo of understanding (MOU) in the spring of 2009. The partnership was meant to integrate students' educational experience with community development, achieve the mutually beneficial goals of community partners, and via the grass-roots efforts of faculty members, sow the seeds of trust in the community. The college's location on Staten Island provided a rich and diverse cultural heritage that would serve as a classroom. Many faculty members had established partnerships with various agencies in the Port Richmond neighborhood, teaching service-learning classes related to the arts, immigration, health, and education. These instructors were already committed and served as exemplars to their colleagues as well as to administrators who had a professional and pedagogical impetus to support their engaged scholarship.

Readiness Assessment
The University of Delaware made effective and efficient use of the Carnegie Classification for Community Engagement application by using it as a readiness assessment tool. As a first step in completing the application, the Community Engagement Commission brought together staff members coordinating existing service-learning courses, directors leading existing centers, and faculty members teaching service-learning and conducting CBR for an institutional retreat. Upon completion and submission of the application and successful awarding of the classification, the commission continued its work to create an action plan to be carried out over the next few years.

Strategic Plans

In 2009 Wagner College began the formal process of organizing and structuring its community-based anchor program known as the Port Richmond Partnership. The Center for Leadership and Community Engagement created a strategic organizational plan that included five priority areas: arts and culture, economic development, education and college readiness, health and wellness, and immigration and advocacy. Each priority area had a lead community partner, a lead faculty member, and a student representative. Two or three broad objectives were articulated in each of the five priority areas. Action teams consisting of representatives from administration, academic affairs, student affairs, community partners, and students operated in each priority area. These teams created benchmarks to measure impact and monitor progress toward the various program objectives.

Cultural Factors

Clearly the land-grant mission of the University of Delaware lends itself to the public mission of higher education and community engagement. Thus, the institution can justify its work in and for the community. At the same time the university is working toward a better understanding and practice of the mutuality of community engagement, which manifests itself as working *with* the community. Meanwhile, the internal culture of the university is highly decentralized. Much of the engaged scholarship thus far has been independent and autonomous. As the Community Engagement Commission continues its work, the university is grappling with the pros and cons of a centralized versus a decentralized organizational alignment.

Meanwhile, the implementation of the Wagner Plan, which has incorporated learning communities and service-learning over a decade, created a cultural understanding, if not a cultural expectation, of engaged pedagogy. Faculty members viewed the plan as part of the institution's curricular fabric and thus did not put up significant resistance. Slow, strategic adoption of engaged teaching and learning was orchestrated department by department, gradually producing faculty advocates. In addition to establishing infrastructure and a coordinating center, Wagner College embraced and used collective leadership to influence the academic culture on campus.

Systemic Factors

The University of Delaware currently has four offices that coordinate community engagement at the university: the Office of Service Learning, the University of Delaware Cooperative Extension, the School of Public Policy and Administration, and the Institute for Global Studies. The Office of

Service Learning is currently staffed by one coordinator who works to broker partnerships between faculty members and community partners. It is relatively unusual for a university of this size to use such a small number of human resources in the coordination of community engagement. In addition to these four offices, the College of Health Sciences has a dedicated staff member who coordinates cocurricular and curricular programs. The coordinator's role includes extensive interaction with the STAR Campus Facility (mentioned in chapter 3), an innovative use of existing physical resources off campus that provides the university a physical presence in the neighboring community. As part of its strategic planning, the Community Engagement Commission is exploring how to organize and coordinate these five offices and whether to continue using a decentralized approach or reconfigure the units into a loosely organized network. In addition the university continues to review the reporting structure and administrative oversight.

Wagner College, while smaller, has implemented a centralized organizational structure based around the Center for Leadership and Community Engagement. The center is centrally located in the campus union building and consists of four staff members: a director, a coordinator for community partnerships, a coordinator for student initiatives, and an administrative assistant. The Port Richmond Partnership uses existing community organizations as sites for cocurricular and curricular programming. The center oversees the Bonner Leaders program (described in detail in chapter 6), the IMPACT Scholars Civic Network, Project Pericles, and the MOVE program—all cocurricular leadership programs that integrate civic engagement through internships and independent academically based research for students. The center reports to and works with the Office of the Dean of Integrated Learning, which coordinates the Wagner Plan and its experiential learning component. Wagner College continues to expand its summer internship and programs. This requires coordination and use of existing student housing and dining facilities that are also often used for outside groups and camps.

As is so often the case with campuses attempting to institutionalize community engagement, policies and procedures regarding promotion and tenure remain a challenge at both institutions. Most institutions continue to reward and recognize faculty teaching and scholarship based on traditional models framed within disciplines. Thus, many promotion and tenure policies do not explicitly address or consider the public purpose of engagement scholarship, often putting faculty at risk when they seek tenure and promotion. The University of Delaware recognized this very real challenge during its readiness assessment and included exploring this issue as one of its action plan goals. Meanwhile, the dean of integrated learning at Wagner College,

Patricia Tooker, characterized this topical area as a "slippery slope" (P. Tooker, personal communication, June 24, 2015) as there is currently no language in the policy; the institution is in the throes of addressing that deficit. That said, Tooker asserted that the informal cultural values of the institution seem to support this work.

Institutional Support

These introductory pages provide a brushstroke of the four factors of influence in action as these two different campuses institutionalize community engagement. Once these efforts are formalized, institutional infrastructure in the form of organizational platforms is necessary to support implementation. Institutional support for community engagement comes in a variety of forms but is more than merely providing programs to establish policies, procedures, and requirements. Table 4.1 shows various examples of institutional support as reported by member institutions in Campus Compact's 2014 national survey.

Infusion

As Table 4.1 illustrates, there are a variety of ways to infuse community engagement into the life of the institution. Many colleges and universities are making community engagement a required component of students' educational experience. In other words some institutions now consider community engagement as essential as other required academic competencies, such as diversity, written expression, quantitative reasoning, and critical thinking and discourse. Thus, schools are determining how to ensure students complete some form of community engagement. Some have a core curriculum with specific learning objectives that must be successfully met over the course of the undergraduate experience. A variety of cocurricular and curricular programs (see chapter 6) that meet community engagement benchmarks or criteria are made available to students to choose from. This approach is academically based, rather than merely requiring students to complete hours of service that may or may not be linked to any specific learning objectives. Other schools have incorporated community engagement in multiple ways as a curricular mainstay that is evident across programs, such as learning communities, service-themed living-learning communities in residential halls, and service-learning courses that are prominent across campus. In this way community engagement is not a specific requirement but rather an integral part of the campus and learning experience.

TABLE 4.1

Institutional Support for Student Community Service, Service-Learning, and Civic Engagement

Characteristic	National (%)	Public (%)	Private (%)
Designates a period (e.g., day of service, service week) to highlight student civic engagement or service activities	72	68	78
Manages liability associated with service placements	70	67	73
Provides or coordinates transportation to and from community sites	64	49	80
Considers service formally in admissions process	34	25	43
Considers service in awarding scholarships	69	69	69
Characterizes and identifies academic service-learning courses	72	68	77
Requires academic service-learning as part of core curriculum in at least one major	64	63	65
Offers community service or civic engagement major or minor	15	15	15
Offers courses on volunteerism	27	27	27
Offers courses on activism or advocacy	52	49	54
Designates service-learning courses on student transcripts	50	45	55
Records service on student transcripts	29	29	33
Gives extra credit for cocurricular community engagement	41	25	45
Requires service for graduation	12	38	11
Gives awards to students for service	77	75	80
Offers minigrants to students for service-related activities	41	33	49
Provides funding (e.g., scholarships, grants, fellowships, education awards) for curricular and cocurricular community engagement	68	62	74
Hosts or funds public dialogues on current issues	80	78	82
Provides physical space and communication mechanisms for peaceful student protest	58	55	62
Provides other space for student political organizations on campus	66	61	72
Other	3	3	3

Note. Data from *2014 Campus Compact Member Survey*, by Campus Compact, 2014, Boston, MA: Author. Retrieved from http://compact.org/wp-content/uploads/2015/05/2014ALLPublicInstitutionsReport.pdf. Used with permission from Campus Compact.

Many departments or majors develop and require some kind of experiential learning. As discussed in chapter 2, some of these experiences are professional preparation practicums focused on working *at* an agency and do not necessarily incorporate the basic tenet of engaged pedagogy of working *with* a community partner. However, more and more disciplinary programs have begun to incorporate and even require engaged pedagogy such as service-learning. Some institutions are now offering majors, minors, or certificates in civic engagement that prepare students as professionals in work related to social and political change.

Other institutions have the entire student body—and sometimes a great number of faculty members—participate in a day of service. These days of service, which may or may not be required, typically occur either at the beginning of the academic year as a bonding experience or as a way to celebrate the Martin Luther King Jr. holiday.

Regardless of the way community engagement is infused into the college experience, adequate infrastructure and organizational platforms must be in place to implement and coordinate these efforts.

Organizational Platforms

The scope of establishing community engagement depends on the size and type of institution. Large state university systems operate differently than smaller liberal arts institutions or community colleges. For the past two decades, institutions have largely relied on campus centers to oversee cocurricular service programs and curricular programs involving service-learning, but the growth and expansion of community engagement have seen these centers take on more and more logistical coordination roles (Welch & Saltmarsh, 2013b). Additionally, it appears that program offices related to other forms of engaged pedagogy, such as study abroad programs, internships, and immersion experiences, are now beginning to fall under an organizational umbrella of community engagement (Beere et al., 2011; Welch & Saltmarsh, 2013b). Engaged scholarship in the form of CBR for faculty members is also becoming more prominent, and this type of research is being consolidated in existing campus centers for service-learning or in new offices and programs that fall under the umbrella of community engagement.

Centers, Institutes, and Offices

Colleges and universities are bureaucratically organized into various centers, institutes, and offices that provide a particular service or program (Beere et al., 2011). High-impact practices, such as service-learning and study abroad programs, are typically housed in a center, institute, or office. These units have a director and staff to oversee operations; are housed under a larger institutional umbrella, such as academic affairs or student affairs; and report to a dean, vice president, or vice provost. Each program has its own budget as well.

For example, Augsburg College has four centers of commitment tied to the civic mission of the college. The Sabo Center for Democracy and Citizenship, with a staff of 17, is the umbrella office for service-learning, cocurricular programs, and civic and public learning. The Strommen Center provides career education and internships while the Christensen Center for Vocation is responsible for assisting students in their theological exploration of vocation. International study abroad is coordinated by the Center for Global Education and Experience. More and more institutions are beginning to revisit their existing organizational alignment of programs and to consider possible restructuring under a broader umbrella, thus creating a new institutional division or office of engagement.

In 2002, under the new presidential leadership of Michael Schwartz, Cleveland State University launched Building Blocks for the Future, a comprehensive strategic plan reflecting a significant shift from a traditional inward focus to an outward alignment with the community. By 2009 the university had undergone organizational realignment to create the Division of University Engagement, led by a vice president for university engagement. This division is made up of the Office of Community Engagement, the Office of Workplace Engagement, and the Office of Inclusion and Multicultural Engagement (White, 2016). Cleveland State University has thus embarked on a significant initiative to become an anchor institution in its geographic area.

Indiana University–Purdue University Indianapolis (IUPUI) recently combined four offices into a comprehensive, campus-wide Office of Community Engagement. The new structure combines the Office of External Affairs, the Community Learning Network, the Solution Center, the Center for Service and Learning, and IUPUI Alumni Relations. Driven by the institution's strategic plan, the new integrated office provides a coordinated approach to professional development and corporate education; neighborhood, school, and family partnerships; volunteerism and service; and a campus-wide culture of engagement. The office is currently focused on developing and implementing professional development and corporate education and family, school, and neighborhood engagement.

Similar structural realignment is occurring in smaller private liberal arts colleges as well. Service-learning and cocurricular volunteer service programs at Macalester College, a small liberal arts college in St. Paul, Minnesota, originally fell under the Office of Mission and Ministry. Over time those programs shifted to student affairs and then later to academic affairs, until institutional reorganization in 2008 created the International Global Center (IGC). Through the administrative oversight of a dean, the IGC now consists of three offices led by individual directors, including the Community Engagement Center, domestic and international study away programs, and internships.

Some colleges and universities, especially faith-based institutions, ponder how a campus center for engagement should interface with the campus ministry. One question relates to how the service component of engaged pedagogy is perceived. Many view the service component of engagement as part of the spiritual mission of charity within faith traditions, which is appropriate. Likewise, many campus ministry programs include critical reflection. Finally, some faith-based programs incorporate an academic component of readings before engagement in the community. Consequently, the mission and work of the two centers often share components (see Figure 4.1). The fundamental difference is the primary mission of campus ministry is faith formation while the primary purpose of the campus center for engagement is the academic and civic mission of the institution network.

Figure 4.1 Interface of campus ministry and engaged pedagogy.

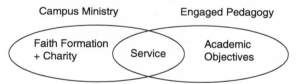

Organizational Models

Pigza and Troppe (2003) described three organizational models for institutionalizing community engagement: concentrated, fragmented, and integrated. Similarly, Sandmann and Plater (2009) described three basic organizational structures supporting engagement: centralized coordinating centers, diffused network units, and hybrid coordinated networks. These structures have been combined here into three broad organizational models: centralized, decentralized, and integrated network.

Centralized Model

As the name would suggest, the centralized model consists of a central office or center focusing on a specific type of community engagement, such as cocurricular programs, service-learning, or CBR. The advantages of this model include visibility and accessibility as well as coordinating programs to minimize redundancy. Limitations include the ability of the center's administrative leadership to work effectively with various stakeholders, ranging from students to faculty members to community partners (Pigza & Troppe, 2003).

The Feinstein Institute for Public Service at Providence College is an example of the centralized model. The institute is organized into five programmatic strands that coordinate all engagement programs on campus. It supports and coordinates service-learning courses on campus. The institute oversees the Smith Hill Annex, a storefront building that provides a venue for campus-community conversations that lead to various community engagement initiatives. Community work-study opportunities provide financial support that allows students to develop their civic leadership skills while working as paraprofessionals at local nonprofit organizations. A broader umbrella of civic engagement in the institute organizes global service-learning experiences and provides funds for student-led initiatives, such as Raise Your Voice projects and the AmeriCorps-sponsored Scholarships for Service, involving 300 hours of service in partnership with the Rhode Island Campus Compact. The institute facilitates partnerships between community organizations and the campus.

Decentralized Model

This model is characterized by programs implemented and coordinated by various offices throughout the campus. One advantage of this approach is the flexibility and specialization of programs afforded to specific disciplines. The decentralized model, however, also allows for redundant efforts across campus and may cause institutional and community partner confusion about where and with whom to coordinate programs (Weerts & Sandmann, 2008). Further, it complicates tasks such as completing applications and surveys for programs or events like the President's Honor Roll for Community Service, as multiple offices need to be involved.

For example, the Office of Research and Economic Development (ORED) at the University of North Carolina–Greensboro (UNC-G) is housed under Academic Affairs and oversees eight independent yet related centers and institutes. While all eight units are involved with the community to some extent, only four are described here. The Institute for Community and Economic Engagement (ICEE) is responsible for coordinating community engagement programming through service-learning, CBR for students and faculty members, and advancing community engagement. The office serves as a strategic mechanism to achieve key institutional, departmental, and programmatic goals that provide student teaching and learning opportunities. The Center for Housing and Community Studies (CHCS) brings together faculty members from multiple disciplines to study these complex social issues related to housing and to provide a point of contact for community partners. This center also serves the region by educating UNC-G students as preprofessionals who provide program evaluation and research in housing and long-term regional sustainable planning. The Center for New North Carolinians (CNNC) supports immigrants and refugees through community-based outreach and advocacy, educational programming, research and evaluation, immigrant and refugee leadership development, cultural brokering, and educational opportunities for faculty members and students. Finally, the Center for Youth, Family, and Community Partnerships (CYFCP) is focused on capacity building for families, service providers, researchers, teachers, and communities to promote the social, emotional, and cognitive development of children.

Integrated Network Model

The integrated model combines the attributes of the concentrated and decentralized models by establishing an overarching umbrella office that provides a central hub for a network of resources and support across curricular and cocurricular offices throughout campus (Beere et al., 2011). This model promotes an interdisciplinary approach with specific departments and a variety of community agencies. It is most common at large public research institutions because of their complex structures. As institutions expand engagement from cocurricular volunteer service and curricular service-learning to include other forms of engaged scholarship and pedagogy, more and more institutions are beginning to reorganize by creating divisions or offices of engagement. Large university systems often have massive administrative hubs coordinating a variety of engaged programs across many campuses. For example, the University of Minnesota system, consisting of four campuses across the state, established a central Office for Public Engagement on the Twin Cities campus that coordinates and administers over 100 programs and offices across all campuses.

Smaller universities have less complex administrative structures. DePaul University, an urban Catholic liberal arts institution, is a good example of an integrated network model. The Irwin W. Steans Center on campus offers various approaches to community engagement. The center works with individual faculty members to create and implement academic service-learning courses that provide direct service, project-based service for teams of students, CBR, and advocacy. In collaboration with the John J. Egan Office of Urban Education and Community Partnerships (UECP), these various forms of academic service-learning can be implemented through grant-funded projects, school-based projects, or departmental programs that have established their own long-standing community partnership with various agencies. The grant-funded projects include conducting research, evaluation, and assessment on behalf of community partners as well as providing technical assistance in capacity building and serving as an incubator for community development projects.

Institutional Architecture

Once institutions have determined the organizational platform to use, they must build an institutional architecture consisting of a structure and policies to guide the work of the center or constellation of centers on campus. This includes reporting lines, budgets, and strategic plans, as well as policy and procedures such as how to designate courses and programs that promote community engagement. A study of campuses receiving the Carnegie Classification for Community Engagement reveals trends of institutional architecture (Welch & Saltmarsh, 2013a, 2013b; see Table 4.2)

TABLE 4.2
Institutional Architecture and Policies for Community Engagement at Institutions With a Carnegie Classification for Community Engagement

Architectural Component	Number	Percentage
Reporting line to academic affairs	107	77.6
Institutional operational funds budgeted for community engagement centers	135	95.8
Campus-wide commitment to community engagement	105	74.5
Central coordinating office on campus	115	81
Community engagement included in the institutional strategic plan	117	83.6
Community engagement courses officially defined and designation process exists	99	70.2

Note. Data from "Current Practice and Infrastructure for Campus Centers of Community Engagement," by M. Welch and J. Saltmarsh, 2013, *Journal of Higher Education Outreach and Engagement, 17*(4), p. 35.

Reporting Lines

Aligning centers responsible for coordinating both cocurricular and curricular community engagement programs with academic affairs rather than student affairs appears to be a slight trend. Campus Compact's 2014 survey revealed that 39% of campus centers for community engagement at public institutions and 41% of centers at private institutions report to academic affairs while 39% of centers at public schools and 35% of centers at private schools report to student affairs. Only 7% of centers at public and 9% of centers at private institutions have reporting lines to both sides of the house while 4% of centers at public and 8% of centers at private schools report directly to the president (see Table 4.3). A smaller study of 147 institutions receiving the Carnegie Classification for Community Engagement revealed that 77.6% (107 institutions) of campus centers for engagement report to academic affairs (Welch & Saltmarsh, 2013a, 2013b).

TABLE 4.3
Reporting Lines for Campus Centers for Engagement

Reporting lines	National (%)	Public (%)	Private (%)
Academic affairs	40	39	41
Student affairs	37	39	35
Both academic affairs and student affairs	8	7	9
President's office	6	4	8

Note. Data from *2014 Campus Compact Member Survey*, by Campus Compact, 2014, Boston, MA: Author. Retrieved from http://compact.org/wp-content/uploads/2015/05/2014ALLPublicInstitutionsReport.pdf. Used with permission from Campus Compact.

Engagement Officers

As illustrated previously with the reorganization efforts at Cleveland State University, it is becoming more common for institutions to create midlevel administrative positions for engagement officers to oversee the coordination of integrated programs that are consolidated under an organizational division of engagement (Beere et al., 2011; Holland, 2009). Because of the primary focus on academic objectives, whether in cocurricular or curricular programs, it may be appropriate to have this position under academic affairs and reporting to the CAO. Such an organizational structure and alignment would have directors of various departments, programs, centers, and institutes report to the engagement officer.

Beere and colleagues (2011) provided a useful overview of the qualifications and roles of an engagement officer. They suggested that this position requires a "full-time, highly regarded, academically qualified person who will command the respect of faculty, staff, and community leaders and who is strongly committed to the public engagement mission" (p. 83). This administrator must be visionary and pragmatic, capable of spanning boundaries. The engagement officer must be a systems thinker who understands the dynamics and culture of both the institution and the community. This administrator should be a pragmatic visionary who understands the dynamics of change and can navigate the cultural and systemic factors of both the academy and community organizations using effective communication and problem-solving skills.

Thus, the qualifications and background of the engagement officer should include experience in community engagement, perhaps as a faculty member doing engaged teaching and scholarship or as a director of centers coordinating some form of community engagement, such as service-learning. Through these experiences this individual would have been afforded ample opportunities to work with community partners in ways that provide insight and understanding into the mission, culture, and challenges of agencies and the stakeholders they serve.

The engagement officer is responsible for advocating and advancing the institutional mission for engagement while serving as the face, or public spokesperson, for on- and off-campus engagement. The officer also brings a sense of legitimacy to the engagement programs by promoting accountability at an administrative level. At the same time the engagement officer must apprise the president and other administrative leaders of progress and activities related to community engagement while brokering partnerships and running interference to circumvent barriers that may interfere with programming. This role also requires monitoring and reporting all aspects of engagement programs. Beyond these responsibilities on campus, the engagement officer must have an understanding of and relationship with the community at large. This administrator is likely to serve as a liaison between community organizations and various centers and institutes on campus. Thus, regular and ongoing conversations and interactions on and off campus with community partners and advisory committees are essential.

Advisory Committees

Another common component of institutionalization infrastructure is establishing an advisory committee of key campus and community leaders. This includes midlevel administrators, such as assistant vice presidents or provosts, deans or associate deans, and some faculty members as well as program directors of various units on campus involved with community engagement. Community representatives typically include executive directors of community agencies that have a history with the institution. These committees also often include student representatives and, at times, members of the community who are constituents of community organizations. Some advisory committees include alumni as well as donors (Welch & Saltmarsh, 2013a).

Financial Support and Budgets

A very real priority during institutionalization of community engagement is financial support. While the range and types of financial support vary by institution, most colleges and universities allocate some internal financial resources to funding community engagement (Weerts & Hudson, 2009). As discussed in chapter 5, the funds provide operational budgets that include staff salaries and benefits, funding for student programs, office supplies, and professional development for staff and faculty members. The size of operating budgets generally reflects the size of the institution and the number of community engagement programs.

Colleges and universities have traditionally relied on federal or private foundation grants to enhance institutional funding of community engagement. However, more and more institutions are turning to the Office of Advancement and Development to generate financial resources through fund-raising and donations. Weertz and Hudson (2009) have conducted extensive research in the area of fund-raising to support community engagement. They cite research studies suggesting institutions are revisiting their typical approaches to advancement and development in light of the growing public interest in community engagement. Potential donors appear to be more likely to invest in programs that make an impact on society and communities rather than merely contribute to institutional initiatives (Grace & Wendroff, 2001; Strickland, 2007). As a result some divisions of engagement or campus centers for community engagement have established development boards in which members are charged with conducting fund-raising and so-called friend-raising. The Haas Center for Public Service at Stanford University has its own development officer responsible for raising approximately 85% of its operating budget through grants and an annual appeal that generates approximately $700,000 each year. Campus commitment to community engagement also appears to appeal to legislative bodies, and as a result engaged campuses often generate greater financial support (Blanton, 2007; Weerts & Ronca, 2006). As community engagement continues to be a major component of institutional missions and programs, colleges and universities are using engagement in their branding and marketing (Weerts & Hudson, 2009). This could also include working with admissions and alumni offices to "tell the story" of community engagement to help attract potential students as well as maintain relationships with graduates who are potential financial supporters of these efforts.

Communication

Campus centers and divisions of engagement must collaborate with offices of development and communication to tell their story across campus and to a broader audience in the community (Beere et al., 2011; Weerts & Hudson, 2009). A combination of messaging reaches a variety of internal and external audiences. There is, however, a delicate dance while telling these stories. Institutions must be sensitive and careful in their depiction of those being served to minimize the possible impression of noblesse oblige or of exploiting underserved groups for the benefits of the institution's public image. Communication of community engagement initiatives should include press releases to local, regional, and national media; newsletters and magazines for alumni; admissions materials; annual reports; and websites. Community partners are also encouraged to discuss their participation as coeducators in their own publications, announcements, and reports. A specific goal tied to communication might be considered and included in the institutional strategic plan (Beere et al., 2011).

Memos of Understanding and Project Agreements

MOUs are not legal contracts. Instead, they are formal written documents articulating an understanding between two parties regarding the nature of a partnership over a specific period, often two to three years. In this case the MOU is between the institution as a whole—rather than an individual faculty member—and the community agency. An MOU typically states that the partnership is educational in nature, spirit, and purpose; that students are entering authentic settings to develop and apply skills associated with formal instructional objectives; and that students are not viewed as employees, paraprofessionals, or consultants. The document usually indemnifies both parties from legal action and enumerates possible risk. Copies of certificates of liability insurance are usually attached to the MOU. An MOU stipulates the duration of the partnership as well as the process to review and consider continuation or termination of the partnership. MOUs are usually maintained on file by the institution's legal counsel office, although staff within the campus center for community engagement may be responsible for initiating and coordinating the process on behalf of instructors, staff, and the community representative.

Other Policies and Procedures

Institutions must also consider ways community partners are supported, recognized, and rewarded for their participation. Some institutions have allocated funds as honoraria while others award adjunct faculty status to representatives of community organizations. Providing access to library resources on campus and presenting awards or certificates are other ways of acknowledging the contribution and participation of community partners.

Other institutional policies and procedures involve teaching assignments and loads. Preparing and coordinating any form of community engagement, whether through engaged pedagogy or research, require significantly more time and energy than traditional teaching. Consequently, institutions must revisit and possibly revise how teaching responsibilities are assigned.

Additional Resources and Support

Institutions need to consider how to organize and provide various types of support and personnel as they plan and establish infrastructural platforms to support institutionalization of community engagement. Coordinating the moving parts of community engagement, such as service-learning courses, creates additional responsibilities and challenges for instructors. Research and applications for the Carnegie Classification for Community Engagement reveal that some institutions have addressed this by providing student assistants (Welch & Saltmarsh, 2013b). Unlike traditional teaching assistants, these student assistants serve as liaisons to community partners, conducting reflection discussions and coordinating logistical tasks, such as processing background checks or timesheets for off-campus work. This type of support is described in more detail in chapter 5.

Centers are now responsible for a considerable amount of logistical coordination so that faculty members can be free to focus on the academic and pedagogical purpose of community engagement. This type of administrative coordination may include conducting risk assessments of potential locations and community agencies, ensuring that required student background checks are completed in a timely fashion, arranging and monitoring administration of required tuberculosis tests for students going into school settings with children, and managing transportation.

Further, faculty members new to community engagement and engaged scholarship will require additional professional development in the form of faculty development workshops and technical support. Faculty development programs are described in more detail in chapter 6. In the same vein many directors of community agencies need to learn how to work with faculty members and students and what community engagement is. Professional development is described in chapter 5.

Assessment

It is imperative to include assessment before, during, and after the institutionalization and implementation process to determine the impact of community engagement within four contexts: among students, among the faculty members, among community partners, and in the institution. As a preface it is important to note that an ironic, culturally entrenched cynicism exists regarding the assessment of engaged pedagogy such as service-learning. Many faculty members assume that engaged service cannot accurately be assessed because it is somehow less academically impactful than traditional teaching and learning methods. They also assume that traditional cognitive assessment of student learning, through exams and written papers, is accurate. However, traditional assessments may in fact merely be determining to what extent students can recall and report information, not to what extent they have understood or applied their assimilated knowledge. Meanwhile, several studies on engaged pedagogy, incorporating a number of dependent variables, have effectively assessed the impact of community engagement on various stakeholders.

In contrast to traditional paper-and-pencil methods of assessment, engaged teaching and learning require that students meaningfully apply what they have learned in realistic and authentic settings and situations. Engaged pedagogy can help students become more sensitive to cultural diversity and more empathic; it can increase students' civic awareness and even shape their spiritual formation. Eyler and Giles (1999) were able to substantiate the impact of service-learning in their now-classic work *Where's the Learning in Service-Learning?* Since then, several rubrics and metrics assessing various dimensions of student development have been created and implemented. The AAC&U created a rubric to assess students' civic engagement. The Multi-Institutional Leadership Study, developed at the University of Maryland, incorporates the social change model of leadership development to assess multiple dimensions of student leadership growth. The community service attitude scale (Shiarella, McCarthy, & Tucker, 2000) reliably assesses students' community engagement experiences in terms of moral obligation, action, ability, awareness, benefits, empathy, norms, reassessment of personal impact, and seriousness of commitment.

Leisey, Holton, and Davey (2012) conducted a study examining impact assessment of university-funded community engagement projects. Their results suggest that institutions of higher education are much more committed to assessing community impact than they were in the past. Waters and Anderson-Lain (2014) analyzed formative and summative assessment tools created and posted online by 121 members of Campus Compact. Their research revealed six consistent, unique themes in the content of the assessment instruments: student leadership, understanding course details, understanding service-learning as a teaching/learning method, course project descriptions, impact on community partners, and student commitment to service-learning. Qualitative approaches, such as analysis of students' reflection comments or journal entries, can reveal affective, behavioral, and cognitive transformation (Dubinsky, Welch, & Wurr, 2012).

Much of the early work on assessing the impact of service-learning can be modified and transferred to a broader assessment of community engagement. Gelmon, Holland, Driscoll, Spring, and Kerrigan (2001) developed a comprehensive and practical guide to assessing service-learning and civic engagement that is still applicable today. They proposed and framed assessment in a matrix that explores four primary questions: "What do we want to know? What will we look for? What will we measure? and How will we gather the evidence needed to demonstrate what we want to know?" (pp. 10–11). This basic matrix is used to assess students, faculty members, community partners, and the institution. Gelmon and colleagues (2001) also described many methods, including pre- and postmeasures, surveys, demographics, interviews, observations, and document reviews.

Student assessment should look at awareness of the community, involvement with the community, commitment to service, career development, selfawareness, understanding of course content, sensitivity to diversity, sense of ownership, communication, and valuing of pedagogy of multiple teachers. Faculty assessment should look at motivation and attraction to engaged pedagogy, professional development, impact on teaching, impact on scholarship, and personal and professional satisfaction. Many faculty members engaged in this type of teaching and scholarship report profound personal and professional satisfaction (Diener & Liese, 2009; Johnson & O'Grady, 2006; Mundy, 2004). Summative assessment for community partners includes exploring the capacity to meet the organizational mission, the economic benefit, and the social benefit while formative assessment examines the nature of interactions with the institution, faculty members, and students as well as overall satisfaction with the process and experience.

Finally, Gelmon and colleagues (2001) enumerate a number of ways to assess the impact of community engagement on the institution itself. These include examining the number and types of partnerships with the community, the prevalence of engaged teaching and scholarship, budgetary allocation for engagement, public relations and image, infrastructure, research, and extramural funding. Adoption by community partners of actual products, or "deliverables," created by students and faculty members reflects social validation (Baer & Schwartz, 1991; Schwartz & Baer, 1991) and a form of authentic assessment in which the theoretical work was actually applied to real-world needs in authentic settings.

A variety of instruments designed to assess community partnerships is presented and described in chapter 8.

Summary

Implementing institutionalization requires infrastructural platforms from which to provide the necessary support for community engagement. Institutionalization is a dynamic and complex interplay of cultural and systemic factors. Preceding chapters have examined community engagement from a macro perspective that included philosophical, pedagogical, and institutional concepts. This chapter has connected that broader perspective to the remaining chapters of this book, which examine operations and programming.

5

INFRASTRUCTURE AND OPERATIONS OF CAMPUS CENTERS FOR ENGAGEMENT

I have begun to think of life as a series of ripples widening out from an original center.

—Seamus Heaney (Cole, 1997)

This quotation by the late Irish poet Seamus Heaney captures the essence of a campus center for community engagement. In the context of this book, engaged pedagogy and scholarship, supported by a campus center or cluster of centers, emanate as ripples into the classroom and the community. And like dropping a pebble into a bowl, the radiating ripples bounce back when meeting the sides of the vessel, literally and figuratively returning to the center. This metaphor nicely represents the mutuality and reciprocity in the tenets of community engagement. Campus centers typically serve three constituency groups: students, faculty members, and community partners. This is evident when one visits virtually any center's website and quickly peruses the pull-down menu of services, resources, and programs. The campus center is generally the entry point for community partners to access the rich resources of higher education.

This chapter begins by presenting guiding principles and practices for centers and then describes basic infrastructure common to campus centers, gleaned from a review of the professional literature and national surveys conducted by Campus Compact, as well as from a smaller research study of nearly half the institutions that have received the Carnegie Classification for Community Engagement (Welch & Saltmarsh, 2013a, 2013b).

Guiding Principles and Practices for Campus Centers

The early professional literature in this burgeoning field has incrementally provided practices and structures to support this work. More than 25 years ago, the National Society for Internships and Experiential Education published a two-volume book that included examples and recommendations for establishing campus community engagement centers (Kendall, 1990). Bucco and Busch (1996) were among the first scholars to recommend specific programmatic frameworks designed to create service-learning programs on college campuses. About that same time Bringle and Hatcher (1996) also enumerated specific infrastructure for service-learning centers. Likewise, Jacoby (1996) published *Service-Learning in Higher Education: Concepts and Practices*, which soon became one of the landmark books of the field as new centers incorporated components from it. Soon thereafter, many centers were showcased in Zlotkowski's (1998) *Successful Service-Learning Programs: New Models of Excellence in Higher Education*. With the growth of programs came a fundamental question, which became the title of a landmark book: *Where's the Learning in Service-Learning?* by Eyler and Giles (1999). The question challenged the growing field to provide empirical evidence of the effectiveness of this pedagogy, paving the way for a scholarship *of* engagement through research on service-learning. Singleton, Hirsch, and Burack (1999) identified six characteristics of organizational structures that shape and define *service-enclaves*, groups of faculty and staff members working on service initiatives in the community:

1. Leadership—Programs and centers must receive intellectual and political support from campus leadership.
2. Integration with teaching and research—The academic value of the service programming and work must be clearly articulated and evident.
3. Institutional support—Centers must receive financial, human, and physical resources that support and enable the programming.
4. Flexibility—Faculty members, staff, and program directors must be able to break from a host of challenges, bureaucratic structure, and policies to quickly respond and mobilize themselves and others to do the work.
5. Visibility—Centers must effectively cultivate ties and partnerships with other entities on campus and in the community at large.
6. Institutional savvy—Centers must understand and work with the campus culture to realize and converge the center's goals with the institutional goals.

The CAS (2015) has published a 12-part set of standards and guidelines outlining ethical and best practices for centers that incorporates and reflects a systems approach. Part 1 addresses mission and advises centers to develop, implement, and periodically review their mission statement to ensure consistency with the institutional mission. A detailed list of six learning objectives in a variety of developmental domains—knowledge acquisition, cognition, intrapersonal growth, interpersonal growth, humanitarian and civic engagement, and practical competence—is provided in part 2, describing educational programming. Part 3 enumerates benchmarks for organizational leadership, including strategic planning, supervision, management, and advancement of the office's mission. Part 4 articulates guidelines for managing human resources and staff members, including student employees, as well as expectations for establishing and maintaining meaningful relationships with community partners. Ethical behaviors are included in part 5, and legal, policy, and governance standards are addressed in part 6. Responsibilities associated with diversity, equity, and access are listed in part 7, and part 8 provides guidelines for internal and external relations. Part 9 outlines adequate and appropriate financial resources for operations and details stewardship of those resources. The need for and use of technology are addressed in part 10. Guidelines for facilities and equipment are provided in part 11. The list of standards concludes with recommendations for assessing center operations and programming in part 12.

Substantial infrastructure in the form of a community engagement unit (i.e., office, center, or division) is a key organizational feature of a highly engaged campus (Etienne, 2012; Hollander et al., 2001; Walshok, 1999; Zlotkowski, 1998). Best practices for centers have emerged over time, and they are now used by the Carnegie Foundation to help establish criteria for the elective community engagement classification. These criteria and other practices gleaned from the professional literature were combined by Welch and Saltmarsh (2013a, 2013b) to create an inventory of platforms and programs that could be used by institutions and centers in strategic planning to compare current structures, practices, and programs with those of other robust institutional centers. The components of the inventory provide a framework for the remaining chapters of this book (see Table 5.1).

Welch and Saltmarsh's (2013a, 2013b) inventory uses a systems perspective to examine the operational infrastructure of campus centers that support and launch an array of community engagement programs. Naturally, the size and scope of the programs are dependent on institution type and size. However, the information presented here applies to the overall roles, responsibilities, and functions of a campus center regardless of its size. The complete version of Welch and Saltmarsh's inventory is in Appendix D of this

TABLE 5.1
Practices and Structural Elements of Campus Centers for Engagement

Practices	Source
Institutional architecture/policy	
Academic affairs reporting line	Battistoni (1998)
Budgeted institutional funds	Carnegie Foundation (2012); Hollander et al. (2001); Walshok (1999)
Campus-wide commitment to civic engagement	Beere et al. (2011); Carnegie Foundation (2012)
Central coordinating center/office	Bucco & Busch (1996); Carnegie Foundation (2012)
Civic engagement in institutional strategic plans	Beere et al. (2011); Carnegie Foundation (2012)
Course designation process	Carnegie Foundation (2012)
Institutional leadership promotes civic engagement as a priority	Carnegie Foundation (2012); Sandmann & Plater (2009)
Institutional mission statement includes community engagement	Beere et al. (2011); Carnegie Foundation (2012)
Official/operational definitions of *service-learning, CBR,* and *engagement*	Carnegie Foundation (2012)
Transcript notation of engaged courses	Carnegie Foundation (2012)
Center infrastructure	
Adequate office space	Walshok (1999)
Advisory/governing board	Carnegie Foundation (2012); Fisher (1998)
Annual report	Welch & Saltmarsh (2013b)
Center vision/mission statement	Fisher (1998); Furco (2002a); Hollander et al. (2001)
Center alumni association	Welch & Saltmarsh (2013b)
Center director background (faculty, student affairs, community)	Beere et al. (2011); Welch & Saltmarsh (2013a)
Center director credential/degree (terminal degree, graduate degree)	Beere et al. (2011); Welch & Saltmarsh (2013a)
Clear internal/external access points to the center	Pigza & Troppe (2003)
Community representative to advisory board	Bringle & Hatcher (1996)
Database tracking system/hardware	Bringle & Hatcher (1996); Carnegie Foundation (2012)
Development officer	Weerts & Hudson (2009)

(Continues)

Table 5.1 (*Continued*)

Practices	Source
Faculty advisory committee/board	Beere et al. (2011); Carnegie Foundation (2012); Fisher (1998)
Faculty liaison to academic units	Bringle & Hatcher (1996)
Full-time administrator	Bucco & Busch (1996); Carnegie Foundation (2012)
Full-time administrative assistant	Bucco & Busch (1996)
Newsletter/Internet updates	Beere et al. (2011)
Support programming staff	Walshok (1999)
Center operations	
Assessment mechanisms/procedures	Carnegie Foundation (2012); Hatcher & Bringle (2010)
Announcements for/provision of resource materials	Bringle & Hatcher (1996)
Community voice/input	Bringle & Hatcher (1996); Carnegie Foundation (2012); Furco (2002a); Hollander et al. (2001)
Research on faculty involvement	Bringle & Hatcher (1996)
Surveys on student involvement	Bringle & Hatcher (1996)
Student course assistants	Bringle & Hatcher (1996)
Course development grants	Bringle & Hatcher (1996); Furco (2002a)
Course syllabi file/database	Bringle & Hatcher (1996)
Faculty involvement database	Bringle & Hatcher (1996)
Faculty awards	Bringle & Hatcher (1996); Carnegie Foundation (2012); Hollander et al. (2001)
Evaluation of community partner satisfaction	Bringle & Hatcher (1996)
Evaluation of student satisfaction with service-learning	Bringle & Hatcher (1996)
Faculty research on service-learning/ civic engagement	Bringle & Hatcher (1996)
Fund-raising mechanisms	Carnegie Foundation (2012); Holland & Langseth (2010); Weerts & Hudson (2009)
Student involvement in creating service-learning courses	Bringle & Hatcher (1996); Fretz & Longo (2010)
Presentations at student orientations	Bringle & Hatcher (1996)
Risk management policy/procedures	Rue (1996)

(*Continues*)

TABLE 5.1 *(Continued)*

Practices	Source
Recognition of student accomplishments	Rubin (1996)
Recognition of faculty accomplishments	Bringle & Hatcher (1996); Rubin (1996)
Student leadership and decision making	Bringle & Hatcher (1996); Furco (2002a)
Transportation coordination/policy	Rue (1996)

Note. From "Current Practice and Infrastructure for Campus Centers of Community Engagement," by M. Welch and J. Saltmarsh, 2013, *Journal of Higher Education Outreach and Engagement, 17*(4), pp. 29–31. Reprinted with permission.

book. It is also available online. Responses to the online version are collected in a growing national database, which allows institutions to compare their results with aggregate results of other types of institutions with and without the Carnegie Classification for Community Engagement.

Role and Function of Campus Centers

The primary responsibility of campus centers is supporting curricular and cocurricular community engagement programs for students. A secondary and closely related purpose is providing support to faculty members and community partners participating in engaged pedagogy and engaged scholarship. As described in chapter 2, campus centers originally focused on cocurricular programs revolving around non-credit-bearing volunteer service projects for students. Over time this focus shifted to include establishing and coordinating curriculum-based engagement such as service-learning. However, not all centers coordinate both. For example, the Center for Community Engagement at the University of Massachusetts Amherst does not administer any cocurricular programs.

In addition to providing these pedagogical and scholarly programs, centers are responsible for logistical coordination, including creating and following policies and procedures (see Table 5.2). As community engagement has evolved, many campus centers have also taken on the role of providing professional development to faculty members as well as coordinating faculty-based work such as engaged scholarship through CBR (see chapter 7). Finally, as more and more campuses include community engagement in the required educational experience of students, centers have begun to take on greater logistical coordination of other forms of community engagement, such as work-study opportunities, internships, and immersion experiences, on behalf of the entire campus. This includes conducting program assessment and evaluation (Welch & Saltmarsh, 2013a, 2013b).

TABLE 5.2
Primary Purpose and Responsibilities of Campus Centers for Engagement

Responsibilities of the center	National (%)	Public (%)	Private (%)
Community partner development	80	75	87
Civic engagement	76	76	79
Community service	76	73	82
Academic service-learning	74	71	79
Student leadership development	60	54	68
Experiential learning	56	50	64
Federal programming	44	43	46
Community work-study	39	31	50

Note. Data from *2014 Campus Compact Member Survey,* by Campus Compact, 2014, Boston, MA: Author. Retrieved from http://compact.org/wp-content/uploads/2015/05/2014ALLPublicInstitutionsReport.pdf. Used with permission from Campus Compact.

Human Resources

Simply put, human resources are people. People working in a campus center for engagement can be categorized into four broad groups: directors, staff, students, and peripheral personnel.

Directors

The center director oversees the operation of the center, supervises the staff, and serves as the manager of the budget. Unless the center has a development officer, the director often assumes a role in fund-raising and grant writing. The director often serves as the face of the center, representing it on and off campus. Thus, unless the center has a dedicated staff member responsible for communication and outreach, many directors must communicate and articulate the mission and work of the center to multiple audiences.

As the field continues to evolve, the role of an engagement officer or director of a campus center for engagement appears to be falling into a new hybrid professional role that Whitchurch (2008, 2013) called "third space professionals." Not to be confused with Cantor's (2010) conceptualization of a hybrid physical setting for place-based education (described in chapter 9), third space professionals do not fall neatly into traditional administrative roles and responsibilities in higher education. Whitchurch suggested that some higher education professionals shift their professional identities in three phases. The first phase is contestation, in which professionals are viewed as outsiders because their duties do not reflect traditional administrative or educational roles and expectations in the academy. Second, these professionals move through the reconciliation phase, in which their new professional identity takes shape and emerges. Third, the professionals reach the reconstruction phase, in which new rules, resources, roles, and responsibilities emerge through collaborative interactions with colleagues that gradually validate the new professional identity. This is particularly applicable to the context of community engagement, as these educational professionals do not necessarily fall under academic affairs or student life. Further, as various forms of community engagement are implemented, coordination and oversight often involve collaboration with other related offices.

Most directors have a graduate degree (see Table 5.3). Their levels of education, however, are not necessarily indicative of the professional pathway they have taken to assume their position (Welch & Saltmarsh, 2013a, 2013b). As discussed in more detail in chapter 9, the professionalization of community engagement in higher education has raised a number of questions, including, How prepared are directors of campus centers to take on this role given the few graduate-level professional preparation programs in this area?

Similarly, the results of Welch and Saltmarsh's (2013a, 2013b) study of 147 campus centers with the Carnegie Classification revealed that the center director typically has a graduate degree and is generally professionally aligned with academic affairs, although the disciplinary background of the administrator varies considerably. Meanwhile, only a third of the respondents had a background in student affairs, and a quarter reported coming from a community leader role. Just over half (53.9%) of the directors have a doctoral degree, and slightly less than half (47%) have a master's degree from a variety of disciplines (e.g., MEd, MBA, MFA, MPA).

Background in a specific discipline may not be nearly as important as foundational understanding of the public purpose of community engagement in higher education coupled with some fundamental knowledge of the mechanics and pragmatics of implementing engaged pedagogy and scholarship. Minimally, directors of campus centers for engagement should have

TABLE 5.3
Center Directors' Highest Level of Education

Degree	National (%)	Public (%)	Private (%)
Doctoral or equivalent	31	25	31
Master's	55	59	51
Bachelor's	11	10	12

Note. Data from *2014 Campus Compact Member Survey*, by Campus Compact, 2014, Boston, MA: Author. Retrieved and adapted from http://compact.org/wp-content/uploads/2015/05/2014ALLPublic InstitutionsReport.pdf. Used with permission from Campus Compact.

some direct experience with engaged pedagogy or scholarship. This would suggest they have an understanding of the rewards and challenges associated with community engagement. Furthermore, a director must be able to navigate town-and-gown culture by being aware of and garnering trust from community partners.

An academic background or faculty appointment empowers a center director with an understanding of academic culture. This understanding allows directors to converse with colleagues and instills directors with a sense of credibility. On the other hand an academic background could create barriers when directors work with community partners. Consequently, center directors with faculty appointments must intentionally work to establish a rapport with community partners and understand the context of their mission in their role as coeducators. Finally, campus directors coming from faculty positions must learn various administrative roles and responsibilities that are not typically part of their autonomous academic experience as a scholar. These roles and responsibilities include recruiting and hiring staff members; supervising personnel and overseeing staff members coordinating various programs; conducting performance reviews of staff members; reporting to institutional leadership and other entities, such as professional associations; managing budgets; raising funds; convening and conducting efficient meetings with staff members and advisory committees; working with development in fund-raising; and being the public face of the office to various audiences.

McReynolds and Shields (2015) designed a professional development framework for center administrators composed of three overarching areas—education, reflection, and communication—and four spheres of knowledge and skills that enable a director to be an organizational manager, institutional strategic leader, community innovator, and field contributor (see Figure 5.1).

Recently, 16 practitioner-scholars formed a learning community to identify and enumerate the essential skills and competencies of a center director (Dostilio, in press; Dostilio & Perry, in press). An initial literature review, coupled with participants' own reflection and self-reports, revealed 100 distinct statements of knowledge deemed necessary for effective center directors. These were categorized into seven functional clusters: committing to social change, leading change in higher education, institutionalizing community engagement on a campus, administering community engagement programs, facilitating students' civic learning and development, facilitating faculty development and support, and cultivating high-quality partnerships.

Staff

The constellation of staff members in campus centers for community engagement varies according to the size and scope of the center's operations.

Figure 5.1 Professional development framework for center directors.

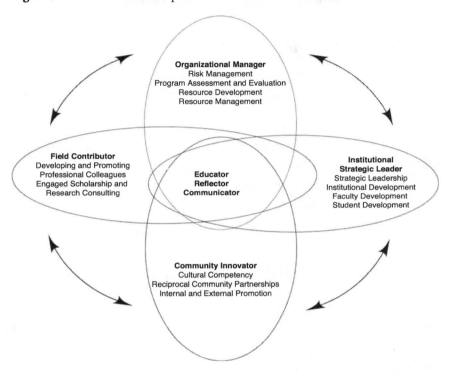

Note. From McReynolds, M., & Shields, E. (2015). *Diving deep in community engagement: A model for professional development.* (p. 12) Boston, MA: Campus Compact. Reprinted with permission.

Typically, the staff includes a full-time associate or assistant director, a full- or part-time administrative assistant (who serves as general office and clerical support), full- or part-time program coordinators or managers, and student workers (who often serve as part-time receptionists, answering the phone or entering data into data management systems) (Welch & Saltmarsh, 2013a, 2013b). Some centers use AmeriCorps volunteers in service to America (VISTAs) as part-time paraprofessional staff members to oversee specific program operations. Program coordinators oversee cocurricular and curricular programs (see Table 5.4). For curricular programs staff members assist faculty members in conceptualizing engaged pedagogy courses or engaged scholarship such as CBR, both of which require arranging partnerships with community agencies. These staff members also typically provide group professional development or one-on-one technical assistance to faculty members. They may also supervise and coordinate students serving as course assistants.

The variance in center staff size is usually due to the number of curricular and cocurricular programs in operation; larger staffs often require a

TABLE 5.4
Staff Constellations at Centers With Carnegie Classification for Community Engagement

	Yes (Percentage) (Number of Responses)	*In progress (Percentage) (Number of Responses)*	*Hope to (Percentage) (Number of Responses)*	*No (Percentage) (Number of Responses)*	*Number of Responses*
Full-time administrator	91.4 (117)	1.6 (2)	3.9 (5)	3.1 (4)	128
Full-time administrator with faculty status	39.4 (50)	3.9 (5)	7.1 (9)	49.6 (63)	127
Full-time administrative assistant	53.1 (68)	3.1 (4)	7.0 (9)	36.7 (47)	128
Part-time administrative assistant, graduate assistant, VISTA	82.0 (100)	3.3 (4)	2.5 (3)	12.3 (15)	122
Advisory/ governing board	71.9 (92)	16.4 (21)	7.0 (9)	4.7 (6)	128
Advisory/ governing board with community representatives	43.0 (55)	20.3 (26)	20.3 (26)	16.4 (21)	128
Advisor/ governing board with student representatives	40.2 (51)	25.2 (32)	18.1 (23)	16.5 (21)	127
Faculty advisory board	56.7 (72)	18.1 (23)	9.4 (12)	15.7 (20)	127
Development officer (either on staff or assigned to support the center)	41.4 (53)	7.8 (10)	13.3 (17)	37.5 (48)	128

Note. Data from "Current Practice and Infrastructure for Campus Centers of Community Engagement," by M. Welch and J. Saltmarsh, 2013, *Journal of Higher Education Outreach and Engagement, 17*(4), p. 37.

single full-time coordinator or manager. However, the size of a campus does not always dictate the size of a center staff, especially if the role of the center is primarily related to networking and brokering partnerships rather than cocurricular programs for students. A case in point is the University of Delaware's Center for Service-Learning, which has a staff of one. A smaller campus center, the Center for Community Engagement at Stetson University, a Carnegie-classified institution, has a staff of four—a director with a master's degree, an assistant director with a bachelor's degree, an AmeriCorps VISTA serving as a community organizer, and another AmeriCorps VISTA overseeing the cocurricular Bonner Leader program. In contrast, a larger campus center, the Center for Public Service at Tulane University, has a total of 25 staff members organized and categorized into administration, faculty programs, academic community engagement, outreach and leadership development, and student support. The administrative unit consists of a full-time director with a doctorate, a departmental administrator, a development officer, a faculty researcher, a research associate, and a project assistant. The center has three faculty program directors, all with doctorates, who oversee the Public Service Fellows program and the faculty seminar programs, and a faculty member from the Department of English serves as a community engagement advocate. The Academic Community Engagement Center has multiple staff members who oversee and manage internships and service-learning.

Students

Many centers use students as leaders who oversee and coordinate cocurricular programs. These individuals typically come up through the ranks, starting as volunteers and gradually assuming leadership roles under the supervision of staff members. As a result these students develop various professional and civic skills such as effective communication, problem-solving, conflict management, and time management, which will serve them well in their personal, professional, and civic lives. Some students may assist with communications by updating social media or capturing activities in photos and videos. As described in chapter 6, student teaching assistants often help faculty members with logistical coordination of service-learning courses. Students may also serve in an advisory capacity as members of various committees and boards. Students often serve as clerical assistants in the center, completing a variety of tasks, such as data entry and reception.

Peripheral Personnel

Peripheral personnel are individuals who are not central to the operation of the campus center. This should not be considered a pejorative title, as it accurately describes the important roles and responsibilities of staff members who do not necessarily contribute to or participate in the daily operations of the center. These individuals are not typically part of the center staff but are often employees of the institution or professionals in fields related to the mission and function of the center.

Advisory Board and Committees

A study of centers at institutions with the Carnegie Classification for Community Engagement revealed that 58% of the respondents had an advisory or governing board, 43% of the centers had advisory committees with community representation, and 40% included students on these steering committees (Welch & Saltmarsh, 2013a, 2013b). The Haas Center at Stanford has a national advisory board as well as a faculty steering committee that meets quarterly. Pitzer College has a steering committee for its Community Engagement Center. Some centers as large as the Lowell Bennion Community Service Center at the University of Utah and as small as the Catholic Institute for Lasallian Social Action (CILSA), which oversees curricular and cocurricular community engagement programs at Saint Mary's College of California, have established development boards of supporters and alumni to help with fund-raising and so-called friend-raising.

Development Officer or Liaison

Weerts and Hudson (2009) conducted a study of advancement and development practices at 15 institutions of various types that had received the Carnegie Classification in 2008. Their study indicated that advancement and development associated with centers for engagement are relatively new phenomena; each institution is "finding its own way" (p. 67) according to its own mission, culture, and organizational structure. Weerts and Hudson's (2009) study also revealed that private liberal arts colleges have been the most successful in their fund-raising efforts while other types of institutions continue to explore development plans. Finally, it appears that the marketing and branding of engagement are an essential part of advancement and development, requiring ongoing collaboration with the institution's communications office and alumni associations. Welch and Saltmarsh (2013a, 2013b) reported that nearly half of the respondents in their study had either a development officer on center staff or a liaison to the institutional office of advancement and development.

Community Partners

The democratic and pedagogical spirit of community engagement views community partners as coeducators. In a sense directors of community agencies working with campus centers could be perceived as virtual staff members as they facilitate the operations and programs that meet the mission and purpose of the center.

Center Alumni Chapters

A few centers have established alumni chapters or affinity groups of former student leaders actively involved in the center. These groups have many potential benefits and uses. Former student leaders have personal experience and insight that may be useful to the center director and staff in shaping or revising programs. Alumni can also serve as resources and mentors to current student leaders by making presentations on how their engaged leadership experiences shaped their professional paths. Relatedly, these former student leaders often hold professional positions and careers in settings that could potentially serve as partners. Finally, this group is a critical mass of individuals with shared experience who can provide financial or in-kind support to programs for current students, thereby supporting the center's mission. The center director or a staff member typically oversees and coordinates alumni chapters and affinity groups.

Informational Resources

Informational resources are broadly defined as written or unwritten knowledge and ideas that influence activities, programs, and operations. Centers use informational resources to guide and support operations. Information is also collected and distributed. This includes tangible mission statements, policies, rules, and regulations as well as curricula or an understanding of skill sets or practices. Centers also collect intangible information, such as cultural values that influence how things are done and why they are done in a certain way. This type of information includes mission or value statements that guide the work and sometimes is embedded in operational tools (discussed later in this chapter). The discussion presented here examines four broad categories of informational resources typically used by campus centers for engagement: policies, educational materials, communications, and data collection and management.

Policies

Every campus center must abide by not only institutional policies but also often legal and professional policies enforced by governmental and community agencies. Policies can also be criteria or benchmarks used to officially designate courses and cocurricular programs as institutionally sanctioned forms of community engagement.

In addition, many centers create and follow their own policies that explain and guide seemingly perfunctory tasks and requirements, such as time lines for submitting course proposals and meeting criteria to be officially designated as a community engagement course. This may include creating and implementing selection criteria for potential community partners. Centers also need to articulate and comply with external policies and procedures such as background checks or tuberculosis tests, which are legally required at many community partner sites.

Educational Materials

Educational materials in the form of brochures, training manuals, videos, and websites are used to educate students, faculty members, and community partners about various programs as well as policies and procedures. These materials include curriculum content used in leadership development for students as well as professional development for faculty members and community partners. It is often left to the campus center staff to develop these materials and resources. However, the center staff also has access to a huge amount of information and resources that has emerged from the field over the past two decades. This information is useful not only for faculty members, students, and community partners but also for center staff.

The National Service-Learning Clearinghouse (gsn.nylc.org/clearing house) is the single most comprehensive online resource available to faculty members. Another excellent online resource is Campus Compact (www .compact.org), which provides sample syllabi, reports, articles, and a list of venues for disseminating research, including professional journals. The AAC&U website has an extensive list of books, reports, and materials that can be used to support faculty members in their engaged work.

Communications

Centers should provide information to audiences outside the center. Among these audiences are campus stakeholders such as institutional leaders, faculty members, and other offices within academic affairs and student life. Many center directors regularly provide campus presidents with talking points for campus leadership, such as trustees, donors, and state legislators. Likewise, centers must communicate information outside the institution to alumni, community partners, funding agencies, governmental agencies, other institutions of higher education, and related professional associations, as well to the general public. This is typically accomplished through press releases, newsletters, social media, and annual reports.

Data Collection and Management

Centers collect and manage information that is used by various units and organizations for different purposes. This information is often demographic—for example, number of students, faculty members, and community agencies involved in community engagement programs—and is used in reports to the institution; reports to accreditation agencies; grant proposals; national surveys, such as those conducted by Campus Compact; and applications to specific organizations, such as the Carnegie Foundation, to receive institutional classification for community engagement. Offices of institutional research (IR) may also request this type of information as part of institutional strategic planning and assessment.

Centers also track and maintain course syllabi and the names of instructors who teach courses featuring community engagement. They maintain records of which community partners and agencies are engaged with instructors in either courses or CBR efforts. Many funding agencies and federal programs require careful tracking of student hours in cocurricular programs, and centers must conduct this tracking.

Operational Tools

Operational tools are tangible objects used in an activity designed to meet specific goals. Technological tools range from complicated computer programs to paper clips to data management programs. Budgets, spreadsheets, computers, directories, files, and motor vehicles are all tools used to manage information related to the operation of the center and its programs.

Tools can also include documents, such as risk assessment inventories and MOUs, that convey information about a community partner site. Instructors can no longer ask students to simply go out and find their own community partner site, owing to a litigious culture and dangerous world; risk assessments and MOUs are now often required to establish a partnership. Many campus centers for community engagement work with institutional counsel to implement and coordinate risk assessment and MOUs. For example, the Service-Learning Institute (SLI) at California State University at Monterey Bay (CSUMB) uses a number of formal documents in establishing and maintaining community partnerships.

The institute's Learning Agreement Form describes the students' specific responsibilities at their service-learning site. The document is signed by the student, course instructor, and site supervisor and kept on file in the SLI for three years. The University-Agency Agreement for Placement of Students serves as a formal agreement between the university and a community-based organization, school district, or government agency that articulates roles and responsibilities for each party, as well as issues of liability and workers' compensation. This agreement may be renewed every five years. Another document related directly to community partnerships is the Community Site Visit Checklist, designed to assess the requirements, risks, and basic safety factors of a community organization site before a student works there. The checklist is completed by a CSUMB staff or faculty member who visits prospective organizations.

Federally funded AmeriCorps programs use a Web-based reporting system (WBRS, pronounced "web-ers") to track student hours in service sites. Although students are expected to report and submit their own information to the database, a center staff person or student worker is often required to monitor the process. Centers are beginning to use commercially developed databases to coordinate how many students are working with specific community partners. Software developers are now visible at professional conferences as vendors or presenters demonstrating their product in the context of program assessment (Hackensmith & Barker, 2015). Information gleaned from these tools is used in a number of ways. It can provide reports to faculty members teaching service-learning courses and to their community partners to help monitor the progress of their partnership. These data are also useful to centers as they prepare and submit reports to the institution and other entities, including the President's Honor Roll for Community Service and the application to receive the Carnegie Classification for Community Engagement.

Thus, the general operation of a campus center for community engagement involves gathering, reporting, and using information with various operational tools to support and maintain the center's mission and its programs to promote community engagement. Operational trends for centers with the Carnegie Classification for Community Engagement are summarized in Table 5.5. This list of operational responsibilities does not include actual programming for students, faculty members, and community partners. These types of programs are presented in detail in the following chapters. The professional literature provides very little information on the actual operational components of campus centers. Therefore, while the data presented here do not represent a comprehensive description of operations at all centers, they do reflect operational trends of centers. In essence, this table provides a useful and concise brushstroke of what campus centers for community engagement do with human, informational, and technological resources.

Physical Resources

Physical resources are geographical locations, settings, or buildings that could include classrooms, community centers, schools, office space, or

TABLE 5.5

Operational Trends for Centers With the Carnegie Classification for Community Engagement

	Yes (Percentage) (Number of Responses)	In progress (Percentage) (Number of Responses)	Hope to (Percentage) (Number of Responses)	No (Percentage) (Number of Responses)	Responses
Manages/coordinates campus-wide community engagement requirements	67.5 (85)	7.9 (10)	5.6 (7)	19.0 (24)	126
Uses mechanisms and procedures to assess learning outcomes	44.5 (57)	35.2 (45)	15.6 (20)	4.7 (6)	128
Uses mechanisms and procedures to assess programs	58.6 (75)	30.5 (39)	10.9 (14)	0.0 (0)	128
Announces and provides resource materials	92.9 (118)	3.9 (5)	1.6 (2)	1.6 (2)	127
Conducts research on faculty involvement in service-learning/engaged pedagogy	35.9 (46)	23.4 (30)	25.0 (32)	15.6 (20)	128
Conducts surveys on student involvement in service-learning/community engagement programs on campus	64.8 (83)	15.6 (20)	14.1 (18)	5.5 (7)	128
Creates and uses student course assistants	34.6 (44)	10.2 (13)	13.4 (17)	41.7 (53)	127
Provides course development grants	62.5 (80)	7.8 (10)	10.2 (13)	19.5 (25)	128
Maintains course syllabi file and database	41.4 (53)	23.4 (30)	16.4 (21)	18.8 (24)	128
Maintains database on faculty involvement in service-learning or community-based pedagogy	54.7 (70)	25.0 (32)	9.4 (12)	10.9 (14)	128
Evaluates community partner satisfaction	66.7 (84)	18.3 (23)	11.1 (14)	4.0 (5)	126
Evaluates student satisfaction with service-learning or community-based pedagogy	63.3 (81)	16.4 (21)	14.1 (18)	6.3 (8)	128
Facilitates faculty research on service-learning or community engagement	50.8 (60)	21.2 (25)	22.0 (26)	5.9 (7)	118

(Continues)

TABLE 5.5 (*Continued*)

	Yes (Percentage) (Number of Responses)	In progress (Percentage) (Number of Responses)	Hope to (Percentage) (Number of Responses)	No (Percentage) (Number of Responses)	Responses
Employs fund-raising mechanisms (grants and donors)	54.7 (70)	14.1 (18)	16.4 (21)	14.8 (19)	128
Involves students in creating service-learning/ community-based courses	38.5 (35)	8.8 (8)	31.9 (29)	20.9 (19)	91
Makes presentations about community engagement and the campus center at new faculty orientation	68.5 (87)	7.1 (9)	13.4 (17)	11.0 (14)	127
Makes presentations about community engagement and the campus center at new student orientation	72.7 (93)	10.2 (13)	5.5 (7)	11.7 (15)	128
Has/implements/ coordinates risk management procedures	53.9 (69)	25.0 (32)	9.4 (12)	11.7 (15)	128

Note. Data from "Current Practice and Infrastructure for Campus Centers of Community Engagement," by M. Welch and J. Saltmarsh, 2013, *Journal of Higher Education Outreach and Engagement, 17*(4), pp. 38–39.

neighborhoods. Minimally, campus centers for community engagement require individual office space for each staff member and space for program activities. Ideally, centers include meeting space with tables, chairs, and a television or computer monitor for presentations as well as social or work space for students. The center must be welcoming and inviting and provide a sense of place for students who often gather there for work-related tasks as well as socializing with peers, doing homework, or just hanging out. The size and scope of the office space vary by the size and scope of the center and its home institution.

The 14,000-square-foot, 3-story Haas Center for Public Service at Stanford University was built in 1993 after the original Public Service Center was relocated from the Owen House. The University of Nebraska at Omaha recently completed the construction of its new 60,000-square-foot Barbara Weitz Community Engagement Center at a cost of $24 million. Other centers comprise a few square feet of office space for a desk, files, and perhaps a conference or work table.

Location, Location, Location

True to the real estate tenet, the physical location of the campus center for engagement, regardless of whether it reports to academic affairs or student affairs, is critical. The value of easy and visible access to the center was included in the early literature (Pigza & Troppe, 2003) and continues to be an important component in the application for the Carnegie Classification for Community Engagement. All constituencies served by the center—students, faculty members, and community partners—must know where the center is and how to find it. Community partners can often become frustrated when they are navigating the maze of buildings and the parking situation on a campus. The Center for Community Engagement at Seattle University is located on the boundary of campus, making it easily accessible to community partners.

Off-Campus Settings

As discussed previously, community engagement initiatives are expanding from temporary, short-term partnerships in various settings to sustained, long-term partnerships through place-based education or anchor institutions. These initiatives frequently entail a physical presence in a specific area of the community or neighborhood. In a sense this approach creates an annex location, expanding the boundaries of the campus center to create either shared space with a community agency or an autonomous office space located off campus. This reframes some of the roles and responsibilities of campus centers and staff members as they often coordinate or oversee these off-campus programs. Some off-campus programming results in the creation of a hybrid center for community engagement. For example, the University of Utah leases the former residence of a city park caretaker to establish a physical presence in a specific neighborhood as an annex office to coordinate the University Neighborhood Partners program, working in collaboration with the Lowell Bennion Community Service Center on campus.

The Sabo Center for Democracy and Citizenship at Augsburg College has implemented place-based partnerships in shared space with the Cedar-Riverside neighborhood of Minneapolis, which borders the campus. The School of Education has created and oversees a charter school located in a nearby housing complex. Nursing students work in a health center, and other students provide English as a second language tutoring at this same housing complex. In addition, the college works with a nearby ecumenical religious center known as the Common Table, devoted to capacity building and community organizing. The Feinstein Institute for Public Service at Providence College acquired a 1,000-square-foot office space in a nearby neighborhood to establish meaningful conversations and partnerships with the community.

Rutgers University chancellor Nancy Cantor refers to these as *third spaces*, a term that connotes the creation of an entirely new physical space, independent of the institution of higher education and its related community organization, that can revitalize a sector of the community while meeting the public and educational mission of higher education (U.S. Department of Housing and Urban Development, 2013a).

Financial Resources

Financial resources are monetary funds that pay for activities, personnel, and equipment. These funds may be part of the institutional budget or flow-through dollars from governmental, corporate, or private sources. Not surprisingly, center directors reported the importance and necessity of institutional funds to support center programming (Welch & Saltmarsh, 2013a, 2013b). In a study of 15 different institutions receiving the Carnegie Classification for Community Engagement, Weerts and Hudson (2009) found that the amount and type of internal funding for community engagement centers vary by institutional mission, size, and culture, with larger public research universities typically having larger and more complex budgets. Budgets typically included staff salaries and benefits, operational funds for student programs, and professional development for faculty. Weerts and Hudson (2009) also noted that institutional funding tended to support academically based programming for developing curricula, courses, and learning objectives around civic themes more so than cocurricular programs. Finally, internal institutional funds tended to be supported by a range of external grants, such as AmeriCorps funding to support student programming. Welch

TABLE 5.6
Centers' Annual Budgets

Annual budget including salaries	National (%)	Public (%)	Private (%)
Less than $20,000	12	15	9
$20,000–$49,000	9	8	10
$50,000–$99,000	16	16	17
$100,000–$249,000	27	28	25
$250,000–$499,000	17	17	18
$500,000–$999,999	9	8	11
$1,000,000+	6	7	6

Note. Data from *2014 Campus Compact Member Survey*, by Campus Compact, 2014, Boston, MA: Author. Retrieved from http://compact.org/wp-content/uploads/2015/05/2014ALLPublicInstitutionsReport.pdf. Used with permission from Campus Compact.

and Saltmarsh (2013a, 2013b) reported that nearly two thirds of the respondents from their survey of 128 centers with the Carnegie Classification have incorporated fund-raising as a mainstay operation of the campus center.

Some larger centers have significant operating budgets that are funded by a combination of institutional dollars, endowments, grants, and fund-raising. For example, the Haas Center for Public Service at Stanford University has a staff member solely dedicated to development and an annual operating budget of $5 million, of which only 15% comes from general institutional funds; the remaining 85% is derived from endowments or gifts. The Haas Center's annual appeal generates approximately $700,000.

Campus Compact's report on its 2014 member survey included a table of the annual budgets of responding centers (see Table 5.6). Just over a quarter of the respondents reported an annual budget (including salaries) in the range of $100,000–$249,000.

Grants

Virtually all centers for engagement rely on some form of grant funding. In fact, grants often make up the bulk of center budgets. For example, only 25% of the annual operating budget of the Sabo Center at Augsburg College in Minneapolis is derived from institutional funds while the remaining 75% of the budget is derived from grants. AmeriCorps programs often provide federally funded flow-through dollars to support cocurricular student programming, such as Jumpstart. AmeriCorps grants also generate dollars to fund VISTAs to serve as program coordinators. Learn and Serve grants, as well as awards from the Fund for the Improvement of Postsecondary Education (FIPSE), also support center programs. Government agencies such as the National Science Foundation announce requests for proposals designed to integrate service-learning with science, technology, engineering, and math (STEM) priorities. Professional organizations such as the AAC&U provide seed grants to institutions and centers for new initiatives related to civic engagement. Large and small private foundations also provide grants. The W.K. Kellogg Foundation has a long history of supporting community and civic engagement initiatives. Local philanthropic foundations also provide grants for programs that demonstrate community impact.

The Lowell Bennion Community Service Center at the University of Utah presents a unique exception in the scenario with regard to grants. While initially receiving a Learn and Serve grant as seed funding in its infancy 25 years ago, the center made a pragmatic decision to avoid pursuing federally funded grants such as AmeriCorps. The exception to this approach was the institution's Office of Financial Aid participation in the AmeriCorps America Reads program, which transferred operational funds to the campus center that housed the program coordinator and managed the budget. The decision not to pursue federally funded grants was based on three primary reasons. First, the center administrator and staff found the bureaucratic logistics aversive and time-consuming, diverting time and energy from other tasks and priorities. Second, the center and its advisory board made a tactical decision to minimize reliance on precarious federal funding that could be reduced or eliminated during national fiscal crises, thus threatening the continuation of programs. Third, and related to the second reason, the center and its board targeted endowed gifts and grants from local foundations as its priorities. Endowments provided the center with greater latitude in programming priorities and coordination.

Endowments

Many centers rely on drawing interest from the principal of endowments that have been provided as gifts to the center. Some centers are actually established with endowment gifts. For example, the Sturzl Center for Community Service and Learning at St. Norbert College was created through the gift of an alumni family in partnership with a food corporation. The Bonner Foundation played an instrumental role in establishing centers for community engagement at Berry College and Oberlin College, with each center bearing the Bonner name. The Community Engagement Center at Pitzer College is the result of gifts and grants from several private and corporate foundations. Endowments are also used to provide financial support for specific programs. The Center for Civic Engagement at Kalamazoo College has three endowments to fund civically engaged student projects that impact the community.

Fund-Raising

Centers rely on fund-raising in addition to extramural funding through grants. Research suggests that donors are inclined to support programs that demonstrate community impact (Grace & Wendroff, 2001; Weerts & Hudson, 2009). Centers coordinate fund-raising efforts internally if they have the staff and resources, or they collaborate with the institution's Office of Advancement and Development. These efforts typically involve reaching out to institution trustees, alumni, and friends. A premiere example of significant financial gifts is the $40 million donation by the Tisch family to the College of Citizenship and Public Service at Tufts University. The college has since been renamed to bear the Tisch family name.

Fund-raising is often included in an institution's strategic plan, as is the case of the efforts to support the Center for Community Engagement at California State Polytechnic University, Pomona. Funds can successfully be raised through annual appeals, galas or events, and social media. The Netter Center at the University of Pennsylvania reaches out to alumni, trustees, and classes to support and sponsor specific programs or individual students participating in internship opportunities. In the fall of 2011, Citizen Alum was created at the University of Michigan as an affiliated program of the American Commonwealth Project. The organization is a national network of campus teams that involves alumni, campus leaders, faculty members, staff members, and current students—as "agents and architects of democracy"(American Commonwealth Project, 2011, p. 2) to provide financial or in-kind support to centers of engagement.

Dispersal of Funds

In addition to obtaining funds for operations, centers often disperse funds as part of their operations. This can include institutional dollars used to provide course development grants for faculty members, funds to buy out a course taught by a faculty member to create a course or pursue an engaged scholarship project, or stipends or honoraria to faculty members successfully completing professional development programs. Centers also disperse stipends, scholarships, or service awards to student leaders coordinating programs or participating in fellowships and internships. Finally, centers may administer flow-through dollars to community partners to support community engagement initiatives.

Summary

This chapter has used a systems approach to examine the infrastructure and operation of centers for community engagement. The information presented here reveals the moving parts, nuts, and bolts of infrastructure that make up a campus center. Campus centers for community engagement are busy hubs of activity that are different from many other offices on campus because they serve three distinct constituencies: students, faculty members, and community partners. Furthermore, the nature of the center's work is substantially different from on-campus units because it requires nimble dexterity in juggling policies and procedures in a culture and setting known for academic autonomy. The next three chapters present the most important work of the campus centers, describing programming to support students, faculty members, and community partners.

PART THREE

PROGRAMS

Program [prō-ˌgram] *noun*

: a plan or system under which action may be taken toward a goal

—Merriam-Webster, 2016

6

ENGAGING STUDENTS

Preparing graduates for their public lives as citizens, members of communities, and professionals in society has historically been a responsibility of higher education. Yet the outcome of a civic-minded graduate is a complex concept. Civic learning outcomes are framed by personal identity and commitments, disciplinary frameworks and traditions, pre-professional norms and practice, and the mission and values of colleges and universities. Civic engagement can take many forms, from individual volunteerism to organizational involvement to electoral participation.

—Association of American Colleges and Universities (2010, p. 1)

This chapter provides an overview of community engagement in cocurricular and curricular programs for students. Colby, Ehrlich, Beaumont, and Stephens (2003) articulated eight basic principles of learning associated with engaged pedagogy through cocurricular and curricular programs in the context of preparing undergraduate students to be educated and engaged citizens:

1. Learning is an active, constructive process.
2. Genuine and enduring learning occurs when students are enthusiastic about their educational experience.
3. Thinking and learning are active and social processes.
4. Knowledge and skills are shaped by contexts in which they are learned.
5. Transfer of knowledge and skill occurs when they are learned in similar settings.
6. Intentional reflection and informative feedback are essential to learning.
7. Students have different levels and clusters of skills.
8. Genuine learning is facilitated by the ability to represent ideas and skills in more than one modality as well as moving to and from those various forms of knowing.

These principles can be applied to a variety of engaged pedagogical methods that vary in duration, outreach, and resources. Engagement opportunities occur along a continuum, ranging from non-credit-bearing, one-time service projects to course-based experiences in the community to complex anchor-based hybrid organizations comprising universities and businesses or health services with a physical presence in the community. Each form has both unique and similar characteristics with a degree of overlap. Some require nominal resources for implementation while others demand significant support in a variety of forms. Programs can be divided into three broad categories: cocurricular, curricular, and degrees or certificates. Providing a rationale for and orientation to the principles of community engagement and the mutuality of partnerships is an essential prerequisite for implementing any of the program types described here. Understanding students' historical and current role in cocreating their community engagement experiences is also important.

Student Roles and Leadership

The application process for the Carnegie Classification for Community Engagement requires articulating the students' role in community engagement. This requirement often nudges administrators, faculty members, and staff to reimagine the students' role. An important aspect of community engagement—beyond educating students as citizens and empowering community partners—is what might be called the hidden curriculum of leadership development for students. Students are not viewed merely as participants or recipients of community engagement but as critical partners and contributors in creating an engaged campus (Fretz & Longo, 2010). This premise was formally expressed in two landmark publications more than a decade ago.

In 2002 a group of 27 students was convened to develop and articulate a vision for student civic engagement. The group produced a document titled *The New Student Politics: The Wingspread Statement on Student Civic Engagement* (Long, 2002). A few years later, Campus Compact published *Students as Colleagues: Expanding the Circle of Service-Learning Leadership* (Zlotkowski et al., 2006), which described identifying and training student leaders and having students coordinate programs, thereby inviting them to be coscholars who worked with faculty members to teach courses, conduct engaged scholarship, and serve as academic entrepreneurs. Many of today's programs for students emerged from *Students as Colleagues*. Fretz and Longo (2010) aptly point out that some of the major initiatives driving the community engagement movement came from students. COOL, for example, was a student-led organization that promoted and helped launch community engagement in higher education. Break Away, an organization that promotes service-oriented spring breaks for college students, was similarly created by students. Vogel and colleagues (2010) noted that even the Teach for America program grew out of a student's senior thesis. Table 6.1 provides examples of various forms of student leadership in community engagement. The remainder of this chapter describes cocurricular and curricular programming as well as civic education and certificate programs and minors designed to prepare civic professionals.

TABLE 6.1
Student Leadership in Community Service, Service-Learning, and Civic Engagement Efforts on Campus

Characteristic	National (%)	Public (%)	Private (%)
Recruiting peers	93	90	97
Assisting in staffing the offices associated with curricular and cocurricular engagement	84	82	86
Assisting with reflection activities	72	66	80
Acting as liaisons to community sites	72	65	81
Serving on campus service, community engagement, and service-learning committees	69	71	69
Playing a lead role in setting the direction of the offices associated with curricular and cocurricular engagement	49	48	51
Acting as guest speakers in service-learning courses	45	48	42
Acting as service-learning course assistants	44	43	45
Recruiting faculty	44	39	49
Acting as service-learning co-instructors	18	19	17
Helping to design academic service-learning courses and create syllabi	16	15	17
Other	7	7	8

Note. Data from *2014 Campus Compact Member Survey,* by Campus Compact, 2014, Boston, MA: Author. Retrieved from http://compact.org/wp-content/uploads/2015/05/2014ALLPublicInstitutionsR eport.pdf. Used with permission from Campus Compact.

Rationale for and Orientation to Community Engagement

Most students are unlikely to understand or even be aware of the public purpose of their college education. They have been socialized to view college as a four-year experience designed to help them find a career. While some may, indeed, be searching for majors and careers that promote the common good and a democratic society, the vast majority of students will need a rationale for and orientation to engaged pedagogy. Some may have done service projects in high school, for church youth groups, or in a scouting organization. But the idea and practice of integrating academically based community engagement into a postsecondary educational experience traditionally comprising lectures, reading, written papers, and exams may be new at best and intimidating at worst. As more institutions formally incorporate community engagement in the educational experience and curriculum, students (and some faculty for that matter) may begin to view engagement experiences as matters of compliance to curricular programs; they may put in the hours just to check off a task required to pass a course or to graduate. To prevent this complaisance, students must fully understand the purpose and process of community engagement in curricular and cocurricular programs.

Students must also understand the principles articulated earlier in this book, including promoting intercultural humility before, during, and after engaged experiences. Engagement involves critical reflection, which can be a new and even intimidating experience for students. It also involves preparing students for their roles as leaders, change agents, and perhaps even paraprofessionals, as opposed to merely coaching them to be consumers of the factoids necessary to pass a course. Preparing students in this way becomes the responsibility of instructors and campus center staff members coordinating community engagement programs. Furthermore, community partners must provide a history and description of their missions, as well as their expectations, protocol, policies and procedures, before the actual activity or project begins. Finally, students should understand their role as what Boyte (2004) called "co-producers" (p. 80) in community engagement. Thus, unlike in traditional pedagogical approaches involving passive accumulation of information to be repeated on papers and exams, in community engagement students are cocreators of their experiences and knowledge. Table 6.2 presents an overview of the common types of cocurricular and curricular programs as reported in the 2014 Campus Compact survey.

Cocurricular Programs

Cocurricular approaches to engagement are generally characterized as voluntary, non-credit-bearing experiences that are mutually beneficial to the

TABLE 6.2
Types and Prevalence of Community Engagement Programs

Characteristic	National (%)	Public (%)	Private (%)
One-day service project	89	87	90
Nonprofit internship	84	79	89
Discipline-based service-learning courses	81	82	80
Service clubs	77	76	77
Alternative breaks	72	60	85
International service opportunities	72	64	81
First-year experience service opportunities	63	51	75
Residence hall–based service	59	53	66
Government internships	58	53	61
First-year orientation to service	55	43	68
Fraternities/sororities	55	57	51
Capstone service courses	54	54	53
Alumni service projects	43	32	54
Learning community concerning service and engagement	45	39	44
Summer service programs	40	36	45
Graduate school service	30	27	34
Intercampus service programs	37	37	38

Note. Data from *2014 Campus Compact Member Survey*, by Campus Compact, 2014, Boston, MA: Author. Retrieved from http://compact.org/wp-content/uploads/2015/05/2014ALLPublicInstitutionsReport.pdf. Used with permission from Campus Compact.

student and to the agencies and those they serve. These experiences are voluntary in that they are not required in a credit-bearing course or program major. Some are literally voluntary in that students do not receive any form of financial support. Other cocurricular programs may provide some form of a stipend, such as federal work-study funds or a voucher that can be used to defray the costs of college. Thus, cocurricular engagement programs are intentionally designed to promote students' civic growth.

Although not directly tied to formal course learning objectives, these cocurricular activities certainly afford learning opportunities. Unlike traditional *extra*curricular activities, which tend to be recreational or social in nature, *co*curricular programs often entail supervision and oversight by a professional staff member and are often housed in the campus center of community engagement. As opposed to traditional student clubs, which are often loose, informal, unsupervised gatherings, engaged cocurricular programs typically include regularly scheduled meetings, seminars, or training that focuses on topics or skill sets related to the activity. A few decades ago, most cocurricular programs were small in scope and could be easily coordinated by a staff member from a campus community service center who had other responsibilities. Today, as cocurricular programs grow in number and complexity, it is common for campus community centers to have one staff member dedicated to coordinating specific types of program activities.

As colleges and universities continue to formalize expectations and requirements for community engagement, some campuses include benchmarks or criteria to formally designate some cocurricular programs as meeting institutional requirements or learning goals. Cocurricular engagement may be developed and maintained by individual institutions or be part of a federally funded program.

Alternative Breaks

Two students from Vanderbilt University created Break Away, a program that provided opportunities for college student volunteers to perform weeklong service projects as an alternative to traditional spring break partying. By 2000 Break Away had become a 501(c)(3) not-for-profit organization with administrative offices at the Center for Civic Education and Service at Florida State University. The organization now involves nearly 200 campuses and over 500 nonprofit partners and provides a basic template for training, organizing, and implementing trips to various locations. Today, many colleges and institutions have created their own alternative breaks, which are typically organized by staff members at campus centers for community engagement. A key and consistent characteristic of the alternative break model is student leadership; students undergo significant training to lead and coordinate their trips and service activities. Participants commit to a week of service free from indulging in alcohol and drugs. Often they do not receive any academic credit for the experience, and they pay for travel, food, and housing themselves.

AmeriCorps—Federally Funded Service Programs

A number of federally funded AmeriCorps programs operate at many colleges and universities. These programs emerged from the Corporation for National and Community Service (CNCS). Most AmeriCorps programs require students to complete 300 hours of service during the academic year by committing to serve a minimum of eight hours per week at a project site.

Students must also complete required training throughout their service, pass a live-scan fingerprinting security check, and be a U.S. citizen or legal permanent resident. Many students receive work-study payment or educational vouchers that can be used to pay the cost of their college education.

Many campus centers for community engagement oversee and coordinate these programs. Often cooperating with offices of financial aid, center staff members recruit, train, coordinate, and supervise college students who receive work-study support to serve as tutors for children in underresourced schools. The tutors are therefore not volunteers working without pay in the traditional sense. Because these are cocurricular programs, the college students do not usually receive any academic credit.

President Clinton established America Reads in 1996 as a national literacy campaign. College students serve as reading tutors to children in schools. A year later, Clinton, in partnership with the National Science Foundation, established America Counts to use college students as tutors to enhance grade-level student performance in science and math. Jumpstart was also created in 1996 and coordinates preschool literacy programs, again using college students as tutors and mentors.

In addition to these specific programs, AmeriCorps education awards have been used in other cocurricular engagement programs. One example is the Justice Corps, created by the California Judicial Branch in 2004. To staff the corps, the Haas Center for Public Service at Stanford University recruits, trains, and places over 270 undergraduates and recent graduates in court-based self-help centers. Participants receive comprehensive training and supervision in providing individualized legal assistance, conducting workshops, and making referrals throughout the year. Similarly, AmeriCorps VISTAs have delivered and coordinated cocurricular civic engagement programs in community settings. Since 2008, for example, Siena College has given VISTA fellows the opportunity to spend the year working with community partner agencies as paraprofessionals.

Bonner Leaders and Scholars

The Bonner Foundation established a partnership with Berea College in 1990 to create a program that provided students in rural Appalachia financial scholarships and service opportunities. Today, the program is the largest privately funded, service-based college scholarship program in the country, with nearly 3,000 students participating at over 60 campuses. Students with financial need receive four years of financial aid and participate in one of two programs to nurture an ethos of service. Students in the Bonner Scholar Program engage in 10 hours a week of community service during the school year

(140 hours per semester) and 280 hours in the summer. The Bonner Leader Program supports students who commit to 300 hours of service throughout their college experience. Student leaders and supervising staff from campus centers attend leadership retreats during the summer. Hoy and Meisel (2008) created the five-level Bonner Model for Civic Development based on a variety of common experiences. The precollege expectation level establishes a foundation of engagement ethics and values. The first-year exploration level allows students to try a variety of service opportunities. The second-year experience level asks students to focus on one issue and geographic area. The third-year example level facilitates student leadership in the coordination of peers and specific projects. The fourth-year expertise level allows students to continue leadership in a specialty area.

Volunteer Service

Some institutions coordinate volunteer service programs and opportunities in which participating students receive no financial support or academic credit. The most common form is a one-time day of service, usually on Saturdays. While these service days are not directly tied to a course or discipline, participants are often exposed to information about the topic or issue being addressed in the activity. Student leaders coordinating the service project will often begin by providing an introductory overview of the underlying issues and explaining the relevance and impact of the day's activity. Representatives from the community organization involved in the service will also talk about the organization's history and mission to provide the group with foundational knowledge. Another traditional component of volunteer service days and projects is reflection, usually led by student leaders, in which participants in the service activity critically consider the need for service and the impact of their efforts, often using a reflection rubric. One such rubric is "What? So What? Now What?" originated by COOL. The reflection process invites students to consider the following questions: What is the issue? What can be done, or what did we do? Why does this matter? and finally, What can or should be done next?

Some campus centers for community engagement coordinate ongoing volunteer opportunities that do not provide any financial remuneration or academic credit throughout the academic year. Since 1987 the Lowell Bennion Community Service Center at the University of Utah has had an extensive student-directed volunteer service network with over 40 programs that fall into five broad categories: education and advocacy, environmental stewardship, health and ability, international service, and social justice. A student leader coordinates these categories, overseeing peers who direct each program in that category. A center staff member supervises and provides extensive leadership training to the student leaders. The student leaders recruit and train peers who commit to volunteering a specific number of hours over the course of the semester. With the guidance of center staff, these student leaders also release requests for proposals (RFPs) to local community organizations. Student leaders review the proposals and select formal community partners under the guidance of center staff.

Academic Student Assistants

An interesting hybrid form of student leadership and engagement has emerged in which students serve as assistants to faculty members and community partners involved service-learning courses. These students are not traditional teaching assistants who grade papers or lead study groups. Instead, they are student leaders who serve as liaisons between the instructor and community partner. They typically coordinate logistical tasks, such as transporting students to and from partner sites, monitoring service hours, and managing forms and other paperwork associated with the engaged learning experience. In this way students are developing leadership skills, such as time management, problem-solving, and effective communication, while also serving as an extra pair of eyes, ears, and hands for both the instructor and the community partner. Some students even conduct reflection discussions with their peers. Faculty members have found this type of support invaluable, as it reduces the amount of additional work common to teaching service-learning courses. In addition, these academic student assistants are getting an in-depth look behind the curtain at the moving parts associated with teaching a community engagement course. These students usually receive comprehensive training, much like the training faculty members receive in professional development programs that prepare them to teach community engagement courses. These assistantships are often paid positions for which students must apply, be interviewed, and be recommended by a faculty member. Assistants typically work 5 to 10 hours a week; some may assist with more than one course and for more than one instructor, depending on the type and size of the class.

Duquesne University has a Community Engagement Scholar program in which student assistants can choose between working primarily with a faculty member and working primarily with a community partner to provide support in community engaged course projects. Scholars attend 40 to 45 hours of training and seminars that include a 2-and-a-half-day retreat, 1-hour weekly seminars each semester, and a service-based seminar in the spring. Seminars provide an overview of the principles and practices of community engagement coupled with reflection. The service-based seminar requires scholars to complete at least 2 hours of direct service each week.

Curricular Programs

Curricular programs are credit-bearing experiences and opportunities that are tied to formal learning objectives in either a course or another academic experience, such as an internship or immersion. These programs typically involve oversight and coordination by a faculty member, thus making them a form of engaged scholarship as characterized previously. Students are not viewed as volunteers as the service they are providing is a form of pedagogy rather than an altruistic act of charity. In this sense, service is tied directly to the instructional and learning objectives of a course, like a written paper or reading assignment is. Many curricular programs have been characterized by Kuh (2008) as so-called high-impact practices owing to the pedagogical significance each approach can have on students' civic learning experience. Many types of programs lend themselves well to civic engagement, including service-learning/community-based learning, undergraduate research, internships, first-year experiences (FYEs), learning communities, diversity/global learning, and capstone courses. Research suggests these high-impact practices facilitate and promote deeper learning as well as self-reported personal and practical development (Kuh, 2008).

Service-Learning

As discussed in chapter 1, service-learning has evolved into a prominent form of engaged pedagogy, becoming a field unto itself with professional organizations, scholarly literature, and conferences. Over time a key role of most centers for engagement became coordinating service-learning on campuses. Two decades ago, Jane Kendall (1990) reported in her book, *Combining Service and Learning*, that 147 terms and definitions have been used to characterize *service-learning*. For some faculty members and institutions, the prefix "service" is problematic in several ways. First, it may connote a spirit of noblesse oblige or charity along with power over others. Second, it is often confused with the concept of service in the academic trilogy and may be viewed as less valued or scholarly. Thus, some programs use other terms, such as *academically based community service* or *community-based learning*. Today, we have well exceeded those 147 terms and definitions as practice of service-learning has grown exponentially. Bringle and Hatcher (1996) defined *service-learning* as

> a course-based, credit-bearing educational experience in which students participate in organized service that meets community needs, and reflect on the service to gain further understanding of course content, a broader appreciation of the discipline and an enhanced sense of civic responsibility. (p. 112)

This definition emphasizes the strategic and purposeful development of experiences in an authentic community setting that facilitates students' cognitive and academic development through reflection and mutually beneficial partnerships.

The National Service-Learning Clearinghouse summarized characteristics of service-learning gleaned primarily from Eyler and Giles (1999). Serving-learning experiences

- Are positive, meaningful, and real to the participants.
- Involve cooperative rather than competitive experiences and thus promote skills associated with teamwork, community involvement, and citizenship.
- Address complex problems in complex settings rather than simplified problems in isolation.
- Offer opportunities to engage in problem-solving by requiring participants to gain knowledge of the specific context of their service-learning activity and community challenges, rather than only to draw on generalized or abstract knowledge such as might come from a textbook; thus, service-learning offers powerful opportunities to acquire the habits of critical thinking (i.e., the ability to identify the most important questions or issues in a real-world situation).
- Promote deeper learning because the results are immediate and uncontrived; there are no right answers in the back of the book.
- Are personally meaningful to participants because of the immediacy of the experience; thus, they generate emotional consequences, challenge values and ideas, and support social, emotional, and cognitive learning and development.

Service-learning courses can provide direct or indirect service to community partners in a variety of ways, as illustrated in Box 6.1.

Like any form of teaching and learning, however, service-learning has its inherent drawbacks and challenges. Eby (1998) wrote a classic friendly critique of service-learning, titled "Why Service-Learning Is Bad," that warrants consideration. Other researchers and practitioners have voiced similar and related concerns that service-learning can be a form of charity, perpetuate negative stereotypes, and minimize complex social issues (Crabtree, 2008; Kiely, 2005). Mitchell (2008, 2013) has developed and presented a perspective of practice using critical theory that brings issues such as power and privilege to the forefront of professional dialogue and practice. These important points should be made as part of students' orientation and rationale for entering into partnership with community agencies.

BOX 6.1
Examples of Service-Learning Courses

College students in a chemistry class learned and applied chemical analysis skills by working with schools and community gardens. Students conducted soil and water analysis to determine the presence of toxins and articulated their results to a lay audience with recommendations for practice. The class collectively reflected on the role of chemists as professionals and citizens in policymaking and focused especially on resolving issues, such as environmental racism, in which underresourced agencies' or communities' exposure to toxins was greater than affluent areas'.

An undergraduate computer science course worked with a local wildlife conservation agency to create apps for mobile devices that identified various animals in a geographical region used for educational curricula.

A graduate-level research methods course provided indirect service to schools and nonprofit agencies by crunching numbers of existing surveys and assessment measures. Students were able to apply their statistical analysis knowledge by helping agencies.

A service-learning course in religious studies focused on food and faith issues by working with community gardens and local food banks. Students provided direct service by stocking shelves, delivering food, and working in gardens. They explored issues of social justice, poverty, and hunger using Christian scripture and tenets. Students critically reflected on society's role (or lack thereof) in caring for the hungry as well as on the intertwined issues of nutrition and other health or social needs.

Students in an Italian class developed their language skills and cultural understanding by meeting with elderly Italian immigrants to create an oral history on a DVD given to the seniors. Students reflected on cultural values, including American views of elders and family.

An urban planning class canvassed a neighborhood to conduct asset mapping and compiled a comprehensive report that can be used by various nonprofit agencies for collaboration when serving the area's residents.

A subset of service-learning that is directly tied to global education experiences is global service-learning (GSL), which has experienced significant growth and interest. GSL not only includes the basic principles of service-learning enumerated previously but also incorporates salient components related to international contexts. *GSL* is defined as

a community-driven service experience that employs structured, critically reflective practice to better understand common human dignity, self, culture, positionality, social and environmental issues, and social responsibility in global context. It is a learning methodology *and* a community development philosophy. It is also a way of being in that it encourages an ongoing, critically reflective disposition. (Hartman, Kiely, Friedrichs, & Boettcher, 2014, pp. 11–12)

Hartman and Kiely (2014) provided an extensive overview of GSL that also includes careful consideration of its limitations and potential drawbacks. They acknowledged the power and potential of carefully constructed and implemented GSL to include critical reflection on power and privilege and a focus on cultural competence to minimize neocolonialism. Campus centers of community engagement must therefore work with colleagues in offices such as international studies to incorporate critical best practices. Following an international service-learning summit in 2013, Cornell University, Duke University, Kansas State University, Northwestern University, and Washington University created Globalsl.org with support from the Henry Luce Foundation. The website offers extensive empirically based resources and information on research and best practices as well as a syllabi wiki and blog. The site also provides information on community development and social justice education focused on power, privilege, race, class, and gender.

The Center for Service and Learning in the Office of Community Engagement at IUPUI provides funds and professional development for faculty members to design and implement international service-learning courses. Elon University and North Carolina Campus Compact developed a useful guide of best practices for international service-learning that can be conducted through alternative breaks as well as semester-long courses.

A study by Niehaus and Kavaliauskas Crain (2013) revealed generally higher gains on a variety of dimensions, including levels of community engagement, for students who participated in international service-learning versus peers in domestic service-learning experiences over alternative breaks. In 2009 Study Abroad for Global Engagement (SAGE) surveyed nearly 6,400 graduates of 22 programs from 1950 to 2007. They examined global engagement through five self-reported domains: civic engagement in domestic and international arenas, knowledge production of various media, philanthropy through volunteering and financial donations, social entrepreneurship by working with organizations whose purpose or profits serve the community, and the practice of voluntary simplicity in one's lifestyle (Paige, Fry, Stallman, Josic, & Jon, 2009). Results revealed positive responses and outcomes in each of the categories.

A recent experimental study was designed as a follow-up to the SAGE study (Murphy, Sahakyan, Yong-Yi, & Magnan, 2014) to determine if there were differences in these same five domains between graduates of study abroad programs and a control group of alumni who did not participate in global study. The study revealed mixed results. Global study participants showed higher levels of civic engagement in international and domestic arenas as well as higher levels of voluntary simplicity. Results also revealed higher levels of philanthropic activity in the arts, education, the environment, human rights, international development, and social justice. The report revealed no significant differences in social entrepreneurship or in knowledge production.

Undergraduate Research

Undergraduate research is also considered a high-impact practice that can be incorporated in curricular programs promoting engaged learning. The Council on Undergraduate Research (CUR) defined *undergraduate research* as an inquiry or investigation conducted by an undergraduate student that makes an original intellectual or creative contribution to the discipline (www .cur.org). However, as described previously, CBR is a "partnership among students, faculty members, and community members who collaboratively engage in research with the purpose of solving a pressing community problem or effecting social change" (Strand et al., 2003, p. 3). What makes this a form of civic and community engagement is the intentional effort to conduct a study that addresses a community need and contributes to the disciplinary field. Research on or about a social issue in the community in and of itself does not constitute a form of engaged pedagogy. This method of inquiry and cocreating knowledge can be conducted by individual students through an independent study project or incorporated into the classroom, often as the "service" in service-learning courses.

Student Leaders in Community Engagement (SLICE) at Saint Mary's College of California is a yearlong program in which individual undergraduate students conduct a CBR project under the guidance of a supervisory committee. The committee comprises an instructor of record, a representative from a community agency, and a staff member from the campus center for community engagement. The project is typically on a topic of interest to the student, who meets with the community partner. The student formulates a research question and methodology with the community partner and writes an action plan to create an empirically based product. The product could be a curriculum, training materials, or a policy brief that the agency can implement in its programming. During the first semester the student works with the instructor of record to review the literature. The students meet as a cohort every other week during a seminar conducted by the campus center staff to learn principles of CBR and engaged pedagogy (Colby et al., 2003) and to monitor the progress of the research action plan. The second semester is used to implement the action plan, field-test the product, and write a final formal research paper that is compiled into a written monograph of all the projects. The students must also orally defend their project to their supervisory committee and make a public oral presentation to the campus community.

Undergraduate research incorporating CBR can also be conducted in a service-learning class by compiling policy briefs through literature reviews or conducting analysis of data that can guide the programs or policies of an organization. For example, Kowaleski (2004) described how an undergraduate research methods course in sociology conducted research on behalf of two local housing authorities. Incorporating research methods learned in class, such as content analysis, observation, interviews, and surveys, student teams were able to provide valuable data documenting program impact on clients of the organizations. In addition to applying assimilated research methods, students were able to work with and for community partners to address pressing programming needs while critically reflecting on salient social issues of poverty and homelessness.

First-Year Experiences

FYEs are typically associated with orientation programs for students entering college. *FYE* is defined as an intentional and comprehensive program designed to assist student transition into college as well as to enhance academic and personal development, provide a cohesive learning experience, nurture student persistence, and promote a sense of community and commitment to the campus (Barefoot, Fidler, Gardner, Moore, & Roberts, 1999). Many FYE activities include voluntary service projects that are often a college student's first experience in community engagement. Barefoot (2008) and Gardner (2008) enumerated a variety of strategies for integrating community engagement activities and programming throughout the campus during a student's first year. Hunter and Moody (2009) described several FYE programs, in addition to service projects, that promote civic engagement, including seminars with discussions, readings, and service activities. The University of Michigan conducts seminars on diversity and social justice in its First-Year Interest Groups. This program emphasizes and incorporates critical dialogue to promote civil discourse on volatile topics, such as stereotypes, power, privilege, and discrimination. George Washington University has first-year theme residential halls that focus on topics such as politics and environmental stewardship.

Much like service-learning, FYEs have become a field of their own, with a national resource center at the University of South Carolina, a growing professional literature, and conferences. As they have for service-learning, many campuses have established an office or center dedicated to the coordination of FYEs. These new centers are noteworthy, as they will influence the infrastructure of institutions, requiring additional coordination between and across offices and centers as more campuses institutionalize civic and community engagement. Hunter and Moody (2009) proposed some guiding principles for operating FYE programs that promote civic engagement. These include clearly articulating the connection of civic engagement and engaged pedagogy with the mission of the institution; clearly defining roles and responsibilities of community agencies, faculty members, and students in meeting mutually defined goals; and involving all stakeholders on a regular basis to seek and provide information and constructive criticism.

Learning Communities

Learning communities are interactive cohorts of students often taking a combination of courses together with multiple instructors. To integrate theory with practice, many learning communities incorporate experiential learning, such as service-learning, which includes reflection on the impact the service has on students and those they serve. De Anza College, a community college in California, has a learning community called Latina/o Empowerment at De Anza (LEAD) in which over 450 students work in small groups known as *familias*, led by student mentors. Students integrate content from courses into community-based projects (Murphy, 2014). Wagner College has made learning communities the cornerstone of its liberal arts curriculum, requiring students to participate in a learning community their first year, one in their sophomore or junior year, and one in their senior year. Learning communities explicitly promote civic engagement, reflecting many of the tenets of engaged pedagogy articulated by Colby and colleagues (2003) at the beginning of this chapter. Wagner College routinely assesses the impact of first-year and senior learning communities each year. Results indicate students consistently evaluate their experience as being very effective, with seniors typically rating their learning community experience higher than first-year students (Wagner College, 2014b).

Living-Learning Communities

Living-learning communities (LLCs) are typically part of a campus residential life program in which students live together in a theme-based hall or floor. Critical elements and best practices of LLCs include peer study groups, a focus on an academic discipline, academic and cultural discussions, and course-related faculty interactions (Nanna, Skillman, & Zgela, 2011). Themes are typically discipline specific, but residential communities are beginning to use learning communities to promote civic engagement

(Welch, 2009). Brower and Inkeles (2010) conducted a comprehensive study of LLCs, surveying more than 24,000 students at 34 institutions from 2004 to 2007. The study found student commitment to civic engagement through LLC-related volunteering activities or service-learning courses more frequent than civic engagement among students living in traditional residential programs.

The Haas Center for Public Service has its own public-service-themed residential hall. About half of the residents are sophomores while juniors and seniors equally make up the rest of the LLC. Students apply for acceptance and attend a fall retreat to discuss basic LLC group expectations. Residents must make a sustained commitment to various forms of service on a specific issue for one year. Additionally, LLC participants attend a winter retreat and end-of-year reflection retreat. Throughout the year residents engage in various formal and peer-facilitated LLC conversations. One formally structured discussion is on ethical principles of service, and another is on exploring professional and career pathways. Residents also participate in at least two student-led 90-minute discussions on various topics, such as power and privilege and intercultural humility. Finally, residents are required to participate in at least one of three direct service events sponsored by the LLC.

Other institutions have an array of LLCs related to community engagement. Colorado College has an LLC called Arts for Social Change in which residents commit to learning about and using the arts for advocacy and activism. Similarly, Oregon State University has an Arts and Social Justice LLC and a Civic Engagement LLC that conduct direct and indirect service projects on campus and in the local community. The Vincent and Louise House at DePaul University invites 10 students to live in an intentional Catholic community that promotes service, social justice, and voluntary simplicity. Since 2002 a total of 11 different academic departments and 19 professors have offered courses as part of the social justice learning community at Columbia College, reflecting the social justice principles of the United Methodist Church.

Capstone Experiences

Kecskes and Kerrigan (2009) provided an excellent overview of capstone experiences in the context of community engagement. Capstones are generally characterized as culminating educational experiences that provide students an opportunity to apply and demonstrate mastery of assimilated knowledge and skills through a project. In their review they examined and described departmental, interdisciplinary, independent, and honors capstones. They also emphasized that effective capstone experiences provide opportunities for students to learn, apply, and reflect on basic civic skills.

In keeping with the fundamental tenets of engaged pedagogy, students have an important role and responsibility in developing and implementing their capstone experience in partnership with community agencies. For example, the capstone experience in the certificate for civic engagement and public service at the University of Massachusetts Amherst requires students to identify a potential project and partner, seek the input and voice of the community in conceptualization, and develop an action plan with specific goals and outcomes.

Immersion Experiences

Immersion experiences are intensive experiences ranging from one week to a full academic year in a local, domestic, or international setting. Historically, immersion experiences were practiced in language acquisition programs by having students travel to and live in countries where English was not the primary language in order to develop language skills and have multicultural experiences (Graham & Crawford, 2012). Immersion is becoming more common in programs designed to incorporate civic and community engagement. As the name implies, the experience is all-encompassing as students often live together in a community setting to gain a sense of place as they learn and work.

From a cognitive development perspective, an immersion experience often creates cognitive dissonance or what Mezirow (1999) characterized as a disorienting dilemma, whereby students' assumptions about complex social issues such as poverty, race, power, and privilege are challenged. This dilemma provides an excellent opportunity for reflection activities that allow students to find meaning in their experience. This experience might be thought of as a "squirm and learn" (Welch, 2010b, p. 5) moment within a dynamic known as the "shadow side of reflection" (p. 1); instructors must accompany their students as they process what they feel as well as what they did and learned.

A common model for immersion experiences is alternative break programs that typically last for one week. Depending on their structure and nature, even short-term experiences can affect both students and community partners. Elder, Seligsohn, and Hofrenning (2007) reported that an immersion experience in the 2004 electoral campaigns had a significant impact on students' engagement indices. Short-term (six- or seven-day) immersion experiences were comparably educationally and civically impactful as traditional semester courses (Bowman, Brandenberger, Snyder, & Smedley, 2010).

The Micah Project at Saint Mary's College of California provides a unique eight-week summer immersion experience that combines essential tenets and purposes of community engagement with faith-based traditions, as described in chapter 2. The title of the program is from Micah 6:8: "What does the Lord require of you but to do justice, and to love kindness, and to walk humbly with your God?" (English Standard Version). Students apply, are interviewed, and are accepted into the program. They live together as a community in shared housing with a modest communal grocery budget in highly economically impacted neighborhoods in the community they serve. Each student works 40 hours a week as a paraprofessional at a nonprofit organization. Student responsibilities include direct and indirect service, such as conducting research for policy briefs, writing grant proposals, or developing programs. Students complete a comprehensive curriculum consisting of readings related to social justice and community organizing. They also engage in deep critical reflection two nights a week facilitated by a member of the college center for community engagement during community time dinner. The reflection discussions integrate readings with the community engagement experience. Students also earn academic credit for participating in and completing the academic exercises and the service. Transportation costs are provided, and students receive $2,500 at the end of the eight weeks to account for wages they may have lost by not having a summer job during the immersion experience.

Internships and Fellowships

Many campuses are using *internships* and *student fellowships* in their community engagement programs for students. These two terms are often treated as synonyms. Traditionally, however, an internship has been associated with preprofessional career development that primarily and unilaterally benefits the student. A fellowship, in contrast, is typically financial support that allows a student a concentrated period to pursue a scholarly activity. Stanford University (2015) defines a *fellowship* as a full or partial tuition payment and a stipend for living expenses awarded as financial support to a student and not provided in exchange for services. A fellowship may indeed nurture a student's career interests and may even serve as a catalyst for further career exploration, but it is not primarily designed to provide a setting and opportunity to practice professional skills to achieve a job.

Over time and with some modifications, both internships and fellowships have begun to incorporate tenets of community engagement to include mutual benefit to the community partner. As described in chapter 2, robust internship and fellowship experiences include learning objectives; ongoing and regular oversight by an educator or staff member from the campus center for engagement and someone with authority at the community agency; and academic exercises, such as readings, reflective journals, papers, or seminars, coordinated by an educator at the institution (O'Neill, 2010). At the same time these experiences must be codeveloped with the community partner so that the academic learning objectives are tied to meeting the partner's specific goals. Therefore, it is important to differentiate these types of experiences from other experiential learning programs, such as student teaching, practicums, and clinicals, as described in chapter 2.

There currently is debate about payment for interns and fellows. In the past some commercial and nonprofit agencies have essentially incorporated interns and fellows as unpaid employees, allowing the agencies to dismiss existing staff. Consequently, federal guidelines under the Fair Labor Standards Act (FLSA) have now been imposed to regulate and monitor paid and unpaid internships. The U.S. Department of Labor (DOL) developed six criteria for differentiating between an employee entitled to minimum wage and a learner or trainee who, while an employee, may be unpaid. The criteria are as follows:

1. The internship, even though it includes actual operation of the facilities of the employer, is similar to training that would be given in an educational environment;
2. The internship experience is for the benefit of the intern;
3. The intern does not displace regular employees, but works under close supervision of existing staff;
4. The employer that provides the training derives no immediate advantage from the activities of the intern; and on occasion its operations may actually be impeded;
5. The intern is not necessarily entitled to a job at the conclusion of the internship; and
6. The employer and the intern understand that the intern is not entitled to wages for the time spent in the internship. (U.S. DOL, 2010, p. 1)

According to the FLSA, if the activity meets the criteria for an unpaid internship, paid employment does not exist, and the intern does not qualify for minimum wage and overtime requirements. Many campus centers for community engagement work in tandem with career services on campus to coordinate and oversee the increasingly complex logistics of internships and fellowships.

As discussed in chapter 9, many students and their families view the college experience as a stepping stone to a job. Similarly, corporate and non-profit organizations often use internships to identify and recruit potential employees. This creates an expectation that colleges and universities will not merely offer but provide internship experiences to students. This expectation, in turn, creates an array of equity challenges, issues, and questions. Owing to curricular demands during the academic year, many students (especially athletes or students in the sciences with many required labs) simply cannot take time away from studies and part-time work that helps pay for their education to complete an internship, and thus, they must seek internships during the summer. However, many of these same students must work during summer months to help cover the cost of school. Therefore, they need paid internships, which may be limited in number. Other questions arise as to whether students should receive academic credit and wages at the same time. Some institutions view this as double-dipping. All institutions must be aware of equity issues to minimize situations in which some students benefit from receiving both credit and payment while others are not afforded the same opportunity.

California Campus Compact implemented a Community Engagement Student Fellowship (CESF) program with its members. The CESF is a four-month initiative designed to give student leaders opportunities to advance community service, service-learning, and community engagement by providing direct service to the community addressing economic development, health disparities, homelessness, and poverty. The fellowship is also designed to give fellows experience to support service-learning programs on a campus and promote access to postsecondary educational opportunities. Students receive a $500 scholarship upon successful completion of at least 50 hours of fellowship service.

The Kenneth Cole Community Engagement Program at Columbia University is designed to prepare students to become leaders in nonprofit and commercial settings by developing practical approaches to challenges and opportunities faced by communities in various settings. The fellowship is co-coordinated by the Office of Student Engagement, the Center for Career Education, the Fu Foundation School of Engineering, and the Columbia College Office of the Dean. It comprises three components. The first is a credit-bearing course focused on community engagement and community building. Readings and guest speakers take an asset-based approach to exploring specific skills related to community engagement and social entrepreneurship. The second component of the fellowship is a series of biweekly meetings and planning sessions between the fellows and program administrators to further strengthen their knowledge in preparation for the third component: a community-based summer fellowship experience. Each fellow works with a community partner 30 hours a week to complete a specific project under the guidance and supervision of staff members from the various coordinating offices on campus. A stipend is provided to each fellow. Fellows meet collectively each week for debriefing and reflection. They live together as an LLC on campus during the summer. Each fellow makes a final, formal presentation at the conclusion of the summer fellowship experience.

In cooperation with the Kathryn W. Davis Foundation, the Projects for Peace program is designed as an ambitious fellowship opportunity for college students. The fellowship is codirected by Middlebury College and

Macalester College and has its administrative home at Middlebury College. Students from colleges across the country are invited to propose a domestic or an international project that promotes peace making and capacity building. Students must conceptualize, design, implement, and assess a project with tangible outcomes, such as access to clean drinking water, mobility for landmine victims, women empowerment through education and social entrepreneurialism, and environmentally sustainable practices. Each student project receives $10,000.

Some colleges and universities provide programs designed to help students reflect and consider their own vocation as well as personal and professional development as part of their engaged learning. Macalester College has two unique approaches to encourage reflection on personal civic engagement as part of students' planning for transitions to civic lives and careers. The Lives of Commitment program has 35 first-year student participants who engage in service each week with immigrant groups and refugees. The students meet twice a month as a group in a seminar and in a one-on-one conversation with a sophomore mentor to explore various themes of vocation using *Let Your Life Speak* by Parker Palmer (2000) as a text and guide. Using the theme of transition based on the experience of the immigrants and refugees they serve, students explore their own vocational commitment over the next three years. Another Macalester program known as Embody the Change was inspired by the work of the late Senator Paul Wellstone and is open to all students. Students commit to weekly small group meetings to learn and practice active listening to draw wisdom from self-knowledge. The small groups use trained peer coaches.

Stanford University created and implemented a Public Service Pathways assessment tool and curriculum to help students explore six specific forms of service that could lead to careers: advocacy, engaged research, direct service, philanthropy, policy/politics, and social entrepreneurship. The pathways are presented and used in the public service LLC. The approach has been shared with other institutions through workshops at Campus Compact conferences, resulting in some collaborative implementation and evaluation (Schnaubelt, Welch, Lobo, & Robinson, 2015).

Civic Education

Thus far, the programs described in this chapter incorporate service and community engagement as either a pedagogy itself or a curricular approach to develop students' sense of civic responsibility during the college experience. These programs typically include skill sets that promote leadership as well as engaged citizenry. Battistoni (2002) published *Civic Engagement*

Across the Curriculum: A Resource Book for Service-Learning Faculty in All Disciplines, which presents eight skills students need to be engaged citizens: political knowledge and critical thinking, effective communication, public problem-solving, civic judgment, civic imagination and creativity, collective action, community/coalition building, and organizational analyses. In addition to the high-impact practices described previously, some colleges and universities also provide explicit instruction to develop students' civic and community organizing skills through courses or programs. In partnership with AAC&U, McTighe Musil (2015) published a curriculum of civic prompts that can be used across disciplines to explore the public purpose of disciplines. Both of these materials were designed to integrate a fundamental set of civic skills in disciplinary study.

Augsburg College and the University of Denver both explicitly incorporated civic education into their cocurricular and curricular programs using public achievement (PA). The community organizing model used in PA was created in 1990 at the Center for Democracy and Citizenship at the University of Minnesota's Humphrey Institute of Public Affairs and has been adopted in several states and countries. The PA model focuses on promoting civic agency and can be implemented in schools, community organizations, or faith-based institutions using a set of core elements and principles threaded through six developmental stages. The nursing program and the teacher education program in the Department of Special Education at Augsburg College are integrating the PA model's civic skills into their professional preparation programs to develop "citizen professionals" (D. Donovan, personal communication, June 23, 2015).

Degree or Certificate Programs

Butin and Seider (2012) argued that colleges and universities have reached an "engagement ceiling" (p. 1) that requires a second wave of engagement efforts in higher education in the form of certificates, minors, and majors in community engagement. Formal programs of study on and about civic skills are needed to prepare professionals who will serve the community after graduation. This approach goes beyond essentially infusing community and civic engagement into the cocurricular and curricular experience of students to achieve what Boyte and Fretz (2011) refer to as "citizen professionalism." While it could be argued that the various forms of engaged pedagogy presented thus far contribute to citizen professionalism, overtly preparing students through curricula and programs responds to what Saltmarsh and Hartley (2011) propose as higher education's larger democratic purpose.

DePaul University offers a minor in community service studies (CSS) that incorporates a variety of courses, primarily service-learning classes, from several disciplines to provide a theoretical framework, an examination of ethics, and an understanding of group dynamics. Students who choose this minor begin their first year performing 20 service hours with a community partner organization in the fall quarter and completing another 30 hours every quarter for their remaining 3 years. Scholars must enroll in the CSS minor program, attend quarterly workshops, and maintain a 2.7 GPA. They compile an electronic portfolio throughout their time in the program. In addition to three core courses, students select their remaining courses in collaboration with the program director.

The University of Massachusetts Amherst has a certificate in civic engagement and public service (CEPS) that uses theory and practical experiences to prepare students to be effective in building a more just and peaceful world. Students can choose from a service-learning track or a community engaged research track and complete a capstone project. The service-learning track includes five to six courses and has five topical emphasis pathways. The community engaged research track has five to six courses, including a required engaged research methods course. Students complete their community engaged research project in the capstone experience.

Summary

Students are at the heart of community engagement. In many respects this stakeholder group played a significant role in resurrecting the public purpose of higher education through volunteer service activities in the 1980s and 1990s. Campuses have responded by providing resources to support cocurricular and curricular programs that engage students and nurture their civic development. These students will go on to become business, educational, and political leaders in the future. Their transformative experiences through community engagement may very well sow the seeds for the future professoriate.

7

ENGAGING FACULTY

When I wonder what it would be like not to do this work—which I do consider sometimes because the demands of it feels too heavy—I imagine I'd feel lonelier and more limited. And without service-learning and civically engaged scholarship, the university would be limited. Conventional ideas about what makes a person an academic—teaching, service, and scholarship—narrow us.

—Janet Kaufman (2009, p. 63)

Engaging faculty is a key component of community engagement. Faculty members are, however, experts in their field of study and do not necessarily have the knowledge or skills to incorporate engaged teaching or scholarship in their classes. Furthermore, most college professors emerged from doctoral work focused on disciplinary content and, for the most part, traditional research methods. Thus, faculty members require significant technical support and socialization to engage with the community. In the early days of community engagement, engaged faculty members essentially made it up as they went along. Over time it became apparent that experiential education offered a profound learning experience for students, but often at the expense of those in the community they were attempting to serve. At times, both faculty members and students entered into community partnerships without adequate intercultural humility or cultural competency (Dunlap & Webster, 2009) and inadvertently created tension. In addition, over time a litigious society fraught with danger and violence required more due diligence, resulting in more legal paperwork, background checks, and health screenings that faculty members alone could not process. However, as faculty members became more adept at implementation and received more support for engaged pedagogy and scholarship such as service-learning and CBR, they suddenly faced the challenge of disseminating their new democratically generated knowledge in journals and at conferences. Gradually, scholarly venues for the scholarship of engagement have emerged only to reveal yet another daunting challenge: including this work in the promotion and tenure review process. To address this challenge faculty members require yet more technical support. This chapter presents the various ways campus centers for community engagement provide programs that serve faculty.

Faculty Development

Engaging faculty essentially requires creating an entirely new epistemology for faculty members. Scholars are experts in their disciplinary field and typically have not had any professional exposure to the public purpose of higher education. In addition, most doctoral programs do not provide any preparation in basic pedagogy, let alone in engaged pedagogy. Given that most doctoral programs do not include the basics of pedagogy in their programs (Doberneck, Brown, & Allen, 2010), continued professional development for faculty members is necessary in the engaged academy. Thus, the primary faculty-related programming of campus centers for engagement is professional development, which is also one of the most—if not the most—demanding aspects of community engagement and responsibilities of centers.

The center staff is usually responsible for providing technical and professional support to faculty members who teach service-learning or embark on community-based scholarship. In a study of centers at campuses with the Carnegie Classification for Community Engagement, 90% of the respondents reported providing one-on-one consultation, technical assistance, and resource materials to faculty (Welch & Saltmarsh, 2013a, 2013b). Approximately 70% of the respondents from that same study reported they provide faculty development programming. Furthermore, in the 2014 survey of its members, Campus Compact reported that just over 75% of responding schools provide faculty development workshops or fellowships, materials to assist faculty with reflection and assessment, and curriculum models and sample syllabi.

McKee and Tew (2013) defined *faculty development* as educational activities specifically designed to help faculty members grow in their professional practice. As the term implies, faculty development is a continual process, and campus centers for community engagement must provide a continuum of programs to support faculty members. At one end of the continuum is programming primarily designed to support academics entering into engaged pedagogy and scholarship. At the other end centers must also provide programming and opportunities for continued professional development and scholarship for more experienced public scholars through fellowships.

Van Note Chism, Palmer, and Price (2013) provided a theoretical overview of faculty development in the context of service-learning. They noted that theoretical foundations for faculty development tend to be developmental in nature, focusing on how faculty members change and grow. These researchers also observed that the most commonly used theoretical models in faculty development emerge from theories of individual learning. These include the developmental model of Lewin (1946) and experiential learning, described by Dewey (1933) and Kolb (1984). Reflective practice, described by Schön (1983) and Eraut (1994), is also incorporated. In their review Van Note Chism and colleagues (2013) synthesized five developmental components common to all theoretical foundations for faculty professional development:

1. Entry point based on need—Faculty members enter into continued professional education because of an external trigger, such as an organizational mandate, or an internal motivation based on personal experience.
2. Plan to change practice—Faculty members explicitly or implicitly contemplate how to revise their professional practice given this new information.
3. Active experimentation—Faculty members incorporate new knowledge or skills on a trial basis rather than adopting and assimilating them on a permanent basis.
4. Observation of impact—Faculty members observe the impact of the experimental implementation of the new knowledge or skills.
5. Reflection and implication—The observation prompts faculty members to reflect on the impact the trial application has and to determine whether to adopt or reject the new knowledge or skill.

These five developmental stages make up a chronology for providing technical and professional support before, during, and after applying new knowledge and skills. This chapter borrows and repurposes a conceptual curriculum consisting of knowledge, skills, and application used by a task force originally intended to propose and articulate core competencies in civic engagement for students (Center for Engaged Democracy Core Competency Committee, 2012) as a framework for engaging faculty. The content, nature, and scope of the knowledge, skills, and application differ over time and according to faculty members' experience. Hoyt (2011) refined this triadic chronology even further by incorporating a theory of systemic chronological adoption from thought to action that consists of five stages: pseudoengagement, tentative engagement, stable engagement, authentic engagement, and sustained engagement. These stages manifest themselves at the individual faculty member level as well as at the institutional level. Over time, through experimenting and experience, faculty members gradually assimilate engaged teaching and scholarship into the core and essence of their teaching and scholarship.

Blanchard and colleagues (2009) developed a comprehensive sequence of the 14 competencies of an engaged scholar. They sorted each competency into three levels of experience and expertise—novice, intermediate, and advanced—as presented in Table 7.1.

This chapter is similarly organized to describe the knowledge, skills, and application of community engagement before, during, and after participation in engaged teaching and scholarship, as illustrated in Table 7.2. Implementation of community engagement means administrators and the staff of campus centers for community engagement must be knowledgeable of basic tenets and strategies to advance this work as well as skilled at facilitating adult learning. Lawler (2003) characterized effective faculty development as a community of adult learners that created a climate of respect, encouraged active participation, built on experience, employed collaborative inquiry, learned for action, and empowered the participants. As discussed in chapter 5, creating, locating, and disseminating community engagement material are primary responsibilities of center staff. In addition, center staff must organize and facilitate various types of professional development. Finally, because academic culture values credentialed experts with background and experience, campus center staff must have credibility in the eyes of the faculty.

Knowledge and Skills

Axtell (2012) compiled a comprehensive set of skills for faculty members to become engaged scholars. Her model consists of two broad domains, each with five categories or competencies (see Box 7.1). The faculty development domain consists of learning skills, obtaining career development, practicing critical reflection, building and sustaining relationships, and navigating and changing the institutional system. The domain of the community engaged scholar includes teaching, research, outreach, professional practice, and administration (see Figure 7.1).

Public Purpose of Higher Education

When engaging faculty, as when engaging students, one must provide a rationale for and orientation to the history and principles of community engagement as well as the mutuality of partnerships. Providing rationale is an essential prerequisite for implementing any of the types of programs described here and should be an essential part of professional development and ongoing technical assistance for faculty members (Jordan et al., 2014).

TABLE 7.1

Competencies for Community Engaged Scholarship

Skill level	Competencies
Novice	Understand the principles and components of community engagement and community-engaged scholarship (CES)
Novice	Understand the various factors of community issues and develop strategies for promoting community capacity building and social change
Novice to intermediate	Apply principles of CES in theory and practice (e.g., in theoretical frameworks, models and methods of planning, implementation, and evaluation)
Intermediate	Work in and with diverse communities through cultural competency and intercultural humility
Intermediate	Collaborate and problem-solve with various community and academic stakeholders and constituencies
Intermediate	Write proposals and obtain grants for CES
Intermediate	Disseminate new knowledge through peer-reviewed publications and presentations articulating CES procedures and products
Intermediate to advanced	Transfer skills to enhance community capacity and to share knowledge and skills with other faculty
Intermediate to advanced	Understand and apply CES benchmarks, concepts, definitions, and principles to scholarly products, outcomes, and measures of quality
Advanced	Understand implications of CES and work with communities in translating the process into policy
Advanced	Balance and integrate the academic trilogy into CES to meet academic cultural expectations in the academy
Advanced	Articulate CES in the promotion and tenure process and serve on promotion and tenure committees
Advanced	Mentor students and novice faculty members in articulating CES in their professional portfolio

Note. Adapted from "Models for Faculty Development: What It Takes to Be a Community-Engaged Scholar," by L. Blanchard, C. Hanssmann, R. Strauss, J. C. Belliard, K. Krichbaum, E. Waters, & S. Seifer, 2009, *Metropolitan Universities Journal, 20*(2), pp. 47–65.

TABLE 7.2

Comprehensive Scope and Sequence of Faculty Development for Engaged Teaching and Scholarship

Characteristic	Before	During	After
Knowledge	Learn the public purpose of higher education Learn the epistemology of engagement Learn about reflection Learn about intercultural humility	Continue professional development Participate in fellows program Participate in professional development learning community	Mentor colleagues Serve on advisory committees Disseminate new knowledge Continue professional growth
Skills	Design and implement engaged teaching (e.g., service-learning) Design and implement engaged scholarship (e.g., community-based scholarship) Establish partnerships with community Design and implement scholarship about engagement	Build community and trust Practice reflection Practice intercultural humility Develop engaged research methodology Develop engaged teaching methodology	Prepare for promotion and tenure review
Application	Coordinate logistics and complete paperwork Join a professional learning community or have a one-on-one consultation	Incorporate new knowledge and skills Begin grant projects	Evaluate and assess engaged teaching/scholarship for students and community Begin professional service in engaged scholarship Research engaged teaching and scholarship

BOX 7.1

Faculty Development Skill Set for Community Engaged Teaching and Scholarship

Engagement Framework
<ul><li>Understand how your own work is connected with broader societal issues</li><li>Place your work on a methodological continuum, ranging from completely community-led to completely university-led</li><li>Understand and articulate the conceptual framework or anchor guiding your work, such as a social justice or equity framework or a public land-grant framework, and articulate how this framework coheres with frameworks others are utilizing</li></ul>
Career Development
<ul><li>Understand historical grounding of CES in higher education</li><li>Understand history of CES in your discipline</li><li>Articulate your engaged work, particularly when it is challenged</li><li>Present work in P & T [promotion and tenure] process</li><li>Develop teaching and research statements that reflect your engaged work</li><li>Assess and document the impact of your work</li><li>Define your CES agenda</li><li>Engage in self-assessment of your CES</li><li>Develop creative ways to "get credit" for CES</li><li>Understand the rigor and standards of CES, regardless of form</li></ul>
Critical Reflection
Power relations and community strengths:<ul><li>See community members and community organizations as equal partners</li><li>Work from critical action, rather than missionary mind-set</li><li>Understand class issues between large institutions and small grassroots organizations</li><li>Understand ways in which your actions/work can potentially undermine a community</li><li>Examine myths, biases, and stereotypes</li><li>See communities in terms of assets</li></ul>Knowledge:<ul><li>Understand limits of your own knowledge/dismantle expert knowledge</li><li>Value community knowledge</li><li>Learn from community knowledge</li><li>Be open to new learning about the community</li></ul>Self-knowledge:<ul><li>Be open to your own transformation</li><li>Use who you are as a person to integrate personal self with academic self</li></ul>

(Continues)

BOX 7.1 (*Continued*)

Critical Reflection

- Understand and articulate what you and the university are able to contribute in a particular situation
- Identify self-interest in CES work
- Practice humility

Accountability:

- See yourself not as an individual, but as part of the institution
- Understand expectations people have of you and the institution

Conflict and ambiguity:

- Live with ambiguity
- Be present in discussion without becoming defensive
- Live with unanswerable questions or questions that have answers that are messy
- Be prepared to make, acknowledge, repair, and recover from mistakes
- Stay in touch with tensions and work through them
- Have conflict and be comfortable with it, embrace it as necessary

Building and Sustaining Partnerships

Communication:

- Communicate about expectations
- Engage in deep listening
- Speak without using jargon
- Read signals about when our requests might overwhelm a community
- Ask questions
- Use language that reflects authentic partnership
- Communicate clearly, without dumbing down language
- Communicate clearly about resources that are available
- Learn from story
- Value story as medium for shared power
- Negotiate about problems in the relationship and about differing priorities

Project management:

- Discuss roles in project
- Be flexible about roles
- [Practice] project management—for example, checking in with partners about project progress
- Bring groups together, and facilitate coworking
- Involve partner from beginning of planning project
- Negotiate differences in rhythm on and off campus
- Transition from consultation to collaboration

Relationship skills:

- Practice perspective taking
- Share authority—intellectual, financial, and so on

Building and Sustaining Partnerships

• Navigate cross-cultural partnerships
• Preserve relationship even when project does not work out
• Behave appropriately in other people's space—be a good guest
• Work through transition of relationship at the conclusion of a project
• Develop/restore trust in you and institution
 	
Community and university:
 	
    • Understand history of community relationship with university
    • Learn basic lay of the land of community, but understand that your knowledge is incomplete
    • Work with community navigator
    • Avoid involvement in community politics
    • Examine power relations
 	
How pieces fit together:
 	
    • Understand and collaborate to achieve mutual benefit
    • See how university and community assets complement each other
    • Listen to interconnections among issues, and also see starting points

Navigating/Changing University Systems
• Act as a buffer between community partners and university systems, procedures, and policies—that is, help to smooth the road for partners' interaction with university systems • Navigate intellectual property policies and protocols • Put into place logistics of partnerships so that community has some control (e.g., over finances of project) • Troubleshoot problems that arise working within institution • Engage in systems advocacy to create policies and procedures that support CES • Identify and coordinate with other CES scholars and partnerships that are doing work related to your project • Help build a culture for CES at the university • Understand and articulate benefits of engagement to academic programs
Engaged Teaching
• Talk to students about service-learning and other community-based learning • Be aware of community opportunities available to students • Understand what your students are able to contribute • Prepare students for multicultural engagement • Develop syllabi for service-learning and other community-based and experiential courses • Develop appropriate assignments for experiential learning • Develop appropriate assessments for experiential learning

(Continues)

BOX 7.1 (*Continued*)

Engaged Teaching
• Structure and facilitate reflective sessions • Respond to student reflections, and integrate academic content • Hold students accountable for their community work • Integrate classroom and community learning experiences • Integrate skill development into understanding of larger social issues • Pull learning out of "bad" experiences • Grant students credit for community work in creative ways
Engaged Research
• Start with community-defined problem/issue, and work with partners to turn it into a researchable question • Build agreement about research questions with community partners • Align community definition of problem with the state of the scientific literature • Link CES project to theory and literature in discipline • Build agreement about appropriate measurement • Reconcile evidence-based interventions with community appropriateness and cultural knowledge systems • Share knowledge about academic research with community partners and learn from knowledge community shares about community's knowledge production systems • Engage in process evaluation with other team members • Work with institutional review board (IRB) to comply with standards in a way that is consistent with participatory research principles and practices • Facilitate community researchers receiving IRB training • Secure funding for research, and collaborate on grant development • Manage tensions between what the funding agency wants and what the community needs • Articulate work so that it is meaningful to communities • Disseminate research results in ways that are meaningful to and benefit communities • Maximize real impact of research, in terms of social and policy change and change within communities and institutions

Note. From *Creating a Community-Engaged Scholarship (CES) Faculty Development Program: Phase One: Program and Skill Mapping,* by S. Axtell, 2012, University of Minnesota Office for Public Engagement, www.engagement.umn.edu/sites/default/files/CES_Faculty_Development_Report_FINAL_000.pdf. Reprinted with permission.

Figure 7.1 Faculty development framework.

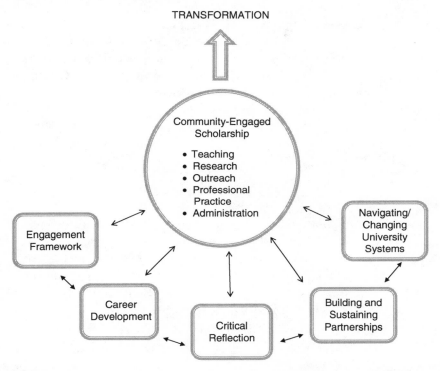

Note. Retrieved from *Creating a Community-Engaged Scholarship (CES) Faculty Development Program: Phase One: Program and Skill Mapping,* by S. Axtell, 2012, University of Minnesota Office for Public Engagement, www.engagement.umn.edu/sites/default/files/CES_Faculty_Development_Report_FINAL_000.pdf. Reprinted with permission from the author.

Such an introduction provides faculty members with a clear understanding of the differences between community engagement and traditional experiential education approaches.

Engaged Epistemology

Understanding engaged epistemology, as discussed in chapter 2, requires reframing traditional principles and practice related to the academic trilogy. Each component of the trilogy must be revisited to fully understand the democratic and public purpose of community engagement. This includes introducing community organizations as partners and coeducators. Faculty members must also be introduced to the idea and practice of integrating research, teaching, and service. Traditionally, each of these components has been viewed and practiced as a separate activity.

Engaged Teaching and Learning

Faculty members need to be educated about the high-impact practices for engaged teaching and learning described in previous chapters. Of these the most pervasive form of engaged teaching and learning is service-learning. Thus, campus centers for community engagement spend a great deal of time, energy, and resources providing information on service-learning. Basic foundational knowledge, coupled with steps and strategies for implementation, must be provided. A foundational understanding of service-learning should include basic best practices (Honnet & Poulson, 1989), such as the following:

- Engage students in responsible and challenging actions for the common good
- Provide structured opportunities for students to reflect critically on their service experience
- Articulate clear service and learning goals for everyone involved
- Allow a voice for those being served to define their goals and needs
- Clarify the responsibilities of each person and organization involved
- Expect genuine, active, and sustained organizational commitment
- Include training, supervision, monitoring, support, recognition, and evaluation to meet service and learning goals
- Ensure that the time commitment for service and learning is flexible, appropriate, and in the best interests of all involved

Faculty members need to know and incorporate five basic components for conceptualizing, implementing, and assessing engaged teaching through service-learning. Using principles of metacognition (Binbasaran Tuysuzoglu & Greene, 2015; Littrell-Baez, Friend, Caccamise, & Okochi, 2015), Welch (2010a, 2014) created the first-letter mnemonic device OPERA for professional development to help novice faculty members incorporate and recall those components (see Figure 7.2).

The letter *O* represents objectives for student learning and for helping community partners reach their aspirations and goals. Instructors must consider not only what they want their students to learn but also how those objectives meet the goals of a community partner, the *P*. This dual consideration indicates a shift from a teaching to a learning paradigm. Some instructors will require help from a campus center for community engagement to identify potential community partners. Others already have established a partnership with an organization or have been contacted by an agency. The *P* component is not just about identifying a placement but also about encouraging faculty members to conduct a site visit to learn about an organization's sense of place, mission, history, and constituencies. This process

Figure 7.2 OPERA rubric for engaged courses.

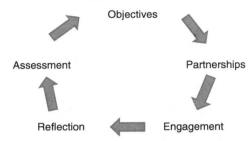

should ideally entail a face-to-face conversation and can be characterized as a courtship process. Can the instructor and community partner become "engaged," or should they respectfully part as good friends because it is not a "match"? In addition, faculty members learn they must select potential community partners in the same way they choose a textbook, as both provide a cognitive foundation for the learning objectives of the course. To help make an informed instructional decision, faculty members are encouraged to ask specific questions during the courtship process (see Appendix D). The responses to these questions will help determine the type of activity students and faculty members will engage in.

The letter *E* stands for engagement. The instructor and the representative of the community agency should collaboratively determine what activities the students will engage in to meet the objectives identified and articulated in the first step. To facilitate this process, the instructor and community partner should develop and follow an action plan enumerating time lines, roles, and responsibilities that integrate learning objectives from the course with the partner's goals.

Reflection is represented by the letter *R* and is ideally conducted before, during, and after the engaged learning experience. Teaching faculty members about reflection, including strategies for conducting and assessing reflection, is often a major component of professional development.

Finally, the letter *A*, for assessment, brings the rubric full circle: Have the objectives of both parties been met? Assessment also includes a summative evaluation of the experience as a whole. This summative assessment may be as simple as asking if the instructor and the community partner found the course constructive enough to repeat in the future. Dempsey (2015) found that the majority of faculty members who received professional development that included the OPERA rubric successfully incorporated its components into course syllabi, showing successful generalization of the rubric and professional development process.

Engaged Scholarship

Novice practitioners should have a fundamental knowledge of Boyer's (1990) reconceptualization of engaged scholarship. From the tradition of participatory action research (PAR) developed by Lewin (1946) emerged the current predominant form of engaged scholarship, known as CBR (see chapter 2). Faculty members should have a basic knowledge and understanding of CBR. Other principles and assumptions regarding community-based scholarship include the community holds specialized knowledge, the community has a unique and valuable vantage point in research, and knowledge production involving academics and communities must be shared (Blanchard et al., 2009). Faculty members should also be able to compare and contrast traditional academic research with CBR.

Scholarship of Engagement

As discussed in chapter 2, there are faculty members and even some graduate students who, rather than practice engaged pedagogy or scholarship, pursue the study *of* engaged pedagogy and scholarship. This can be a mutually beneficial effort in which the research conducted by faculty members or graduate students can provide valuable information to campus centers of community engagement for evaluating the impact of programs. Center staff, possibly in collaboration with the IR office, can work with faculty members to design and conduct research that will make a contribution not only to the field but also to center operations. The assistance from campus centers provides direct benefit to faculty members conducting research as they pursue promotion and tenure. The scholarship of engagement can and should also be afforded to graduate students conducting research for their theses or dissertations. For example, a doctoral dissertation conducted at Portland State University examined what factors motivate community partners to engage in community-based scholarship (Norvell, 2010). This research won a dissertation award at the annual conference of the IARSLCE in 2010.

Reflection

Reflection is a significant component of engaged teaching and learning. Given its centrality to nearly all conceptualizations of service-learning and community engagement as a whole, reflection and its uses continue to offer practitioners and scholars opportunities for discussion and debate. Dewey (1933) suggested intentional consideration of thoughts, feelings, and actions promotes meaningful learning and cognitive growth. He described reflection as "active, persistent and careful consideration of any belief or supposed form of knowledge in the light of the grounds that support it, and the further conclusions to which it tends" (p. 6). Dewey's reflective theory of inquiry is supported by Schön's (1983) characterization of reflection as "a continual interweaving of thinking and doing" (p. 281). Hatcher and Bringle (1997) argued that reflection connects intentionality on a student's part with intentionality on the instructor's part to link the student's experiences with instructional objectives. Yet despite its appeal on multiple levels and the general acceptance of its importance, most faculty members do not know what reflection is or how to effectively incorporate reflection into curricula or assessments (Dubinsky et al., 2012). Thus, it should be included in professional development programs.

In addition to knowing what reflection is, faculty members must also have the skills to practice it. Many faculty development workshops are devoted entirely to reflection.

Like students, faculty members also need rubrics and frameworks to effectively engage in reflection. One theoretically based user-friendly reflection rubric is the ABCs of reflection (Dubinsky et al., 2012; Welch, 1999). The rubric is based on the theoretical framework of Hondagneu-Sotelo and Raskoff (1994), who emphasize three main components of reflection: what students learn (cognition); what and how students feel (affect); and how students behave before, during, and after learning experiences (behavior). Using this rubric, students reflect on and articulate the affective dimension of the experience, such as emotions and attitudes. They also reflect on their behaviors before, during, and after the experience. In this way they contemplate how they probably will behave in a specific circumstance before the learning experience, how they actually behaved during the experience, and how they might or hope to behave in the future as a result of the experience. Finally, students articulate how they made concrete connections to class content to demonstrate the cognition that has occurred through the experience. Reflection can also involve large and small group discussions or dyads. Faculty members can also learn how to use written reflection in and outside classroom settings.

Assessment

Faculty members must also learn how to assess the impact of the service on both the students and the community partner. Assessment is traditionally conducted through final exams or papers, but the authentic application of skills to meet both the instructional objectives of the course and the goals of the community partner requires additional assessment approaches. The most basic and straightforward process is to simply determine if the activities or products of the students' work satisfactorily accomplished what the agency hoped it would. In this way faculty members conduct a type of authentic assessment by observing if students are able to assimilate and apply course content in a meaningful way and within real-world context. Similarly, instructors can incorporate a satisfaction survey by asking community partners to rate their level of satisfaction on various aspects of the service experience, such as student performance, professionalism, timeliness, responsiveness to feedback, and accuracy of work. Chapter 8 provides an extensive description of other procedures and tools that can be used to assess the impact of engaged teaching and scholarship on community partner agencies.

Other dimensions of student development can also be assessed. Faculty members can conduct content analysis of written reflection. The ABC method described previously can be used to assess students' cognitive growth (Dubinsky et al., 2012; Welch & James, 2007). Instructors might also consider implementing pre- or postmeasures of various variables, such as cognitive mastery of specific content or attitudes toward a topic or issue (e.g., diversity, race, or socioeconomic status).

Intercultural Humility

As discussed in chapter 3, intercultural humility or cultural competency is a key concept and practice for faculty members and students alike. Professional development must include providing a basic understanding of intercultural humility's meaning and importance in community engagement. Cultural issues can be presented in two contexts: as part of the town-and-gown cultural conflict or in the anthropological context of culture, race, ethnicity, and gender differences. Intercultural humility requires an intentional awareness of the inherent power and privilege associated with higher education. This awareness is achieved through self-reflection and self-critique to recognize unintentional and intentional racism and classism (Ross, 2010). Beyond assimilating facts about cultural differences and practices, cultural humility promotes an understanding of the social, political, cultural, and economic dynamics that affect beliefs and behaviors of members in a particular community.

Dissemination

Professional development programs for faculty members should also include exploration of dissemination venues. Faculty members should be encouraged to consider ways of publishing and presenting on their engaged teaching and research. Through professional development, engaged faculty members must come to recognize and understand that they can integrate their teaching, research, and service in the alternative paradigm of engaged epistemology. Instructors should consider how to translate their engaged scholarship into articles for peer-reviewed journals and professional conferences. This requires approval from their IRB, and therefore, engaged faculty members should consider applying for IRB approval as a prerequisite, before teaching a course or embarking on CBR projects with community partners. Most professors are unaware of peer-reviewed journals outside their own discipline that publish articles on engaged pedagogy and scholarship. Campus centers for community engagement must assist faculty members as they consult the professional journals and conferences listed on the Campus Compact website.

Preparation for Promotion and Tenure Review

Because many institutions of higher education do not yet recognize and reward engaged teaching and scholarship, it is important that campus centers help faculty members prepare to articulate this work and advocate for their promotion and tenure review. Early on, faculty members should be encouraged to "write what they teach and teach what they write" in ways that address important social issues, as well as to make contributions to a disciplinary field. Through their writing, faculty members can integrate their teaching, research, and service in ways that will serve them well during promotion and tenure review. Many campus centers for engagement provide one-on-one consultations to explore how to articulate engaged teaching and scholarship in articles for peer-reviewed journals or for presentations at peer-reviewed professional conferences.

Many campus centers for community engagement also offer guidance to faculty members in preparing for promotion and tenure review. This guidance can be provided through workshops, one-on-one consultations, and various resource materials. Gelmon and Agre-Kippenhan (2002) published a user-friendly and pragmatic guide for faculty members preparing for promotion and tenure review. Their tips have stood the test of time even as new approaches have emerged. In partnership with Imagining America, Ellison and Eatman (2008) produced a comprehensive report about promotion and tenure related to engaged scholarship. The report included a resource guide and examples to assist faculty members in the arts, design, and humanities in preparing for the review process. The following items should be considered for inclusion in a faculty member's personal statement or dossier.

Introduction to Engaged Epistemology

Initially, a scholar's personal statement or preamble to his or her review portfolio should define *engaged scholarship* and *engaged teaching*, using references cited in the opening chapters of this book. Of particular value is Colby and colleagues' (2003) characterization of engaged pedagogy. Introducing the concept of engaged epistemology is necessary and vital because the review committee will likely be unfamiliar with it. This introduction should overtly articulate how engaged teaching or scholarship meets review criteria.

Theoretical Foundations

Faculty members should provide a theoretical framework for teaching and scholarship that not only reflects tenets of engagement but also is consistent with the discipline or area of work. For example, Dewey's (1933) work on experiential education to promote a democratic society will resonate with social scientists. Vygotsky's (1978) social development theory presents a constructivist approach to teaching and learning. Fry and Kolb's (1979) articulation of four elements in experiential learning reflects basic tenets of the scientific method and is consistent with experimental perspectives in the sciences. Another theoretical foundation for engaged research is Lewin's (1946) PAR. Critical theory is another framework for consideration and includes the work of Paulo Freire (1970), feminist theory (hooks, 2000), and critical race theory (Delgado, 2012). The faculty at faith-based institutions should consider using tenets related to social justice and the institution's particular faith tradition; Catholic institutions of higher education, for example, might use Catholic social thought (DeBerri & Hug, 2003; Krier Mich, 2011).

Institutional Mission

Many promotion and tenure reviews require faculty members to describe how their teaching, research, and service reflect the institutional mission. It is incumbent on the scholar under review to consult and incorporate language from the mission statement as discussed in chapter 3.

Dissemination

Most important, faculty members should document how their engaged scholarship is disseminated through peer-reviewed journals and conferences. Some campus centers for community engagement conduct workshops on where and how to publish or present scholarly work on engaged teaching and scholarship. Most scholars are familiar with publishing and presentation venues in their own discipline but are unaware of other peer-reviewed dissemination possibilities specifically focused on engaged scholarship. Campus Compact provides a comprehensive list of professional journals and conferences as possible dissemination outlets for faculty members. Other centers actually host writing retreats during which faculty members can escape from routine settings and distractions to focus on writing for concentrated periods. These retreats provide structure as well as a collegial group of like-minded peers also dedicated to this work.

Forms of Faculty Development Programming

Chapter 5 reported results from national surveys indicating that providing faculty development was a major role and responsibility of campus centers for community engagement. Programs for faculty development can take many forms, ranging from one-on-one consultation to informal brown bag lunch gatherings to formal yearlong learning communities to individual grants and fellowships (see Table 7.4). Professional development continues past intermediate levels of knowledge and experience; faculty members can advance their scholarship through participation with professional associations. Development includes being a good citizen of the field by assuming leadership roles in various organizations and associations.

Resource Library

Faculty development requires a vast library of resources available to faculty members on a loan or check-out basis. Many campus centers for community engagement subscribe to key professional journals, such as the *Michigan Journal for Community Service Learning*. There is a huge, and somewhat overwhelming, professional literature on community engagement. A list of suggested readings is presented in Box 7.2. While some of these readings may appear dated, these suggested books are considered landmark publications in the field.

As mentioned in chapter 5, the National Service-Learning Clearinghouse (gsn.nylc.org/clearinghouse) and Campus Compact (www.compact.org) provide excellent resources. Additional information can be found through the AAC&U.

Some centers have begun to catalogue or even produce their own training videos and Web-based instructional modules. The CILSA at Saint Mary's College of California coordinates service-learning, community engagement, and social justice courses and has created a series of introductory training videos on its YouTube channel that can be watched anytime, anywhere, and by anyone. Illinois State University developed five Web-based professional modules made available to the faculty during the summer (Presley, 2011). The topics of the modules reflect the essential knowledge base necessary for engaging faculty: What Are Civic and Community Engagement?, Why Incorporate Civic and Community Engagement?, Innovative Pedagogy for Incorporating Civic and Community

TABLE 7.4
Forms of Faculty Development

Resource library	*Books, articles, videos, online resources, and handbooks readily available on an as-needed basis*
One-on-one consultations	Specialist in engaged teaching and scholarship meeting individually with a faculty member
	Initial logistical coordination of community partnerships, including course action plans, MOUs, student transportation, background checks, tuberculosis tests, oversight of student/research assistants, IRB research approval
	Ongoing technical support throughout professional development and faculty application of knowledge and skills
Informal workshops	Typically a voluntary drop-in meeting (sometimes during lunch as a brown bag gathering) to learn about or discuss a specific topic related to community engagement
	Webinars
Formal workshops	Often a required meeting or series of meetings designed to present new knowledge or skills
	Preconference workshops
	Institutes
Learning communities	Regularly scheduled, ongoing gatherings of a long-standing cohort of participants to discuss readings, practice, and ideas and possibly create a plan or product related to community engagement courses or CBR
	Book clubs
Grants	Financial support to develop engaged teaching or scholarship that may include a course buyout relieving an instructor of his/her responsibility to an existing course to focus on the development of a new course or scholarly project with ongoing one-on-one technical support
Fellowships	An award and title given to a faculty member for scholarly pursuit in a given topical area with ongoing one-on-one technical support or with the support of a cohort of scholarly fellows for a sustained period
	Sometimes an advocate or champion of community engagement across campus, conducting conversations or discussion groups

BOX 7.2
Suggested Readings for a Resource Library

Community-based research

Community-Based Research and Higher Education: Principles and Practice (2003), by Kerry Strand, Sam Marullo, Nick Cutforth, Randy Stoecker, and Patrick Donohue

Community engagement

Colleges and Universities as Citizens: Issues and Perspectives (1999), by Robert G. Bringle, Richard Games, and Edward A. Malloy

Educating Citizens: Preparing America's Undergraduates for Lives of Moral and Civic Responsibility (2003), by Anne Colby, Thomas Ehrlich, Elizabeth Beaumont, and Jason Stephens

Civic Responsibility and Higher Education (2000), edited by Thomas Ehrlich

Deepening Community Engagement in Higher Education: Forging New Pathways (2013), by Ariane Hoy and Mathew Johnson

Civic Engagement in Higher Education: Concepts and Practices (2009), edited by Barbara Jacoby

Engaging Departments: Moving Faculty Culture From Private to Public, Individual to Collective Focus for the Common Good (2006), by Kevin Kecskes

A Crucible Moment: College Learning and Democracy's Future (2012), by the National Task Force on Civic Learning and Democratic Engagement

Engaged scholarship

Scholarship Reconsidered: Priorities of the Professoriate (1990), by Ernest Boyer

Service-learning

The Advances in Service-Learning Research Series, edited by Shelley H. Billig and associates, published by Information Age Publishers

Research on Service-Learning: Conceptual Framework and Assessment, Vols. 2A and 2B (2012), by Patti Clayton, Robert G. Bringle, and Julie A. Hatcher

Why Service-Learning Is Bad (1998), by John Eby

Where's the Learning in Service-Learning? (1999), by Janet Eyler and Dwight Giles

Building Partnerships for Service-Learning (2003), by Barbara Jacoby

Service-Learning Essentials: Questions, Answers, and Lessons Learned (2015), by Barbara Jacoby

Looking In/Reaching Out: A Reflective Guide for Community Service-Learning Professionals (2010), by Barbara Jacoby and Pamela Mutascio

Students as Colleagues: Expanding the Circle of Service-Learning Leadership (2006), by Edward Zlotkowski, Nicholas V. Longo, and James R. Williams

Engagement, Political Engagement: Beyond Politics, and Innovative Partnerships for Service-Learning.

One-on-One Consultation

Ongoing technical support should be provided through one-on-one consultation with either staff from the campus center for community engagement or friendly peers as colleagues with experience serving as mentors. This support includes logistical coordination of the various moving parts associated with developing and implementing engaged courses and scholarship, such as partnership agreements, background checks, or tuberculosis tests for students when necessary. Consultation also provides the hand-holding necessary to reassure and support faculty members as they embark on this new and complex form of teaching and scholarship.

Informal Workshops

Many centers provide informal workshops open to all faculty members. For example, the campus center for community engagement at Elon University hosts monthly brown bag discussions on various topics related to community engagement; participants bring their own lunch.

   While not traditional workshops per se, some gatherings hosted by campus centers allow faculty members and community partners to meet each other before they become "engaged." One such gathering is a speed-dating event during which faculty members looking for potential community partners circulate among tables at which representatives of community agencies are seated. If the instructional objective(s) or research agenda of a faculty member is compatible with the aspirations and goals of the community agency, the two continue the conversation in an effort to develop a partnership.

Formal Workshops

Formal workshops can be an hour, a full day, or several days of training and are usually components of faculty development cohorts or learning communities. Workshops are also often required components of faculty fellowships and grants. Workshops generally focus on a specific topic or skill and often include readings from either an article, a book, or a training manual specifically developed for the professional development event. Ideally, workshops are interactive and involve hands-on activities and discussion. Some centers host a full-day institute that introduces key concepts, principles, and components of engaged teaching and scholarship as a part of the formal institutional process of designating courses that meet the criteria for community engagement. A full-day institute creates a concentrated focus on content that informal brown bag lunch workshops typically cannot provide.

The Center for Service and Learning in the Office of Community Engagement at IUPUI sponsors and coordinates a variety of professional development opportunities under its Communities of Practice programs. The Public Scholarship Faculty Learning Community is a cohort of faculty members from several disciplines that devotes a year to exploring public scholarship to cultivate engaged faculty research agendas and to form a network of engaged faculty members on campus. Participants develop an action plan for promoting engaged scholarship on campus by sharing the current literature and research on public scholarship and community-engaged research.

The center allocates funds to support faculty community fellows working on community-based projects with the Great Indy Neighborhoods Initiative (GINI). In addition, the Boyer Scholars receive support to enhance their scholarship on service-learning or civic engagement. The Faculty Liaison Program is designed for faculty members with documented experience in teaching service-learning classes. Participants promote the campus mission of civic engagement in their department or school by advocating service-learning and engagement of students in the community. The liaisons also provide and strengthen professional networks between academic faculty members and the center staff and use internal and external resources to increase support for service-learning and civic engagement and to develop a cadre of faculty leaders in service-learning. The Faculty Fellow in Service-Learning Program is for faculty members with experience teaching service-learning classes and is designed to deepen their practice, cultivate leadership to advance civic engagement, and increase departmental and campus support for engaged teaching and scholarship by developing a cohort of master teachers. Finally, in partnership with the Office of International Affairs, the International Service Learning Teaching and Learning Circle provides a monthly venue to discuss issues and topics related to developing, implementing, and assessing service-learning programs in international and cross-cultural settings.

Learning Communities

Learning communities are organized groups of colleagues who make a long-term commitment to learn about a specific topic. The semistructured groups typically have a facilitator who uses readings and other materials to generate discussions. One example is the Faculty Civic Seminar, which is part of the Brooklyn Public Scholars Project, conducted in partnership with the City University of New York and Kingsborough Community College (Cahill & Fine, 2014). The Faculty Civic Seminar provides an interdisciplinary "sanctuary" (p. 69) where 25 like-minded faculty members can pursue public scholarship through engaged coursework.

Book clubs are another type of learning community in which a group discusses information presented in a specific book. A couple of professional development learning communities have collectively published edited volumes designed to be used by other learning communities committed to community engagement. In 2009 a cadre of kindred spirits at a large public research university met in each other's homes to share their personal and professional stories related to civic engagement. The stories, from an array of academic disciplines, were collected and published as *Finding Meaning in Civically Engaged Scholarship: Personal Journeys, Professional Experiences* (Diener & Liese, 2009). Similarly, faculty members at a faith-based institution reflected on their own commitment to community engagement in higher education in an edited volume titled *The Spirit of Service: Exploring Faith, Service, and Social Justice in Higher Education* (Johnson & O'Grady, 2006). Both books illustrate the reflective practitioner dimension of professional development presented here and could be used in a learning community book club.

Stanford University's Haas Center for Public Service launched an innovative professional development learning community for graduate students with the explicit goal of grooming the future engaged professoriate. The Graduate Public Service Program comprises 15 to 20 graduate students from all schools and disciplines. The students meet biweekly for a two-hour dinner seminar with guest speakers and discussion forums on community engagement related to their own interests and projects. They also commit to helping with one Haas Center project, such as a program evaluation or curriculum development. Each participating graduate scholar receives $1,000 per quarter.

Grants and Fellowships

Grants are financial awards that serve either as an incentive or as pay for resources that can be used to develop community-based courses or scholarship projects. Faculty members typically apply for grants, providing a proposal articulating the purpose and design of their course or research project. The funds are sometimes used to compensate faculty members for the additional time and energy spent in developing a new community engagement initiative. Other times the funds are used to buy out a course, meaning a graduate student or adjunct instructor takes on the responsibility of teaching a course so that the scholar has more time for project development. Finally, grants may be specifically allocated to support community-based activities or to create a product that can be used by a community organization for capacity building.

Fellowships are similar to grants in that they typically provide financial support to develop an engaged course or engaged research project. A faculty member receiving the financial award also receives the title of fellow, which has a certain amount of prestige on some campuses. Some fellowships come with an expectation or responsibility to meet a specific goal or advance a particular agenda. In the context of community engagement, faculty fellows are often academic exemplars and role models who champion community engagement to their peers. A faculty fellow may even be charged with specific duties, such as convening learning communities or conducting workshops.

For example, the Office of Vice President for Academics at Stanford University created and implemented a fellowship called the New Engaged Academic Professional Scholar. The fellowship is awarded to five professors, not based on their discipline or department but rather to create a community of engaged practice that can promote engaged scholarship.

The Steans Center for Community-Based Service Learning at DePaul University awards up to three Community-Based Research Faculty Fellowships each academic year. Each fellowship supports a full-time DePaul University faculty member interested in conducting CBR designed for community capacity building with one or more community organizations and includes at least one undergraduate or graduate student research project linked to a course. Fellows receive a $3,000 stipend, a funded research assistant for three consecutive terms, and financial support to present at an academic conference in the United States.

Examples

The following examples illustrate implementation of the various forms of faculty development designed to promote the application of knowledge and skills related to engaged teaching and research. The professional development opportunities at Duquesne University, a small Catholic liberal arts institution, nicely depict the range of forms described previously. The Center for Community-Engaged Teaching and Research at the university hosts a library of materials readily available to faculty members and offers one-on-one technical assistance in course design and identification of community partners. Faculty development includes excursions and site visits to neighborhoods and community partner organizations. Faculty members who hold the Gaultier Community Engaged Teaching Fellowship, sponsored by the Office of the Provost and Center for Community-Engaged

Teaching and Research, share their successful strategies for teaching community engagement, assist emerging engaged teachers, and disseminate promising practices to colleagues to promote community engagement. The center also hosts a variety of events: a monthly open house called Community Uncorked, an engaged research inquiry group, a fall workshop titled From Learning Objectives to Evidence of Student Learning, a spring workshop on preparing for promotion and tenure, an intensive one-day institute on designing courses that focus on community engagement, and a two-day summer writing retreat.

The University of Minnesota participated in an innovative pilot project, sponsored by the CCPH through a grant from the U.S. Department of Education's FIPSE, to develop a nine-month, competency-based faculty development cohort (Jordan et al., 2014). The components of the cohort reflect most of the knowledge and skill sets presented in this chapter. The project was guided by four principles: professional development should be competency based, professional development should be interactive and participatory, community partners should be involved, and projects should focus on individual and institutional change. The cohort members consulted with a mentor individually and attended professional development workshops as a group. Mentoring and workshops focused on the competencies articulated by Blanchard and colleagues (2009). Participants discussed action plans and reflection sheets during mentoring sessions. The faculty development program culminated with a capstone project designed using an action plan. Participants conducted formative and summative evaluation with community partners. Pre- and postsurvey results suggest increased knowledge and confidence on the part of the cohort participants.

Continued and Ongoing Application of Faculty Programming

Programming for faculty members extends beyond initial education and support to novice academics and includes advancing engaged teaching and scholarship over time. Many campus centers for community engagement, sometimes in collaboration with an institution's center for teaching and learning, provide an array of professional enrichment opportunities for advanced and experienced faculty members. Support staff may also suggest specific activities and roles for veteran faculty members to consider.

Advisory Boards and Mentoring

Experienced faculty members can play a useful role by serving on a campus center's advisory board. In this role faculty members can use their own experience and insight to help advance and guide the work of the center and their colleagues. In addition, advanced engaged scholars may be asked to mentor novice scholars through professional development cohorts or learning communities.

Professional Associations and Professional Service

Faculty members should be encouraged to continue their professional development through membership in and participation with professional associations and organizations for community engagement. Attending and presenting at conferences sponsored by these professional associations are legitimate forms of advanced professional development. As an example, two professors with doctoral degrees at Oregon State University, Dana Sanchez, a wildlife ecologist, and Suzana Rivera-Mills, a Spanish linguistics scholar, are actively involved in the Society for Advancement of Chicanos/Hispanics and Native Americans in Science (SACNAS), a professional association dedicated to encouraging Chicano/Hispanic and Native American college students and professionals to attain advanced degrees, careers, and positions of leadership in science through outcome-based programs. Sanchez learned about engaged scholarship by attending the Emerging Engagement Scholars Workshop and the Engaged Scholarship Conference and then shared her new knowledge with her colleague. She and Rivera-Mills have infused engaged scholarship into their STEM research and teaching, working with indigenous groups' traditional ecological knowledge. Rivera-Mills noted that engaged research redefines *faculty scholarship*, shifting it away from traditional power dynamics: "Our role shifts from pure application of academic expertise to reciprocal interaction with communities. Traditional duties of teaching, conducting research, and performing service may all be interwoven with aspects of the engaged project" (Sanchez & Rivera-Mills, 2014).

Engaged faculty members should be advised that they can also meet professional service expectations for promotion and tenure by serving on committees or advisory boards for professional associations. These professional service roles provide continued professional development by allowing faculty members to work and learn with preeminent leaders of the field.

The IARSLCE hosts an annual conference and publishes a refereed online journal. The association has a robust program supporting graduate students interested in pursuing engaged teaching and scholarship. It provides professional development for graduate students, trains nationally recognized scholars in the field as mentors, and offers awards for dissertations on engaged teaching and scholarship. Many doctoral students in IARSLCE have gone on after graduation to assume scholarly or administrative roles at prestigious engaged institutions.

Imagining America is a consortium dedicated to advancing the public and civic purposes of the humanities and arts. It publishes reports and a peer-reviewed e-journal as well as convenes national conferences, regional meetings, and institutes. New American Colleges and Universities is a national consortium of selective small to midsize independent colleges and universities advancing the integration of liberal education, professional studies, and civic engagement. It hosts summer institutes and programs for students. As mentioned in chapter 1, the AASCU sponsors the American Democracy Project (ADP), a consortium of campuses focusing on public higher education's role in preparing students to be informed, engaged citizens in a democratic society. Like other professional associations, the ADP hosts conferences, provides a number of resources, and coordinates several civically engaged projects for both faculty members and students.

Summary

The primary ways to engage faculty members are ongoing technical support and professional development. While faculty members are experts in their fields, most have little to no experience or knowledge of engaged pedagogy and engaged scholarship. Clearly, effective engaged teaching and scholarship can occur only through well-prepared and supported faculty members willing to do and interested in this complex work. Although they are demanding, engaged teaching and scholarship can and do serve as a catalyst for promotion and tenure if faculty members are advised and supported in the scholarly dissemination of their work. Until colleges and universities formally recognize and reward faculty members for this type of work, faculty must also be prepared to be effective self-advocates as they articulate their engaged work during the promotion and tenure review process. Campus centers for community engagement must include promotion and tenure review preparation in programming for faculty members. Finally, faculty members can continue their professional development by becoming actively involved in professional associations committed to community engagement.

8

ENGAGING COMMUNITY PARTNERS

Yes, the community-campus partnership is about organizations, it's about students, but it is about common values that are much deeper. What we're learning to do, whether we're students or whether we're a non-profit, is doing something that is actually moving us as a community, a path of achieving progress along the context of what we care about.

—Anonymous community partner (Sandy, 2007, p. 10)

[Community partners] want us [academics in higher education] to treat them as partners, not supplicants. They want us to seek first to understand and then be understood. They want us to recognize that they have the capacity to teach us as well as learn from us. And they want us to appreciate that our future, as well as theirs, is dependent upon our work together.

—James C. Votruba (cited in Beere, Votruba, & Wells, 2011, p. 193)

Partnerships with community agencies have evolved significantly over the years. Early on, but to a lesser extent today, instructors teaching service-learning courses often assigned students to find community sites on their own and emphasized putting in hours. This approach reflected a unilateral and student-centric experience, often with little or no benefit for cooperating community agencies hosting the students. Over time attention has shifted to ensure that these experiences have a positive impact on the community (Blouin & Perry, 2009; Schmidt & Robby, 2002). Today, a combination of philosophical, pedagogical, logistical, and legal issues is reshaping the way institutions and campus centers for community engagement work with the community. Consequently, campuses are beginning to embrace a more collaborative approach and are broadening their perspective, using community agencies as coeducators and partners rather than mere placement sites. Community partnerships require a philosophical and pragmatic shift from doing *for* community agencies to doing *with* these organizations (Ward & Wolf-Wendel, 2000).

While it is necessary and prudent to establish truly reciprocal partnerships, this process is rarely neat and tidy (Jones, 2003). Institutions of higher education and their centers for community engagement are grappling with many legal and logistical challenges that were not as pervasive or apparent two decades ago, when community engagement was in its infancy. Many community agencies require background checks of non–staff members working on site. In addition, institutions of higher education are requiring certificates of insurance from community agencies and risk assessments of potential partnership sites. As mentioned in chapter 4, colleges and universities are establishing complex and institutionalized partnerships with community agencies that require significant infrastructure and resources. Campus centers for community engagement are becoming more and more responsible for coordinating these efforts related to community partnerships. In essence campus centers have taken on logistical and legal coordination so faculty members can focus on providing rich engagement activities for both students and community partners. This chapter highlights all the moving parts in the process and the ways that campus centers for community engagement establish and maintain meaningful partnerships with community agencies.

Partnership Principles

Bringle and Hatcher (1996) enumerated several best practices for working with community partners, including presenting and publishing with representatives from community agencies, recognizing the contributions of community partners with an award, collaborating with community partners in writing grant proposals, educating community partners on engaged pedagogy, and initiating site visits and meetings with community partners.

In 2001 Gelmon and colleagues wrote about key concepts and principles that characterize meaningful community partnerships, and these remain germane today. They include the capacity to fulfill the organizational mission, economic benefit, social benefit, efforts to establish and maintain the relationship, high-quality interaction and communication, satisfaction with the partnership, and sustainability of the partnership. Similarly, Holland (2005a) suggested that participants in campus-community partnerships should explore and expand separate and common goals; understand the capacity, resources, and expectations of all partners; plan carefully for mutual benefit; share control of activities and decisions; and continually assess processes and outcomes.

Benchmarks and Trends

The application for the Carnegie Classification for Community Engagement requires documentation of partnerships with community agencies using a response grid that articulates the purpose of the partnership, duration of the partnership, number of students and faculty members involved, funding sources, and impact on the institution as well as the community agency. The application also requires documentation of collaboration on scholarly products and a narrative of efforts to connect with community agencies as well as ways to sustain and improve partnerships.

The trends of community partnerships presented here come from three sources: the 2014 Campus Compact survey of its members plus two related surveys of community engagement centers with and without the Carnegie Classification. The first related survey was conducted in 2012 (Welch & Saltmarsh, 2013a, 2013b), and the second survey was conducted in 2014 (Welch & Saltmarsh, 2015). Data from these three surveys provide useful insight into trends. Further, it is interesting to compare the responses of campus centers with the Carnegie Classification with those of centers that do not have the classification.

Examples of various types of community partners are presented in Table 8.1, and the various ways community partners are involved in student learning and engagement activities are presented in Table 8.2.

Welch and Saltmarsh (2013b) revealed that the aspiration for community programming is high compared to what already exists or is in process. This finding suggests that institutions continue to strive toward improvements in their work with community agencies. Table 8.3 reports responses from this survey.

TABLE 8.1
Types of Community Partner Organizations

Description	National (%)	Public (%)	Private (%)
Nonprofit, community-based organization	97	97	99
K–12 school	96	97	89
Faith-based organization	78	71	87
Government agency	75	80	71
International community or organization	72	70	74
Other higher education institution	70	77	64
For-profit business	69	75	63
Other	4	4	3

Note. Data from *2014 Campus Compact Member Survey*, by Campus Compact, 2014, Boston, MA: Author. Retrieved from http://compact.org/wp-content/uploads/2015/05/2014ALLPublicInstitutionsReport.pdf. Used with permission from Campus Compact.

TABLE 8.2

Community Partner Involvement in Student Learning and Engagement Activities

Activity	National (%)	Public (%)	Private (%)
Come to class as guest speakers	93	94	92
Provide feedback on the development/ maintenance of community engagement programs	82	81	83
Provide reflection on site in community setting	76	74	78
Act as uncompensated coinstructors	54	55	52
Participate in the design and delivery of community-based courses	44	44	45
Serve on campus committee that determines learning goals or engagement activities	37	43	31
Assist in creating syllabi or designing courses	32	33	32
Act as compensated co-instructors	27	25	29
Other	2	2	1

Note. Data from *2014 Campus Compact Member Survey*, by Campus Compact, 2014, Boston, MA: Author. Retrieved from http://compact.org/wp-content/uploads/2015/05/2014ALLPublicInstitutionsReport.pdf. Used with permission from Campus Compact.

TABLE 8.3

Community Partner Programming Through Centers With Carnegie Classification

Program Option	Yes (%) (Number of Responses)	In progress (%) (Number of Responses)	Hope to (%) (Number of Responses)	No (%) (Number of Responses)	Number of Responses
Presentations/publications with partners	57.8 (74)	10.9 (14)	16.4 (21)	14.8 (19)	128
Awards to community partner	47.7 (61)	7.0 (9)	19.5 (25)	25.8 (33)	128
Collaborative grant proposals with community partners	67.2 (86)	9.4 (12)	16.4 (21)	7.0 (9)	128
Education of community partners on engaged pedagogy	64.8 (83)	19.5 (25)	9.4 (12)	6.3 (8)	128
Site visits/meetings initiated with partners	89.8 (115)	6.3 (8)	2.3 (3)	1.6 (2)	128
Community incentives and awards	33.1 (55)	4.2 (7)	16.3 (27)	46.3 (77)	16
Funding for community partners to coteach courses	9.5 (12)	4.0 (5)	25.4 (32)	61.1 (77)	126

Note. From "Current Practice and Infrastructure for Campus Centers of Community Engagement," by M. Welch and J. Saltmarsh, 2013, *Journal of Higher Education Outreach and Engagement, 17*(4), pp. 42–43. Reprinted with permission.

Open-ended responses to the 2012 survey revealed a number of other community partner programming elements. As a result the number of response items for community partner programming was increased in the second phase of the study to include these newly identified program components. However, the item regarding funding for coteaching included in the first survey was inadvertently omitted in the second phase of the study.

Table 8.4 shows the responses from 55 institutions with the Carnegie Classification and 37 institutions without the classification received during the second phase of the study (Saltmarsh & Welch, 2013). In general, centers with the Carnegie Classification had slightly higher response rates for actual implementation than centers without the classification. Nonclassified respondents, however, were slightly higher on the practice of providing awards to outstanding community partners and using agreement forms and action plans for service-learning courses. Otherwise, there is a fairly consistent application of these practices, suggesting more and more campus centers are incorporating these methods and procedures.

The most prevalent activity reported in both surveys and both categories of institutions was initiating site visits and meetings with community partners. This reflects a clear trend away from the early practice in which students essentially found their partners on their own and toward intentionally identifying appropriate partners and communicating with them. The least prominent practice for both groups was providing professional development opportunities for community partners, with a moderate percentage of centers without Carnegie Classification indicating no plans to do so. This suggests either that many centers are unaware of this practice and its potential benefits or that they lack the resources to offer such development opportunities. Topics of professional development for community partners might include writing grant proposals, raising funds, or using social media. The largest discrepancy between the responses of the classified and nonclassified centers was on the practice of collaborative assessment of partnerships, with only 30% of the nonclassified centers reporting any sustained efforts on assessment.

Another priority activity is grant writing, with just over three fourths of respondents indicating that their center already does this or is in the process of starting to. Eighty-five percent of centers provide opportunities to educate partners on engaged pedagogy. In the area of collaboration on scholarship, nearly 70% of respondents indicated that the center offers opportunities for collaboration on presentations and/or publications with community partners. Conversely, far less common is compensation for community partners as coeducators; less than 10% of respondents reported currently providing funding for community partners to coteach courses.

TABLE 8.4

Comparison of Community Partnerships on Campuses With the Carnegie Classification and on Those Without the Classification

Our community engagement center has	*Carnegie Classified*				*Not Carnegie Classified*			
	Yes	Hope to	No	*n*	Yes	Hope to	No	*n*
Written presentations/ publications with partners	46 83.6%	6 10.9%	3 5.5%	55	26 70.3%	3 8.1%	8 21.6%	37
Given awards to outstanding community partners	30 54.5%	13 23.6%	12 21.8%	55	14 37.8%	8 21.6%	15 40.5%	37
Written collaborative grant proposals with partners	37 67.3%	12 21.8%	6 10.9%	55	27 73.0%	3 8.1%	7 18.9%	37
Educated partners on engaged pedagogy	39 72.2%	11 20.4%	4 7.4%	54	23 62.2%	2 5.4%	12 32.4%	37
Initiated site visits/ meetings with partners	51 92.7%	3 5.5%	1 1.8%	55	33 89.2%	1 2.7%	3 8.1%	37
Created community incentives and rewards	24 43.6%	14 25.5%	17 30.9%	55	12 32.4%	10 27.0%	15 40.5%	37
Provided community agency orientation to classes	45 81.8%	5 9.1%	5 9.1%	55	29 78.4%	3 8.1%	5 13.5%	37
Created agreement forms or action plans for each service-learning class	27 50%	17 31.5%	10 18.5%	54	23 62.2%	5 13.5%	9 24.3%	37
Provided orientation/ training sessions on how to work with faculty members/ students	29 52.7%	14 25.5%	12 21.8%	55	14 37.8%	6 16.2%	17 45.9%	37

	Carnegie Classified				Not Carnegie Classified			
Provided collaborative assessment of partnership activity	30 54.5%	19 34.5%	6 10.9%	55	11 30.6%	11 30.6%	14 38.9%	36
MOUs or formal agreements with partners	31 57.4%	12 22.2%	11 20.4%	54	20 55.6%	8 22.2%	8 22.2%	36
Connected community agencies with career development programs to create greater student awareness of employment opportunities	29 52.7%	13 23.6%	13 23.6%	55	19 51.4%	7 18.9%	11 29.7%	37
Provided professional development for community partners	23 41.8%	17 30.9%	15 27.3%	55	11 29.7%	8 21.6%	18 48.6%	37
Provided professional development for community engagement	28 53.8%	12 25.0%	11 21.2%	51	11 30.6%	5 13.9	20 55.6%	36

Note. Data from "Current Practice and Infrastructure for Campus Centers of Community Engagement," by M. Welch and J. Saltmarsh, *Journal of Higher Education Outreach and Engagement, 17*(4), pp. 25–55.

A consistently reported shortcoming or challenge is conducting research on the effectiveness and impact of community partnerships. This is partially due to the limited technical, human, and financial resources necessary to conduct robust research. Center directors are busy administrators who often make conducting research a challenge or impossibility. It may also be the case that center administrators do not have the skills to conduct research of this nature. Using IR offices or graduate research methods courses might be a viable approach to addressing this challenge. The remainder of this chapter provides additional exploration of survey responses regarding partnerships between campus centers for community engagement and community agencies.

Separate and Complementary Roles

Engaged teaching and scholarship reflect a shared democratic process in which partners from community agencies are viewed and treated as coeducators. Community partners bring public expertise to the partnership while faculty members bring scholarly expertise. Thus, some of the shared roles and responsibilities articulated as best practices in the literature vary in the extent to which they are actually implemented (Littlepage & Gazley, 2013).

Coteaching

Results from the surveys presented in the previous section reveal that relatively few institutions use community partners as coinstructors for actual courses. This seems to be in part because of a couple of pragmatic challenges. First, representatives from community agencies have day jobs that can interfere with scheduling courses on campus. Second, there may not be room in the budget to pay partners for their participation. Despite these challenges, community partners can make significant contributions to the classroom experience. Making guest presentations during a class session is a relatively uncomplicated, short-term activity that does not require a great deal of time, energy, or cost. Inviting community partners to conduct or participate in reflection activities is another useful way of incorporating their expertise and insight into the academic component of the course.

The Public and Community Service Studies Program at Providence College uses representatives from community partner agencies as co-instructors. Community partners who worked with Providence College felt respected by and respectful of the faculty members they worked with, and they added that students appreciated the presence, insight, and praxis community partners brought to the classroom.

Presentations and Publications

Nearly 70% of the survey respondents reported that community partners are included as coauthors of publications or as copresenters at professional conferences. This statistic suggests a significant trend toward the democratization of knowledge in higher education, which has traditionally been exclusively dominated by scholars. It also reflects the concept of critical pedagogy, espoused by Freire (1970) over 40 years ago, which asserted that laypeople can provide authentic insight and perspective.

For example, Heidi Bajaras at the University of Minnesota has worked with a community partner organization serving Hmong families. In that partnership a community organizer from the agency voluntarily completed online training to meet the university's IRB requirements for doing research. Her research role made a meaningful contribution to the research design and protocol. She also conducted interviews and analysis of the results. Together, Barajas and the community organizer published an article (Barajas, Smalkoski, Kaplan, & Yang, 2012) on the collaborative project and presented at a local conference (Barajas, Smalkoski, Yang, Yang, & Yang, 2010).

One question that arises from the practice of collaborative scholarship is, Does such scholarship truly matter to practitioners and partners in the community? While it may not have the same professional impact or meaning as it would to tenure-track faculty members, it appears that collaboration does make a difference. Bajaras explained,

> I do think it matters to partners in place-based work because it not only acknowledges them as experts, but also supports their own professional development and frames their expertise in expanded arenas. In this case, the organizer decided to go to graduate school and had not considered that before—and he also moved into a different job that he also likely would not have considered. I also think that dissemination looks different and teaches an expanded way of considering who has knowledge and expertise if the partner can be in the room. I always talk with organizations I work with about publication and presentation. More would happen if they had more time in terms of copublishing and sometimes if funding for partners was available for both time writing and travel. (H. Barajas, personal communication, January 23, 2015)

Community Partner Awards and Recognition

Over half of the centers responding to the survey indicated they give recognition awards to their community partners. These awards can vary from framed certificates to plaques or trophies to cash. This practice clearly suggests an intentional effort to acknowledge the relationship between the institution and the agencies.

University Neighborhood Partners (UNP) at the University of Utah provides a Community Resident in Action Award to a member of the community. The two-year award provides $5,000 per year so that community residents can offer their knowledge and expertise in campus-community partnership projects. The award also provides visibility for the role of community residents in community partnerships both on and off campus while responding to community interests and needs. Recipients have expertise and interests that match the interests and needs of a planned or ongoing initiative. They have also demonstrated commitment to community work through some level of involvement in the project.

Professional Development for Community Partners

In many respects much of the professional development relevant to community partners is similar to that for faculty members described in chapter 7. Community partners must have an understanding of the public purpose of higher education and the tenet of the mutual benefits of community engagement projects. With this understanding community partners are afforded a voice and agency in the process of establishing and maintaining partnerships with the college or university. However, survey results reveal that conducting professional development for community partners is not common.

Saint Mary's College of California hosts a professional development workshop, on a topic such as trends in using social media or grant writing, for community agencies each semester. These workshops are organized by staff members at the college as a thank you for the community agencies' participation in a partnership with the college. In addition to the workshop, the director or representative of the community agency receives a complimentary library card to access the campus library, which is at no cost to the college. A tour of the library and the services available to community partners is provided. Following a buffet lunch, representatives from the community agencies attend a speed-dating event in order to meet faculty members teaching community engagement courses. If an instructor and community partner determine there is potential for partnership, they schedule subsequent meetings and an on-site visit to develop a course activity plan. Institutional funds cover the cost of the luncheon.

Partnership Preparation

Professional development also helps community agencies prepare for and understand the role and goal of student engagement. Many agencies do not have a clear understanding of the purpose or format of the experience; initially, they think college students are coming to their site simply to log community service hours. Professional development can educate community partners on the difference between cocurricular volunteer service and formal instructional experiences that are course-based and credit-bearing. In addition, partners may gain insight on the difference between required practicum experiences in professional preparation programs, such as education, nursing, and social work, and civic engagement, which is designed to promote students' sense of civic awareness and duty. Professional development may also include an overview of the demographics of millennial college students. Finally, and perhaps most important, professional development for community partners can include how to understand and work effectively with faculty members. Like faculty members, community partners learn that initial conversations are a courtship process that may lead to either becoming engaged or amicably choosing not to pursue the relationship. Thus, community partners are afforded agency and voice. Like faculty members, community partners should learn how to talk to faculty members about possible partnerships for course-based activities and CBR and to campus community engagement staff members or student leaders about establishing cocurricular partnerships. A list of topics to discuss with faculty and center staff members is presented in Appendix G.

Community partners must also have an opportunity to reflect on their programmatic goals and objectives as well as to consider the various forms of community engagement. Like faculty members, community partners can be given a rubric and planning worksheet, such as the OPERA rubric described in chapter 7 (see Appendix F). This allows directors of agencies and their staffs to explore the components of community engagement partnerships before they commit to one. During this exploratory process, community agencies become aware of the various cocurricular and curricular methods for engaging students described in chapter 6. They can make informed decisions on the basis of their goals as to whether they want to pursue a one-time day of service, semester-long service-learning class, or an internship. This professional development also helps representatives from community agencies understand possible research projects they might consider undertaking with faculty members conducting CBR.

Memos of Understanding, Course Agreements, and Action Plans

As discussed in chapter 5, MOUs are used to describe the partnership between the institution and the community agency. It is also becoming more common for centers to coordinate individual course agreements and action plans with the agency and the instructor. These documents ensure that both parties are on the same page in terms of what service is provided by the students and faculty members. These agreements enumerate a time line of specific actions and activities to achieve a goal or create a deliverable product.

The use of these types of forms represents a significant shift from earlier practice, which was much more informal or casual. While this trend might make the partnership process seem less intimate, many community agency representatives report that the formality is beneficial to them and may even strengthen the partnership. Some boards of nonprofit organizations appreciate the documentation because it indemnifies both parties against risk. Agencies can also document formal relationships, which often strengthen grant applications and help secure additional funding sources, such as private foundations.

Assessment of Community Partnerships

Assessing community partnerships is an ongoing challenge. Only half of the Carnegie-classified centers and 30% of the nonclassified centers reported some degree of collaborative assessment of partnerships (Welch & Saltmarsh, 2013a, 2013b). Most centers use a simple satisfaction survey to assess community partnerships. Formal and robust assessment procedures and experimental research to determine the actual impact on the organization and those they serve are less common and more challenging. This is likely because of the pragmatic challenges associated with conducting assessment. However, part of the conundrum is also understanding and articulating what is meant when we talk about assessing community partnerships.

Assessing community partnerships is a broad concept with several foci. Bandy (2012) noted the need to distinguish between assessing the impact a community engagement experience has on community partners and their constituencies and assessing the partnership between agencies and institutions of higher education. The former assessment could include looking for impact at three levels: micro (individuals in the organization or those it serves), meso (organizational efficiency and capacity building), and macro (social structures, laws, policies) (Marullo et al., 2003). The latter assessment could include reflecting on the mutual respect of community time, obligations, and resources (Gelmon et al., 2001) as well as shared power in decision making, open communication, and conflict resolution (Dostilio, Edwards, Harrison, Kliewer, & Clayton, 2011; Dumlao & Janke, 2012).

IUPUI has actively pursued creating and implementing two formal tools to assess their community partnerships. The first tool, created by the Center for Service and Learning in the IUPUI Office of Community Engagement, is known as the SOFAR model to support campuses and communities in improving communication and network building. SOFAR is an acronym representing five of the key stakeholders in community-campus collaborations: students, organization staff, faculty members, administrators and staff members on campus, and residents in the community. The second tool is collaborative relationship mapping (ColRM), a graphic reflection and assessment process intended to increase partners' capacity to understand and assess underlying relationships and networks. ColRM is a flexible instrument that can also gather assessment and research data to document partnerships and the development of human and social capital invested in the process. The ColRM also assesses subsets of collaborative relationships in the partnership, including personal relationships, social networks, factions, and coalitions.

The Office of Community Engaged Learning, Teaching and Scholarship (OCELTS) at Loyola University in New Orleans created a rubric to assess community engagement partnerships in 2013 with the input of the university's Community Partner Council (CPC). The rubric is organized into five broad areas: basics, relationships, capacity, outcomes, and assessment. These areas are assessed across four qualitative tiers: well-institutionalized partnerships, building quality and commitment, building quantity and critical mass, and priority areas for improvement.

Place-Based and Anchor Programs

Community partnerships have traditionally been course-based, consisting of short-term experiences. Students and faculty members typically spent anywhere from 10 to 15 weeks working with an agency. While useful in the short term, this approach does not allow for long-term, sustained partnerships. Plus, many of the engaged projects provide direct service and do not necessarily build capacity for the agency or the community it serves. Institutions of higher education and partners are now conceptualizing and implementing long-term partnerships in which colleges and universities have a physical presence in specific neighborhoods.

Place-based education (PBE) was originally developed in K–12 settings to promote environmental education and community development in the 1990s through initiatives such as the Annenberg Rural Challenge. PBE uses the local community and environment to teach concepts in language arts, mathematics, social studies, science, and other subjects across the curriculum. Over time PBE has migrated into higher education as a form of community engagement. Sobel (2004) presented two operating principles of PBE that reflect basic tenets of civic engagement: maximize shared ownership through partnerships and engage students in real-world projects in the local community. Real-world learning experiences promote a connection with the community, emphasizing not merely a geographical setting but a cultural sense of place as well. The active learning that targets goals identified by members of the community contributes to the civic development of students.

Anchor programs are located in specific neighborhoods, dependent on the partner organization involved, and "cannot move" (Axelroth Hodges & Dubb, 2010, p. 2). These programs generally focus on economic development, education, and health partnerships. They often involve universities and hospitals in the same geographical area and are referred to as "eds and meds" programs. Unlike the other forms of community engagement described thus far, anchor programs sometimes involve a major financial commitment, through capital or low-income loans, by the institution of higher education in partnership with local foundations. These partnerships transcend traditional direct service to promote capacity building for community agencies and organizations (Maurrasse, 2007). Two major resources have emerged in the past decade to assist institutions of higher education and their neighbors in implementing anchor programming.

Anchor Institutions Task Force

The Anchor Institutions Task Force (www.margainc.com/initiatives/aitf) is a think tank that develops and disseminates information to help colleges and universities create mutually beneficial anchor institution-community partnerships. One major focus of the task force is on partnerships between higher education and medical centers to address health issues in the community. A second area of emphasis is economic and community development. Anchor institutions provide teaching and learning opportunities focused on critical needs in the community. Anchor program activities include an urban nutritional literacy initiative; college access and readiness; community arts; academic and cultural enrichment programs in schools, including K–12 STEM education; an institute to support and empower local faith-based and nonprofit organizations to increase community capacity building; and a variety of educational opportunities for students through volunteer service, service-learning courses, and summer internships.

The Netter Center at the University of Pennsylvania serves as an anchor institution and participates on the Anchor Institutions Task Force. In this role the center created the *Anchor Institutions Toolkit: A Guide to Neighborhood Revitalization* (Netter Center for Community Partnerships, 2008), which can be downloaded from its website. The toolkit provides exploratory questions that guide institutions and community partners in developing goals and using assets on campus and in the community to rebuild and revitalize the community while meeting the academic mission of the university. Goals and tools are organized efforts to improve neighborhood safety, improve housing, promote local business and economic development, and enhance existing public school programs.

Democracy Collaborative

In 2005 the University of Maryland created the Democracy Collaborative (www.democracycollaborative.org) as a research center to promote the public purpose of higher education, civic engagement, and community revitalization through anchor programs. Establishing university-community partnerships is a major goal of the Community-Wealth.org project in the collaborative. While honoring the public purpose of higher education, the project also takes a pragmatic view of the necessity for such partnerships. The project's website notes that it is in the best interest of institutions of higher education to not only work with but also support local community organizations, as they can serve as an infrastructural base for community-based economic development while meeting the college's civic and public mission. Courses, academic departments, and research within the institution of higher education can be used to create and disseminate new knowledge and provide learning opportunities for students while serving the community. In partnership with the Cleveland Foundation, the Democracy Collaborative established a major anchor program involving universities, hospitals, and cultural institutions in Cleveland's University Circle area. The program is targeting employer-assisted housing, improvement of local public schools, and community development.

Innovative Community Partnership Programs

The following profiles provide an overview of some innovative partnerships between institutions of higher education and communities. These illustrate most of the best practices reported in the surveys, enumerated in the professional literature, and described in this and previous chapters. All programs reflect the democratic purpose and process of mutually beneficial partnerships with community partners. These programs also depict the four factors of cultural, systemic, top-down, and bottom-up influences on the institutionalization of community engagement as well as demonstrate the platform infrastructure and programs described in earlier chapters. Two examples are from large urban public universities, and one is from a smaller private, faith-based liberal arts institution.

Netter Center for Community Partnerships, University of Pennsylvania

The University of Pennsylvania was one of the first institutions to make an intentional effort to reach out to and include community neighborhoods as coeducators and partners. Thus, the Netter Center at Penn (www.nettercenter.upenn.edu) has a long history as a hallmark model for other institutions. Its website provides an overview of its unique and comprehensive approach to working with community partners. The Netter Center evolved from the West Philadelphia Partnership and the Office of Community Oriented Policy Studies, both created in 1983. In 1985 four undergraduate students created a summer job training corps, known as the West Philadelphia Improvement Corps, as part of an honors course. Originally an after-school program at a local elementary school, the project grew and evolved. In 1992 the university made an institutional commitment by creating the Center for Community Partnerships to coordinate the revitalization of this neighborhood. The center coordinated only four service-learning courses that first year. Today, 60 to 65 courses are taught each year.

Since its inception, the Netter Center has worked with faculty members and students to address various critical issues in the community in partnerships with schools, community organizations, and faith communities. The center coordinates three main approaches to community engagement: academically based community service, direct traditional service, and community development. The center's three core operational tenets, which reflect its spirit and practice of reciprocity and its academic mission of advancing new knowledge, set it apart from other campus centers. These tenets, found on the center's website, are as follows:

1. Penn's future and the future of West Philadelphia/Philadelphia are intertwined.
2. Penn can make a significant contribution to improving the quality of life in West Philadelphia/Philadelphia.
3. Penn can enhance its overall mission of advancing and transmitting knowledge by helping to improve the quality of life in West Philadelphia and Philadelphia. (Netter Center for Community Partnerships, 2012)

The Netter Center now oversees 15 community-based programs, ranging from nutritional education programs in schools to nonprofit and faith-based organization empowerment projects to public service summer internships. It has approximately 50 staff members (including an executive director and three associate directors) as well as a national advisory board and advisory boards for faculty members, community partners, and students.

A major component of the Netter Center programs is the use of existing K–12 schools as place-based community partners. University Assisted Community Schools (UACS) provides programs during and after the school day, in the evenings, and throughout the summer at three K–8 schools and two high schools. This approach is an efficient use of existing physical resources. One or two Netter Center staff members oversee and coordinate the programs at each school. Programs are delivered through a coordinated effort of cocurricular volunteer programs and curricular programs, such as academically based service-learning courses. UACS programs include college access and career readiness; a community arts partnership; a health science educational pipeline; a STEM-based, hands-on educational program; reading and literacy; and an after-school athletic/recreation program that provides mentoring as well as sports. UACS programs extend into the summer, providing academic review and support coupled with college and career mentoring, extracurricular activities, and paid internships to provide real-world job experiences.

The Agatston Urban Nutrition Initiative (AUNI) works in a total of 20 Philadelphia public schools, serving more than 10,000 students every month with nutritional literacy programs. The program includes cooking labs, gardening clubs, and fruit stands managed by students through service-learning courses. The Nonprofit and Communities of Faith Nonprofit Institute works with local organizations and church congregations to build capacity through community-based technical support. Finally, the Penn Program for Public Service Summer Internship is a 12-week summer program in which a dozen or more undergraduates tackle real-world problem-solving in the West Philadelphia–Penn community, working in schools, hospitals, and other community organizations.

University Neighborhood Partners, University of Utah

The University of Utah created University Neighborhood Partners (UNP) in 2001 to promote civic engagement in an under-resourced geographical area of Salt Lake City and to increase access to higher education for its residents. Residents and representatives of community organizations challenged the university to establish a physical presence in the neighborhood. Responding to that challenge, the university leased the former residence of a city park caretaker from the city at no cost for 10 years and converted it to office space. The interior of the house was renovated by volunteers and through donations from local businesses. The university provided a modest operating budget that included paying for three full-time staff members when the office and program were inaugurated in April 2003. Four priorities were collaboratively identified through community and campus interviews and town hall meetings:

1. Increase the capacity of organizations and others to work effectively in the areas of housing, job training, small business development, health, and the environment
2. Provide greater educational and employment opportunities for youth
3. Develop greater skills and opportunities for resident leaders to be able to address local issues
4. Find ways to overcome mistrust and conflict stemming from differences of income, ethnicity, religion, race, and political affiliation, which divide the community and make it difficult to pursue common goals

These goals are addressed through community engagement courses, programs, and research fellowships.

Today, with a full-time staff of 12, UNP directs three broad clusters of partnership programs: community capacity building, community leadership, and educational pathways. Within the community capacity building category are six programs, including the Start-Up Incubator, which assists emerging micro nonprofit organizations and small businesses. The community leadership cluster has five programs, including the Mestizo Arts and Activism project, in which local high school students work with university faculty members to research and document social issues in the neighborhood through arts and activism. There are 13 programs under the educational pathways umbrella. University interns meet with parents and families to learn how to deal with family issues, such as bullying, nutritional literacy, and financial preparation for college, in the 2nd Cup of Coffee program that meets at a local school.

The Community-Based Research Grant Program supports CBR for a faculty member serving as a principal investigator or for a team of investigators. The program is designed to create and implement mutually beneficial research conducted by faculty members and a community partner. The vice president for research provides one or two annual grants of up to $20,000 for the projects. The UNP Community Scholar in Residence and Community Resident in Action assist university and community partners in designing and implementing mutually beneficial projects.

Seattle University Youth Initiative

Seattle University, a Jesuit liberal arts institution, launched an ambitious initiative, known as the Seattle University Youth Initiative (SUYI), with a nearby elementary school and a housing program through its Center for Service and Community Engagement. While its programs are much smaller in scale than the programs at the University of Pennsylvania, Seattle University is incorporating best practices and ensuring the mutual benefit and reciprocity that characterize effective community partnerships. An asset map of the region that is the focus of SUYI revealed more than a dozen parks, several recreation and community centers, three community gardens, two libraries, five public health centers, seven food banks, and over two dozen religious institutions. Despite these assets, the neighborhood suffers youth violence, a significant academic performance gap, and poverty. One of the university's neighborhood partner sites is the Yesler Terrace Housing Development, a multiunit low-income program owned and operated by the Seattle Housing Authority, which received a Choice Neighborhood grant from the Department of Housing and Urban Development. Other neighborhood project sites are the nearby Bailey Gatzert Elementary School, Washington Middle School, and Garfield High School.

After three years of discussion and planning, SUYI was launched in February 2011. The program provides education and support systems for 1,000 neighborhood youths and their families as well as meets the academic mission of the university through advocacy, social entrepreneurship, service-learning, and CBR by students and faculty members. The program was designed and implemented in a neighborhood near the campus to meet three specific goals: children will graduate from high school prepared to succeed in higher education and life; university students, faculty and staff members, and alumni will contribute to a just and human world by expanding campus engagement into the neighborhood; and partners will advance the field of community engagement in higher education by disseminating promising practices learned from the project (www.seattleu.edu/suyi/vision). The program has 21 staff members and an advisory board that collaborates with nearly 50 public and private organizations.

In the 2012–2013 academic year, over 1,200 college students provided direct service to the neighborhood, and 43 faculty members and 838 students participated in service-learning courses. Through a new Faculty Fellows Program, nine faculty members conducted CBR. The after-school program provided over 35,000 hours of educational support, contributing the highest academic growth rates in the city of Seattle. When the Seattle Housing Authority successfully obtained the Choice Neighborhood grant, the initial three-year, $6.3 million investment in Yesler Terrace was leveraged into nearly $37 million in additional funding for housing, education, and health care. Eight neighborhood organizations worked with the university to provide summer learning to over 300 children, resulting in over 27,000 hours of academic enrichment.

In addition to outreach programs at Yesler Terrace, SUYI participants have worked with a nearby elementary school to extend the school day by two hours for nearly 200 students. This extension includes an after-school science education club. The university also worked with eight community organizations in the summer of 2013 to provide summer learning opportunities to more than 300 neighborhood children. These opportunities included kindergarten orientation, math and reading enrichment, media arts, and college readiness. In a partnership with Seattle Public Schools, the Seattle University College of Education created a "Middle College" on the university campus designed for promising high school students struggling in traditional educational settings. The initiative has also hosted several job fairs for neighborhood residents. Finally, these efforts include the Just Serve program, in which university students are paired with students from a local high school to do community service and explore social justice issues (Seattle University, 2014).

Meanwhile, the Center for Service and Community Engagement also coordinates campus-wide efforts focusing on community engagement with over 75 community agencies and organizations. The center provides technical support to the faculty through one-on-one consultations as well as workshops. Resources and information on how to establish community partnerships for service-learning are also provided. In addition, faculty members can access funding and technical assistance for community-based scholarship that can be linked to courses. The center is also responsible for student placement coordination, orientation, hours tracking, risk releases, and background checks.

Summary

Community partnerships have become more formalized over the years. Increased infrastructure is necessary to ensure quality experiences for students, faculty members, and community partners. Campus centers for community engagement are taking more responsibility in establishing and coordinating robust partnerships. There appears to be a concerted effort to make these relationships truly reciprocal and mutually beneficial partnerships. A lingering challenge is that little to no research has been conducted to empirically determine the effectiveness and outcomes for community agencies. In the meantime campus centers for community engagement continue to expand their roles and responsibilities associated with the dynamic process of establishing, maintaining, and assessing community partnerships. More and more institutions and their neighboring communities are working toward establishing long-term, sustained partnerships in local neighborhoods.

9

PROMISE, PERIL, AND PROJECTIONS

This new paradigm of scholarship, I believe, holds enormous potential for colleges and universities. With this broader definition, it would be possible for a university to describe with more confidence and courage its own distinctive mission, working out the formulas and the relationships between those forms of scholarship that fit uniquely that particular campus.

—Ernest Boyer (1997, p. 78)

Increasingly, the campus is being viewed as a place where students get credentialed and faculty get tenured, while the overall work of the academy does not seem particularly relevant to the nation's most pressing civic, social, economic, and moral problems.

—Ernest Boyer (1997, p. 85)

American higher education has never been static. For more than 350 years, it has shaped its programs in response to the changing social context. And as we look at today's world, with its disturbingly complicated problems, higher learning, we conclude, must once again adapt. It would be foolhardy not to reaffirm the accomplishments of the past. Yet, even the best of our institutions must continuously evolve. And to sustain the vitality of higher education in our time, a new vision of scholarship is required, one dedicated not only to the renewal of the academy but, ultimately, to the renewal of society itself.

—Ernest Boyer (1990, p. 81)

Each of these quotations by Ernest Boyer accurately depicts the promise, peril, and projections of community engagement in higher education. Clearly, community engagement has made numerous gains over the past 30 years, evolving from a movement to a legitimate academic field while advancing the public purpose of higher education. Indeed, many of the rich resources of the academy have been used to address critical social issues, as Ernest Boyer advocated. There is a great deal of promise for the future of community engagement. At the same time the field faces considerable peril that could slow, detour, or potentially end its progress. Both the promise of and the peril facing community engagement in higher education generate projected next steps for research and practice. This concluding chapter examines the promise, peril, and projections of community engagement in higher education.

Promise

What started as a small movement in the 1980s has evolved into a robust professional field and productive educational partnerships between higher education and the communities. O'Meara (2011) noted succinctly, "There's more of it" (p. 181). She was referring to the growth of community engagement in at least three interrelated areas: first, campuses continue to provide infrastructure to support faculty members and students in this work; second, a growing body of literature and research has made a dramatic impact on realizing the public purpose of higher education and the institutionalization of engaged pedagogy and scholarship; and third, there is continued professionalization and proliferation of engaged teaching and scholarship in disciplinary associations and the professional research literature. In addition to these three areas, however, we can begin to see promising trends in other areas.

Campus Centers

Proliferation of campus centers for community engagement indicates that the field is growing (Ray, 2014). More and more colleges and universities are establishing an office or hub to coordinate curricular and cocurricular programs. There were only a handful of centers doing this work 25 years ago. Today, Campus Compact has over 1,400 members, which in turn suggests there are at least that many centers overseeing some aspect of community engagement. This means institutions of higher education are allocating financial, physical, and human resources to sustain these efforts. As a result, more courses are incorporating forms of engaged pedagogy and scholarship than ever before. The early pioneers and champions for community engagement could hardly have imagined such growth in such a short period.

The Carnegie Classification for Community Engagement appears to have served as a catalyst for institutional recommitment to the public purpose of higher education. It has created a sense of the legitimacy and credibility of this work. However, despite the classification's utility, out of 4,726 Title IV degree-granting postsecondary institutions in the United States, only 361 campuses have the classification (National Center for Education Statistics, 2012). Many applied for but did not receive the classification; still, the 361 campuses with the designation represent only 7% of all American colleges and universities. While gains have been made, it is clear that there is much more work to do.

Research

Although community engagement is firmly grounded in theoretical foundations, initially little was actually known about putting theory into practice, and a generation ago there was virtually no empirical evidence of engagement's impact. As the field continues to grow, we now have scholars proposing and pursuing research agendas to substantiate and guide engagement work. Best practices based on the professional literature now guide the administrators and staffs of campus centers for community engagement, which in turn guide faculty members, students, and community partners.

Over the past 25 years, research on, about, and for engaged scholarship has grown exponentially. A growing body of literature is contributing to the development of best practices as more research is being conducted on the impact of community engagement on students, faculty members, and community partners. However, there is still much to do.

Research centers, like the NERCHE, the Higher Education Research Institute (HERI) at the University of California–Los Angeles, and CIRCLE, have been established to advance the study of community engagement. The IARSLCE was created to provide a peer-reviewed venue for scholars to publish and present their work and thus make a contribution to the field. The National Serving-Learning Clearinghouse, Campus Compact, and the AAC&U are providing an almost overwhelming amount of empirical information for practitioners and scholars.

Professionalization

The professionalization of the field was highlighted in chapter 1. The previously listed associations and organizations have taken a leading role in advancing the field. As this book was being written, Campus Compact was culling best practices to generate a set of competencies that will be used in the further professionalization of the field. In addition, the Council for the Advancement of Standards in Higher Education (CAS, 2015) compiled a useful and comprehensive set of 12 standards and guidelines. These, in turn, can be used to prepare a new generation of campus center directors. Such training efforts may lead to professional certificates, licenses, or, possibly, degrees. In the meantime Doberneck and colleagues (2010) proposed and described professional development programs at the graduate level to prepare the next generation of engaged scholars. From their review of the literature, they made nine recommendations to support graduate students as emerging engaged scholars:

1. Utilize intentional and collaborative voices of community partners and experts from professional associations in creating graduate professional preparation programs for engaged scholarship

2. Learn about the multiple forms of and various applications of engaged scholarship
3. Intentionally integrate teaching, research, and service as a seamless way of thinking, being, and doing that nurtures personal and professional meaning
4. Develop skill sets that include ethical research, effective communication skills to facilitate community partnerships, appropriate methodologies, intercultural humility and cultural competency, evidence-based practice, extramural funding, and publishing
5. Find, negotiate, and use a "community" or home for engaged scholars on campus for support and a common voice to advocate engaged scholarship
6. Envision engaged scholarship across the various stages of one's career
7. Advance a culture of understanding and acceptance of engaged scholarship among colleagues and across campus
8. Participate in cross-disciplinary and cross-institutional collaboration with others
9. Contribute to the growing professional development and field of engaged scholarship

Doberneck and colleagues' (2010) review also described current initiatives designed to support and prepare the emerging engaged professoriate. A decade ago, Imagining America launched the Publicly Active Graduate Education (PAGE) Fellows program, which provided mentoring opportunities for graduate students who aspired to be engaged scholars. The National Outreach Scholarship Conference created and hosts the annual Emerging Engagement Scholars Workshop, in which graduate students work with mentors and attend panel discussions on engaged pedagogy and scholarship. The Houle Engaged Scholars Program is a collaborative effort by North Carolina State University, Pennsylvania State University, and the University of North Carolina at Chapel Hill to support a cohort of graduate students in becoming engaged scholars. Professional certificates in service-learning and community engagement are offered at Portland State University and Michigan State University.

Despite these proposals and initiatives, O'Meara (2011) also noted a limited number of graduate programs on and about community engagement. This challenge is exacerbated by the continued socialization of the traditional academic trilogy and the competitive individualization and disciplinary focus of scholarship with little to no attention to the public purpose of the academy.

Democratization of Education

The growth of community engagement has contributed to the democratization of education (Harkavy & Hartley, 2012). Admittedly, the process is far from perfect, as addressed later in this chapter. However, the proliferation and pronouncement of best practices have, in many cases, resulted in truly reciprocal and mutually beneficial efforts by the academy and community agencies to cocreate knowledge. More faculty members and their students are recognizing the value of public expertise and community knowledge in engaged teaching and scholarship. Further, organizations and those they serve now have a voice in designing and implementing programs that contribute not only to students' learning and faculty scholarship but also to the common good of the community itself (Post, Ward, Longo, & Saltmarsh, in press). These changes reflect a shift from the expert model to the community of experts advocated by Cantor and Englot (2014). Students are no longer merely the recipients of knowledge; through their community-based efforts, they are cocreators. Gradually, community engagement is shifting from an enabling, charity model to a model of empowerment. Through culturally competent conversations between scholars and community, the collaborative work of programs such as Public Achievement and anchor-based community partnerships has begun to empower community organizations and their constituencies.

Critical Voice and Perspective

The democratization of education has also given voice to the traditionally marginalized. These emerging voices in turn nurture a critical perspective of power and privilege in two contexts. First, the inclusionary practice of involving community partners and their constituencies in projects promotes a true partnership. This practice requires intercultural humility on the part of scholarly experts; that is, these experts must acknowledge and relinquish some of their power to the public. Second, the growing diversity of the new engaged professoriate has prompted reflection on and reexamination of preconceived notions of knowledge and knowledge creation. The traditional positivist approach to scholarship has been called into question as complex social and cultural factors are considered from a democratic and inclusive lens. Saltmarsh and Hartley (2016) refer to this as a new collaborative, or public, scholarship; it has emerged from feminist, postmodern, postcolonial, and critical race theories. They argue that these public scholars represent the emerging engaged academy, which promotes engaged teaching, learning practices, research, and scholarship that transcend the traditional disciplinary, rational expert approach of scholarship and advance democratic knowledge that benefits society as a whole.

New Collaborative Institutional Models

Institutions of higher education are coming to recognize that their traditional structure is not always conducive to advancing a public mission or implementing community engagement. Institutional structure includes not only historical constructs like academic calendars and disciplinary silos but also the actual physical location of engaged scholarship. Saltmarsh and colleagues (2015) wonder whether institutions new to engagement should conform to existing structures and forms or attempt to create new and innovative approaches that may, in turn, be devalued by academia. As previous chapters attest, much of community engagement is becoming place-based and anchored in actual geographic neighborhoods off campus. But a truly democratic approach to community engagement also demands new models, or what Rutgers University chancellor Nancy Cantor describes as a "third space" that is co-owned and shared by universities and community organizations (Cantor, 2010; Cantor & Englot, 2013; Cantor & Englot, 2014; U.S. Department of Housing and Urban Development, 2013a). The future of community engagement may involve what has been called a *communiversity*, in which communities and higher education institutions share bricks and mortar.

Peril

While there have been strides in advancing community engagement, the movement has not yet met its full potential (Saltmarsh & Hartley, 2011), leaving the public purpose of an engaged academy in peril. Weisbuch (2015) argued there are at least four challenges to what he called "public" engagement. The first challenge is economic feasibility. Engagement requires financial resources, but myriad other needs across campuses are also competing for limited funds. Second, applying the humanities in this work continues to be a hurdle. Unlike many professional disciplines that have a tradition of applying knowledge and skills in authentic settings as part of the educational experience, the humanities primarily remain a robust intellectual exercise. Many departments and faculties within the humanities struggle to envision how complex and abstract ideas can be used to serve the community. Third, creating coherence and permanence of programs and research is difficult, given that the academic calendar is transient and nearly all forms of engagement are confined to semesters. Engagement efforts are often person-specific, meaning the programs are dependent on one individual's work rather than on an institutionalized program. In addition, many programs move from one community partner organization to another over time, often because of leadership changes in the organizations and the rotation of faculty members through course assignments. The recent tendency to focus on specific neighborhoods or topical challenges may help stabilize engaged programs and partnerships. Fourth, institutionalizing engaged learning and scholarship continues to be difficult owing to a lack of reward structures in the promotion and tenure system.

Cultural and Systemic Change in the Institution

Change is difficult; however, the difficulty is often due to a lack of awareness or knowledge rather than to the change itself. In other words people and places will not change, or even be motivated to change, if they do not perceive the need for change. Thus, administrators, faculty members, staff, and students must be informed of the public purpose of higher education. High-level administrators are usually preoccupied with the bottom line of running an institution. Community engagement is likely not even on their radars, even though it may be a viable strategy for addressing some challenges they face.

Administrators and faculty members alike are experts in a discipline and have little to no understanding of the public purpose of higher education and the way community engagement can meet that purpose and enhance the teaching, research, and service provided by the institution. An institution cannot promote and practice community engagement if there is no foundational understanding in the institution of what engagement is. Therefore, both administrators and faculty members must learn what this work is and why it is important. The challenge is determining how this learning will take place.

At the same time, even if institutional leaders and faculty members understand community engagement and its importance, various cultural and systemic factors conspire to impede institutionalization. As discussed in chapter 3, cultural factors include values, beliefs, traditions, and attitudes that have a powerful effect on behavior. These cultural variables are expressed in policies and procedures. The predominant cultural framework of higher education is constructed as a positivist, expert model. The reward and recognition structure primarily supports traditional forms of scholarship. Until new ways of thinking and doing are accepted, engaged scholarship will continue to be viewed as countercultural and will not be rewarded; thus, scholars will be reluctant to pursue this work. In addition, systemic factors, such as financial, physical, operational, and human resources, can either impede or stimulate community engagement. Lacking these resources makes it difficult, if not impossible, to implement community engagement programs, but when combined, these resources provide the necessary infrastructure and platforms for launching engagement programs.

Disciplinary Guildism

Related to the deeply entrenched culture of higher education is what Benson, Harkavy, and Hartley (2005) termed *disciplinary guildism*. A focus on narrow disciplinary specialization and benefit persists within the academy. Indeed, a disciplinary lens is useful, important, and even necessary for creating new knowledge. However, the pervasive practice of exclusively creating new knowledge for the intellectual benefit of a disciplinary field alone, coupled with the individual scholar's professional advancement toward tenure, does little to promote the public purpose of higher education. Because of this disciplinary guildism, faculty members have greater loyalty to their discipline than to the broader mission of the institution and higher education as whole. Cantor and Englot (2014) envision and advocate for a shift from disciplinary silos to collaborative public scholarship.

While many scholars continue to embrace and support engaged pedagogy and scholarship, most institutions of higher education still operate on a commodified, expert model. Boyte and Fretz (2011) agreed that the current engagement movement has much to offer with regard to teaching and learning and the potential to redirect higher education toward its original public purpose: to prepare young people to work together to solve problems and build community capacity to nurture a healthy democracy. However, they also argued that the "civic movement has ghettoized activities in discrete programs or centers and, in the case of service-learning, often times isolated efforts of single faculty members within academic departments. This model is proving to be unsustainable" (p. 83). What these scholars call for is an intentional return to the original larger purpose of democratic engagement, which will transform the institution of higher education and promote a democratic society. This clarion call represents the circling pathway returning to the public purpose of higher education depicted in chapter 1.

Commodification of Higher Education

Another challenge is the commodification of higher education. Students are seen and socialized as consumers, only looking for an education that will lead to a career. Many students, families, and politicians are looking to higher education not as a pathway to becoming an engaged citizen in a just and democratic society but as a route to a career that, in turn, stimulates the economy. Colleges and universities are forced to juggle honoring their civic and public purpose and effectively attracting and retaining students. The painful and plain fact is that many potential students and their families are simply looking for a return on their investment that leads to a career rather than an educational experience that prepares young adults to be good citizens.

Historically, few students attended college with the hope of economic advancement since only the well-to-do could afford college in the first place (Covaleskie, 2014). However, immediately following World War II, thanks to the GI Bill, over 2 million veterans entered college and another 6 million entered technical schools. Employers could now use educational attainment to screen potential employees. This began to change the reason for attending college from getting an education to getting a job. Kimball (2011) affirmed this historical shift, arguing that since World War II college has become a consumable good, a product to be purchased. He went on to suggest that colleges are both producer and consumer. Colleges produce an educational product that students consume. At the same time colleges vie with other institutions for customers in the form of students. In turn students have begun to "package" themselves as a product both to colleges attempting to recruit them and later to businesses and organizations as potential employees.

Dorn (2011) found that Americans now understand the public purpose of higher education to be providing degrees that lead to jobs. He noted American higher education's original purpose—to promote civic virtue and a commitment to the public good—but also acknowledged that political, social, and economic forces, including the rise of commercialism, in an emerging urban, industrial, class-stratified society reframed higher education's priorities to focus on preparing professionals for careers rather than on preparing citizens to create a just and democratic society.

This trend is confirmed by a comprehensive study conducted by the Georgetown University Center on Education and the Workforce titled *The Economic Value of College Majors* (Carnevale, Cheah, & Hanson, 2015). Key findings of the study indicate that 35% of current jobs require a bachelor's degree or higher. The average entry salary of full-time, year-round, college-educated employees is $33,000, rising to an average of $61,000 over the course of their careers. Among the 15 major groups, 26% of college graduates major in business and 20% major in STEM subjects. An entry-level STEM major can earn $43,000 annually in contrast to entry-level majors in the arts, humanities, and liberal arts, who typically earn $29,000.

One way to address the current focus on students' careers is to emphasize that a college experience provides a pathway to a meaningful personal and civic life as well as to a professional life. AAC&U attempted to reiterate this point with its Core Commitments initiative designed to nurture students' personal and social responsibility. Stanford University has launched intentional programming efforts to help students explore six related professional pathways of service that could lead to a career. Macalester College has started learning communities in which students explore ways they can use their values and skills as engaged citizens in their vocation.

Similarly, Cantor and Englot (2014) suggested higher education move from "meritocracies to cultivators of talent" (p. 5). Colleges and universities should assess and recruit students because of their potential rather than because of test scores. Cantor and Englot (2014) argued that institutions of higher education should be recognized for the type of student they accept and nurture rather than for the type of student they reject. This reframed emphasis on potential is especially critical for students who come from underresourced backgrounds, without the financial support to attend college despite their academic potential. Grooming student potential will require new thinking and work with high schools and community colleges to cultivate admission candidates.

Decontextualized Learning

Another challenge to engaged teaching is the potential danger of decontextualized learning, in which information is passively ingested by students rather than experienced in authentic settings. Eby (1998) articulated this concern in his landmark essay "Why Service-Learning Is Bad." Saltmarsh and Hartley (2011) also suggested that much of the work of civic engagement has been unilaterally driven by institutions of higher education "grounded in an institutional epistemology that privileges the expertise in the university and its application externally, through activities in the community" (pp. 18–19). They characterized the current framework of civic engagement as focusing on activity and place and argued that many of the current efforts in community engagement still embody an expert model in which higher education institutions are producers of knowledge in a partnership with communities that are knowledge consumers.

Saltmarsh and Hartley (2011) suggested reframing our current understanding and practice of civic engagement as democratic engagement that "seeks the public good *with* the public and not merely *for* the public" (p. 20). This reframing requires reciprocity that integrates academic knowledge with public knowledge so that all participants—faculty members, students, and community partners—are actively involved in a collaborative process of discovery and action that embodies the democratic ideal proposed by Dewey (1933) and Boyer (1990, 1996). Working with the community allows students an opportunity to be immersed in an authentic learning environment where they can assimilate and apply cooperative and creative problem-solving as part of their own educational experience while empowering the community. Engaged teaching and learning represent a shift to a focus on purpose and process and reframe our understanding and practice in several dimensions.

This shift is also a move from a deficit or pathological model of need to an asset-based model incorporating not only the rich resources of the academy described by Boyer (1997) but also the community's assets to achieve a common good. Democratic engagement further embodies a shift from a unilateral application of knowledge to the multidirectional flow of cocreated knowledge. The distinction between knowledge producers and knowledge consumers is minimized, authority in the cocreation of knowledge is shared, and the academy moves from the proverbial ivory tower to an ecosystem of collaborative, public problem-solving. These changes result in not merely the generation and dissemination of knowledge in a scholarly field but also actual community transformation.

Promotion and Tenure

Of all the challenges facing the advancement of community engagement in higher education, the issue of recognizing and rewarding faculty members in promotion and tenure review continues to be a major barrier. Cantor and Englot (2014) point out that promotion and tenure review still use traditional and narrow concepts of "what counts" as scholarship (p. 6). The engagement work of the increasingly diverse professoriate with ties to the community should be considered. O'Meara (2011) pointed out that significant effort has been made over the past 20 years to support faculty members in the promotion and tenure review process through articles, resources, and even the conferences of professional associations. Despite the growth of the field and practice, faculty culture and governance are still confused and often reluctant to view engagement work as scholarly.

O'Meara (2010) conducted extensive research on this issue and reported three observations related to faculty rewards and recognition in the context of community engagement. First, the tenure system and process have generally remained static over time with little or no revisions other than implementing post-tenure review, starting and stopping the tenure clock, and expanding the definition of *scholarship* using Boyer's (1990) model. Second, the results for engaged faculty members seeking promotion and tenure are mixed. On average nearly 75% of faculty members achieve promotion and tenure. However, women and faculty members of color tend to experience more difficulty in the process than their White male colleagues.

HERI conducted a study with more than 16,000 respondents from more than 260 institutions. Results revealed that regardless of demographic factors, such as type of institution, rank, gender, and race, nearly half of the respondents reported integrating community engagement into their teaching and scholarship (Eagan et al., 2014). These data suggest a desire and an expectation on the part of the new professoriate, with a slight trend of more female instructors and faculty members of color participating in some form of community engagement. Further, engaged scholarship has increased since the study was first conducted in 2004–2005 (see Table 9.1). Thus, it is incumbent on administrators, search committees, community service center staff, and other policymakers to consider how and to what extent nearly half of faculty members' scholarly needs and expectations are being supported through faculty programming and professional development as well as how their scholarship is recognized and rewarded in the promotion and tenure process.

These data also reveal two interesting demographic trends. First, many respondents are from diverse backgrounds, and second, an equally large percentage is not on the tenure track. The former demographic factor is significant and represents Saltmarsh and Hartley's (2016) collaborative, or public, scholarship. The second trend suggests that many non-tenure-track faculty members are doing this type of teaching. These findings are consistent with current trends noted by Plater (2011), who cited the work of leading scholars and reports documenting that more and more faculty members are part-time contingent. Their adjunct status may in fact be professionally liberating as these instructors are not as preoccupied or concerned with whether their engaged work will have a negative impact on their future promotion or tenure. This growing demographic may prove to be a viable pool of candidates for faculty members to identify and groom for engaged teaching and learning. Institutions should revisit existing promotion and tenure policies and procedures as well as determine mechanisms to support these scholars, or they will seek other institutions that will provide that infrastructure of support.

O'Meara's third observation—somewhat related to the first—is that research suggests nontenured faculty members view the review process as ambiguous and consequently difficult to navigate. For example, many promotion and tenure systems tend to favor individual, siloed scholarship over the interdisciplinary work that much of engaged scholarship incorporates. Another prominent assumption in existing standards is that engaged scholarship is not as rigorous or "scholarly" as other traditional forms of scholarship. O'Meara (2010) concluded that not all faculty members experience difficulty in the promotion and tenure process. This is because these individuals have essentially "figured out for themselves how their public work will fit into the unique career they are building at a particular institution and in their field" (p. 277).

Litigation and Logistics

Like many engaged faculty members, directors of campus centers for community engagement felt called to facilitate quality learning opportunities in the community that make a difference in the lives of students and the

TABLE 9.1

Faculty Responses to the Survey Question: During the Past Two Years, Have You Collaborated With the Local Community in Teaching/Research?

		2004–2005 (%)	*2013–2014[a] (%)*	*Percentage change in response*
All baccalaureate institutions		42.4	48.8	6.4
Institutional control	Public	44.0	50.4	6.4
	Private	38.3	46.4	8.1
Academic rank	Professor	40.4	45.0	4.6
	Associate professor	46.9	52.5	5.6
	Assistant professor	45.5	51.1	5.6
	Lecturer	35.9	45.0	9.1
	Instructor	35.6	46.0	10.4
Tenure status	Tenured	43.2	48.2	5.0
	On tenure track but not tenured	46.8	51.1	4.3
	Not on tenure track but institution has tenure system	38.6	47.9	9.3
	Institution has no tenure system	34.4	48.1	13.7
Sex	Male	41.1	46.3	5.2
	Female	44.1	52.4	8.3
Race/ethnicity	American Indian	53.4	86.8	33.4
	Asian	40.9	46.8	5.9
	Black	40.4	42.4	2.0
	Hispanic	38.1	55.2	17.1
	White	42.3	48.4	6.1
	Other	47.4	53.4	6.0
	Two or more races/ethnicities	44.7	57.1	12.4

Note. From *Undergraduate Teaching Faculty: The 2013–2014 Faculty Survey*, by M. K. Eagan, E. B. Stolzenberg, J. Berdan Lozano, M. C. Aragon, M. R. Suchard, & S. Hurtado, 2014, Los Angeles, CA: Higher Education Research Institute, University of California, Los Angeles. Reprinted with permission.

[a]Based on responses from 16,112 full-time undergraduate teaching faculty members at 269 four-year colleges and universities.

constituencies community partners serve. However, dedicated campus center administrators quickly learn that part of their job is shielding faculty members and students from the mundane aspects and mechanics of this work while at the same time ensuring that adequate policies and procedures are in place to make community engagement a seamless process.

Early on in their historical review of the field, Stanton and colleagues (1999) noted "the dilemma of institutionalization," citing that some pioneer practitioners worried that formal structures of service-learning would "corrupt" the pedagogy, "robbing service-learning of its power to develop students and communities" (pp. 144–145). The early phase of engagement was dominated by a strong sense of activism, purpose, and even spirituality; there was virtually no discussion or consideration of legal issues. In Jacoby's (1996) landmark book *Service-Learning in Higher Education*, a single sentence on the topic is offered in one chapter (Scheuermann, 1996) and only two full pages on legal issues appear in another chapter (Rue, 1996). Similarly, in Zlotkowski's (1998) formative edition *Successful Service-Learning Programs: New Models of Excellence in Higher Education*, a single bullet point devoted to risk management was included in a list (Henry, 1998), while the chapter by Fisher (1998) noted that student leaders received training on not just the "center's value system, but liability constraints" as well (p. 214).

Even today, many instructors lament the increasing levels of logistical coordination and paperwork and the need for risk management in a world that is not only increasingly dangerous but also litigious. The world has always been a dangerous place, but over time it has become scarier and more litigious in many respects. Many community partners now require waivers of liability. Diligence in risk management is in fact an ethical and moral responsibility and ensures the positive impact of the community engagement experience, not solely for the student and instructor but also for the community partner and the constituencies it serves. By managing risk in our community engagement projects, we contribute to and practice an ethos of "do no harm."

While overseeing mundane tasks such as risk management may seem cold and clinical, the effort affords protection to students, faculty members, and community partners alike. Similarly, while MOUs between institutions of higher education and community agencies appear to add a layer of bureaucracy, the language of these documents clearly articulates roles and responsibilities in order to ensure accountability and mutual benefit to all parties. Course agreement forms outlining specific roles, tasks, and time lines for students and instructors put everyone on the same page. In fact, these legal security blankets allow both students and instructors opportunities to focus on the deeper aspects and dimensions of the experience in the classroom or at the community site.

Projections

Looking ahead, many trends, issues, and questions need to be explored and answered. The field will continue to build on the foundational work that has taken place over the last 30 years.

Engaged Scholarship

Derek Barker (2011) of the Kettering Foundation offered a number of observations and suggestions for the field of community engagement as it continues to evolve. Current efforts to refine and clarify the public purpose of higher education and engaged epistemology must continue. These efforts, in turn, can address the apparent disconnect between theory and practice, rhetoric and reality. Engaged scholars must continue constructing a common lexicon for their work. This growth can and will be facilitated by integrating and connecting engaged epistemology with other related topics and issues, such as multicultural diversity, environmentalism, globalization, and economic disparity at the global and local levels. This integration and epistemological shift will move community engagement beyond traditional service to political action.

Furthermore, engaged scholarship has the potential to double dip in addressing the critical issues of diversity and equity and expanding to involve STEM programs of study and research. Harkavy, Cantor, and Burnett (2015) published a white paper presenting a theoretically based rationale for incorporating community engagement into STEM programs as a way of addressing both critical social needs and issues of diversity and equity in the sciences. Their recommendations build on previous initiatives and efforts by the National Science Foundation. The foundation convened two global conversations on this topic, one at the University of Pennsylvania and another at Durban University in South Africa. These strategic activities help to generate an aura of scholarly credibility that deflects preconceived notions that engagement is charity.

Programs, Purpose, and Place

Programs are a double-edged conundrum. Numerous pages of this book describe programs for faculty members, staff, and communities. These constituencies and their institutions understand what programs are, as well as the logistical utility of program delivery. We know programs deliver resources that meet the educational and public purpose of community engagement. At the same time, as conveyed throughout this book, programs can be problematic when they perpetuate engagement at the margins of the institutional mission. In addition, programs are often delivered to a specific place without a full appreciation of that location's sense of place and purpose. Many programs continue to merely place students in a setting without a full, deep, and rich sense of place that embodies the neighborhood. While some institutions are, indeed, attempting to promote and practice community engagement, much of that effort continues to be halfhearted tokenism that has little meaningful impact on the community (Fitzgerald, Bruns, Sonka, Furco, & Swanson, 2012). To realize the full potential of community engagement, more institutions will need to seriously explore ways to incorporate anchor-based approaches and evolve into new hybrid forms that reflect the true public purpose of higher education, generate real impact on the community, and cocreate new knowledge.

Centers

We have a brushstroke portrait of campus centers for community engagement, but there is much more to learn. For example, we know a primary role of centers is to provide faculty development, but we know little about the processes, formats, content, or outcomes. Similarly, we have a cursory profile of center directors, but we do not know the professional pathway they took to assume that role. These questions point to a need not only for continued research but also to continue the professionalization of the field to prepare competent professional administrators. CAS (2015) provided a useful blueprint for designing empirically based centers.

Centers will continue to evolve with new roles, responsibilities, and expectations. Consequently, we can project that they may ultimately look very different from how they did in their early days and how they do today.

Professionalization

Similarly, we can project that center directors will emerge from doctoral programs explicitly dedicated to preparing the new engaged professoriate and a new engaged administrator who ably bridges the academy, student life, academics, and the community. Research will continue to provide insight into best practices and specific skill sets that professional directors will need to incorporate into their work. Learned professional associations are likely to develop standards that can and will be used for accreditation purposes.

Research

Although strides have been made in research on the impact of engaged teaching on students' development, many questions remain. To what extent does community engagement maintain student retention rates? How do these experiences contribute to career choices and outcomes? Did early community engagement experiences motivate the new professoriate to pursue engaged teaching and scholarship? We have limited information on the longitudinal effects of community engagement on students.

Furthermore, although research has increased and improved overall, much more theoretically driven research is needed in a variety of related topical areas, including impact on faculty members, institutions, and the community (Clayton, Bringle, & Hatcher, 2012a, 2012b).

It is reasonable to project that as research efforts continue to grow, professional personnel in campus centers for engagement and doctoral students may be used to assist with that research.

Conclusion

Engaging higher education has evolved from a movement to a very real presence on campus. Much of the engagement work, events, and activities over the past 30 years represents a return to the original public purpose of higher education. More and more institutions have created and installed infrastructure that provides a platform from which to launch engaged teaching and scholarship among students, faculty members, and community partners. In addition, a new field of community engagement has emerged, along with a growing body of literature and best practices. We are on the cusp of the emergence of an exciting new professoriate dedicated to working with students who pursue personal, professional, and civic purpose to enrich their lives. Overall, higher education indeed appears to be on a trajectory to return to its public purpose. Equally important, if not more so, community engagement has enhanced, if not downright improved, the pedagogical quality of the educational experience. While many institutions may be reticent to pursue Boyer's public purpose owing to complex economic and social pressures, they would be well served by promoting and practicing a pedagogy of engagement that prepares students for meaningful personal, professional, and civic lives.

APPENDICES

Following is an illustration of a systems framework for implementing the institutionalization of community engagement.

Resources	Examples	Need	Have	Seek	Funds	N/A
Human	Midlevel administrative oversight (e.g., chief academic officer, engagement officer, vice provost for engagement)					
	Development officers and communications office representatives					
	Center, institute, and program directors					
	Program staff					
	Executive directors of community organizations					
	Advisory board or steering committee					
	Faculty members					
	Students and student leaders					
	Community members					
	Other?					

Resources	Examples	Need	Have	Seek	Funds	N/A
Information/ policies	Institutional mission statement					
	Asset maps and assessment rubric results					
	Policy and procedure manuals (e.g., course designation process)					
	Promotion and tenure criteria					
	Professional literature					
	Professional development					
	Operational definitions					
	Campus Compact (state or national)					
	Other?					
Physical	Center(s) office space on campus					
	Residence halls					
	Classrooms					
	Community partner sites					
	Community centers, schools, and parks					
	Shared annex space(s) in the community					
	Other?					
Fiscal	Institutional funds and operational budget					
	Grants					
	Development office, gifts, and in-kind resources					
	Tuition tiers					
	Special fees					
	Other?					

Resources	Examples	Need	Have	Seek	Funds	N/A
Operational	Organizational alignment flowchart and reporting lines					
	Asset maps and assessment rubrics					
	Strategic plan					
	Risk management assessment and policy					
	Memos of understanding					
	Data management systems and IT services (e.g., phones, computers)					
	Other?					
Offices/units	President's office					
	Academic affairs					
	Student affairs					
	Residential life					
	Campus communications					
	Advancement and development					
	Mission and ministry					
	Athletics					
	Other?					

Massachusetts Civic Learning and Engagement Assessment Framework (Student Learning Framework)

Goal: To Prepare Individuals for the Role of Citizenship

The goal of the Preparing Citizens Outcome of the Vision Project is to prepare individuals for effective democratic participation, which in turn promotes growth of healthy communities, global economic vitality, social and political well-being, and democratic human interactions.

The student learning framework includes four key objectives and corresponding student learning goals that campuses should pursue to achieve the overall goal of preparing students for the role of citizenship. The framework draws directly from *A Crucible Moment's* "Framework for Twenty-First-Century Civic Learning and Democratic Engagement" and the Civic Engagement VALUE Rubric of AAC&U's LEAP (Liberal Education and America's Promise) initiative (LEAP'S Civic Engagement VALUE Rubric). Each objective corresponds with several learning outcomes listed in this appendix. This document may be used to begin the conversation of how to assess students' civic learning and engagement.

Objective 1: Civic and Democratic Knowledge: Foster the knowledge students need to assume the roles and responsibilities of citizenship through formal curricula, cocurricular activity, and community engagement	Objective 2: Civic and Democratic Skills: Foster the development of the personal and life skills students need to become responsible citizens and active participants in democratic life	Objective 3: Civic and Democratic Values: Engage students in opportunities to clarify and further develop personal civic and democratic values	Objective 4: Civic and Democratic Action: Involve students with experiences in civic action to foster engagement in the practice of democracy

Outcomes	*Outcomes*	*Outcomes*	*Outcomes*
Familiarity with key democratic texts and universal democratic principles, and with selected debates—in the United States and other societies—concerning their applications	Ability to seek, engage, and be informed by multiple perspectives	Respect for freedom and human dignity	Integration of knowledge, skills, and examined values to challenge injustice and address its root causes
Historical and sociological understanding of several democratic and social movements for change, both in the United States and abroad	Ability to use scientific reasoning to understand social issues	Capacity for empathy, open-mindedness, tolerance, and appreciation for diversity	Capacity and commitment to work collectively with diverse others to address common problems
Understanding one's sources of identity and their influence on civic values, assumptions, and responsibilities to a wider public	Ability to use critical inquiry and quantitative reasoning to identify a problem, research solutions, analyze results, evaluate choices, and make decisions	Commitment to justice and equality	Practice of working in a pluralistic society and world to improve the quality of people's lives and the sustainability of the planet
Knowledge of the diverse cultures, histories, values, and contestations that have shaped the United States and other world societies	Ability to read, write, speak, listen, and use communication media effectively	Commitment to ethical integrity	Ability to analyze and navigate systems (political, social, economic) in order to plan and engage in public action
Knowledge of multiple religious traditions and alternative views about the relation between religion and government	Ability to effectively work in groups to deliberate and build bridges across differences in order to reach collaborative decisions	Capacity for compromise, civility, and mutual respect	Moral and political courage to take risks to achieve a greater public good

Outcomes	Outcomes	Outcomes	Outcomes
Knowledge of the political systems that frame constitutional democracies and of political levers for influencing change	Ability to reflect on experience to gain insight and guide action	Responsibility to a larger good	
Knowledge of rights and responsibilities of the individual citizen within wider community	Ability to assume leadership and followership roles that best support democracy and civic life		

Note. From *Preparing Citizens: Report on Civic Learning and Engagement* (pp. 25–26), by Study Group on Civic Learning and Engagement, 2014, Boston, MA: Massachusetts Department of Higher Education, www.mass.edu/preparingcitizensreport.

Action Plan Template

GOAL

Activity	People/units involved	Operational tools needed	Funds needed	Location of activity	Begin date	End date	Product/ outcome

Institutional Community Engagement Readiness Inventory

Part 1: Institutional Architecture and Policy Context
Our community engagement center has

An academic affairs reporting line	Yes	Hope to	No
A student affairs reporting line	Yes	Hope to	No
A joint academic/student affairs reporting line	Yes	Hope to	No
Budgeted institutional funds	Yes	Hope to	No
Community engagement in institutional strategic plans	Yes	Hope to	No
Community engagement in accreditation criteria	Yes	Hope to	No
A course designation process by peer review/committee	Yes	Hope to	No
Extramural grants used for funding of center staff	Yes	Hope to	No
Extramural grants used for funding center programs	Yes	Hope to	No
Official/operational definitions of *service-learning, CBR,* and *community engagement*	Yes	Hope to	No
Community engagement as an institutional priority that is intentionally linked to the institutional priority of diversity and inclusion	Yes	Hope to	No
Community engagement as an institutional priority that is intentionally linked to the institutional priority of student success	Yes	Hope to	No
Community engagement as a formally recognized scholarly work in the faculty reward process	Yes	Hope to	No

Part 2: Center Infrastructure
Our community engagement center has

Adequate office space to meet program needs	Yes	Hope to	No
An advisory/governing board	Yes	Hope to	No
An advisory/governing board with community representation	Yes	Hope to	No
An advisory/governing board with student representation	Yes	Hope to	No
An annual report	Yes	Hope to	No

A vision/mission statement	Yes	Hope to	No
An alumni association	Yes	Hope to	No
Clear, physical internal/external community entry points to the center	Yes	Hope to	No
Database tracking system/software	Yes	Hope to	No
A development officer on staff	Yes	Hope to	No
A staff member who functions as a liaison to the institution development officer	Yes	Hope to	No
Career development professionals on staff	Yes	Hope to	No
A staff member who functions as a liaison to the career development center	Yes	Hope to	No
A faculty advisory committee/board	Yes	Hope to	No
A faculty liaison to academic units	Yes	Hope to	No
A full-time administrator	Yes	Hope to	No
A full-time administrator with faculty status	Yes	Hope to	No
A full-time administrative assistant	Yes	Hope to	No
Newsletter/web updates	Yes	Hope to	No
Institutional funds for part of the operational budget	Yes	Hope to	No
Institutional funds for the entire operational budget	Yes	Hope to	No
Institutional funds to support programming staff	Yes	Hope to	No
An operational budget that provides support for student staff/leaders	Yes	Hope to	No
Work study or service scholarships as financial support for student staff/leaders	Yes	Hope to	No
Student leaders to oversee programs	Yes	Hope to	No
Student leadership and decision making	Yes	Hope to	No

Part 3: Center Operations

Our community engagement center

Has mechanisms/procedures to assess learning outcomes	Yes	Hope to	No
Has mechanisms/procedures to assess programs	Yes	Hope to	No
Has mechanisms/procedures to assess program impact on community partners	Yes	Hope to	No
Shares assessment data with community partners	Yes	Hope to	No
Announces/provides resource materials	Yes	Hope to	No
Conducts research on faculty involvement in service-learning and engaged pedagogy	Yes	Hope to	No

Conducts surveys on student involvement in service-learning and civic engagement	Yes	Hope to	No
Has student course assistants	Yes	Hope to	No
Provides course development grants	Yes	Hope to	No
Has a course syllabi file/database	Yes	Hope to	No
Has a database on faculty involvement in service-learning and engaged pedagogy	Yes	Hope to	No
Evaluates community partner satisfaction	Yes	Hope to	No
Evaluates student satisfaction with service-learning	Yes	Hope to	No
Evaluates student satisfaction with cocurricular programs	Yes	Hope to	No
Facilitates faculty research on service-learning and civic engagement	Yes	Hope to	No
Has fund-raising mechanisms (e.g., grants and donors)	Yes	Hope to	No
Involves students in creating service-learning courses	Yes	Hope to	No
Makes presentations at student orientations	Yes	Hope to	No
Publicizes faculty accomplishments	Yes	Hope to	No
Has risk management policies and procedures	Yes	Hope to	No
Formally recognizes student accomplishments	Yes	Hope to	No
Formally recognizes faculty accomplishments through awards and celebrations	Yes	Hope to	No
Has a student transportation policy	Yes	Hope to	No
Is positioned strategically to catalyze wide organizational change across campus	Yes	Hope to	No

Part 4: Center Programming for Faculty

Our community engagement center has

One-on-one consultation/support to faculty	Yes	Hope to	No
Faculty fellowships/grants	Yes	Hope to	No
A faculty advisory committee	Yes	Hope to	No
A certificate or designation as for engaged faculty members upon completion of professional development programs	Yes	Hope to	No
Faculty development funds (e.g., for attending conferences)	Yes	Hope to	No
A faculty mentor program	Yes	Hope to	No
A faculty recognition award for engaged teaching or scholarship	Yes	Hope to	No
Release time for course development	Yes	Hope to	No
Faculty development off campus at conferences/workshops	Yes	Hope to	No

A yearlong faculty learning community on campus that meets on a regular basis	Yes	Hope to	No
A book club/discussion group	Yes	Hope to	No
Weekend faculty retreats for faculty development	Yes	Hope to	No
Writing retreats for community engaged scholarship	Yes	Hope to	No
Workshops on campus	Yes	Hope to	No
Events featuring outside experts/speakers	Yes	Hope to	No
A summer institute on engagement	Yes	Hope to	No
Opportunities for faculty to explore ways to expand student civic learning and civic action beyond service, tied to a broad institutional commitment to the civic purposes of higher education	Yes	Hope to	No

Part 5: Center Programming for Students

Our community engagement center has

Opportunities for independent student community engagement research	Yes	Hope to	No
Publications or campus presentations of independent student research related to community engagement	Yes	Hope to	No
Opportunities for student leadership in campus-based community engagement programs, community service and civic engagement requirements	Yes	Hope to	No
Opportunities for student internships related to community/civic engagement	Yes	Hope to	No
Opportunities for student study abroad related to community/civic engagement internships	Yes	Hope to	No
Opportunities to meet with employers who demonstrate corporate social responsibility	Yes	Hope to	No
Cocurricular programs and opportunities	Yes	Hope to	No
Majors with service-learning courses	Yes	Hope to	No
A major in service-learning	Yes	Hope to	No
A minor/certificate with service-learning courses	Yes	Hope to	No
A minor/certificate in service-learning	Yes	Hope to	No
Living-learning communities, residence halls, or floors for service or civic engagement	Yes	Hope to	No
A domestic alternative break	Yes	Hope to	No
An international alternative break	Yes	Hope to	No
A break experience tied to a course	Yes	Hope to	No

An alternative weekend immersion experience	Yes	Hope to	No
Digital storytelling/social media as a tool for community engagement	Yes	Hope to	No
Art (music, drama, photography) as a tool for community engagement	Yes	Hope to	No
Programming to assist students in identifying transferable employment skills gained from community engagement activities	Yes	Hope to	No
Service-learning/CBR student scholars	Yes	Hope to	No
Paid student assistants for service-learning courses	Yes	Hope to	No
A minimum of 10-hour training for student assistants to service-learning courses	Yes	Hope to	No
A student recognition award	Yes	Hope to	No
Student leader retreats and/or training sessions before the school year	Yes	Hope to	No
Student input on leadership training	Yes	Hope to	No
Student-led facilitation of training sessions	Yes	Hope to	No
Student advisory committee to the center	Yes	Hope to	No
Opportunities to translate service activity into civic learning and civic action	Yes	Hope to	No

Part 6: Center Programming for Community Partners
Our community engagement center has

Presentations/publications created with partners	Yes	Hope to	No
An award for outstanding community partners	Yes	Hope to	No
Written collaborative grant proposals with partners	Yes	Hope to	No
Partners educated on engaged pedagogy	Yes	Hope to	No
Site visits/meetings with partners	Yes	Hope to	No
Community incentives and rewards	Yes	Hope to	No
Community agency orientation provided in service-learning classes	Yes	Hope to	No
Agreement forms or action plan for each service-learning course	Yes	Hope to	No
Orientation/training sessions on how to work with faculty or students	Yes	Hope to	No
Collaborative assessment of partnership activity	Yes	Hope to	No
MOUs/formal agreements with partners	Yes	Hope to	No

Community agencies connected with the career development programs to create greater student awareness of employment opportunities	Yes	Hope to	No
Professional development for community partners	Yes	Hope to	No
Professional development for community engagement	Yes	Hope to	No

Part 7: Center Director

Has the director attended any professional development institutes devoted to service-learning or community engagement?	Yes	Hope to	No
Has the director published or presented on service-learning or community engagement?	Yes	Hope to	No

Part 8: Professional Affiliations

Mark any of the following organizations your institution is a member of or participates in:

_____ American Democracy Project

_____ America Reads/Counts

_____ Anchor Institutions Task Force

_____ Association of American Colleges and Universities (AAC&U)

_____ Bonner Leaders

_____ Bringing Theory to Practice

_____ Campus Compact

_____ Coalition of Urban and Metropolitan Universities

_____ Coalition of Urban Serving Universities

_____ Community-Campus Partnerships for Health (CCPH)

_____ Community College National Center for Community Engagement

_____ Engagement Scholarship Consortium

_____ Imagining America

_____ International Association of Research on Service-Learning and Community   Engagement (IARSLCE)

_____ Jumpstart

_____ The Democracy Commitment

_____ The Research University Civic Engagement Network (TRUCEN)

Which, if any, would you like to learn more about?

_____

Which, if any, would you like to be or should be a part of ?

_____

Mark any of the following activities or resources that the community engagement center makes use of:

_____ American Democracy Project

_____ America Reads/Counts

_____ Anchor Institutions Task Force

_____ Association of American Colleges and Universities (AAC&U)

_____ Bonner Leaders

_____ Bringing Theory to Practice

_____ Campus Compact

_____ Coalition of Urban and Metropolitan Universities

_____ Coalition of Urban Serving Universities

_____ Community-Campus Partnerships for Health (CCPH)

_____ Community College National Center for Community Engagement

_____ Engagement Scholarship Consortium

_____ Imagining America

_____ International Association of Research on Service-Learning and Community Engagement (IARSLCE)

_____ Jumpstart

_____ The Democracy Commitment

_____ The Research University Civic Engagement Network (TRUCEN)

Part 9: Curricular Impact

A. Total number of *all* undergraduate courses taught per academic year = _____

B. Total number of service-learning/engaged courses taught per academic year = _____

Percentage of service-learning/engaged courses taught per year (i.e., B divided by A × 100) = _____

C. Total number of *all* full-time faculty = _____

D. Total number of full-time faculty teaching service-learning/engaged courses = _____

Percentage of faculty teaching service-learning/engaged courses per year (i.e., D divided by C × 100) = _____

E. Total number of academic departments = _____

F. Number of academic departments with one service-learning/engaged
course = _____

Percentage of departments teaching service-learning/engaged courses per year
(i.e., F divided by E × 100) = _____

Note. From *Institutional Community Engagement Readiness Inventory,* by M. Welch and J. Saltmarsh,
2015, Boston, MA: New England Resource Center for Higher Education.

Top 10 Things for Faculty Members to Discuss With Community Partners

1. Define and describe the engaged activity.

    Be sure to explain if you are doing service-learning or community-based research. Differentiate this from volunteering or other forms of professional preparation practicums.

2. Share your syllabus and instructional objectives.

    Clearly define and describe the instructional goals this activity will meet.

3. Discuss possible projects.

    After you have discussed your syllabus and instructional objectives, explore possible projects by asking the partner what goals or projects (avoid using deficit-based language such as "needs" or "issues") on the back burner they've always wanted to pursue. See if the goals and aspirations are a match.

4. Describe your student skill level.

    Indicate if these are undergraduate or graduate students. Clarify if they are majors or if they are taking this class as an elective. Describe if they are at an introductory level or an advanced capstone level of learning.

5. Explain the time line.

    Do the math: Most engaged courses are 12- to 15-week semesters. There will be ramp-up time as well as winding-down time toward final exams. Discuss start and end dates. Explore the number of hours per week students will be working at the site. Indicate when any semester/holiday breaks occur.

6. Consider capacity.

    Explore how many students the partner can supervise and support.

7. Clarify roles.

    What are the roles and responsibilities of the instructor, partner, site supervisor, and students?

8. Outline orientation process.

    Establish when, where, and how students will be oriented to the community partner site, mission, history, population served, and project. Include policies and protocols students must know and follow.

9. Identify and determine communication channels.

    Clarify who will be the primary contact person and provide contact information and best times and mechanisms for communication. Determine if a student assistant will be serving as a liaison, and if so, provide his or her name and contact information.

10. Create and sign a course agreement form.

    The course agreement form articulates who does what, where, and when. It includes the instructional objectives and the partner objectives, describing the deliverables for the project.

Template OPERA Worksheet for Community Partners

Objectives
On this worksheet or on poster paper or whiteboard brainstorm and list three to four goals you and your organization have. Brainstorm list:
Prioritize each goal and then select and describe one goal. Articulate the goal as a tangible, measurable, observable outcome or product. Selected goal:

Partnership
Imagine what type of partnership might help you meet your goal. Review the possible partnership formats and mark the top two: _____One-day service event with student volunteers _____12–15 weeks of a small group of students from a course related to the goal _____Yearlong assistance from a small group of student volunteers _____A yearlong student intern serving as a paraprofessional _____A yearlong graduate student with background/experience in research _____A summer project with a small group/team of students working two to three months _____A summer project for one student intern working two to three months

Engagement
Describe what the student(s) or team would be doing to help you reach the goal.

Start date:
End date:
How many hours a week?
How many days a week?
How many students can we handle?
Who would supervise/coordinate student(s)?
What information, policies, and procedures need to be included in an orientation?
Would a student assistant to help coordinate the project be helpful? Y   N
Is a background check necessary? Y   N
Is a tuberculosis test or other health screening necessary? Y   N

Reflection

What kinds of issues or topics do you think the student(s) should reflect on and consider? Why?
Where, when, and how might that reflection take place? With whom?
Share this with the campus center or course instructor at the end of the activity.

Assessment
1 = Poor   2 = Marginal   3 = Good   4 = Excellent

Formative evaluation:

Punctual and professional students	1	2	3	4
Helpful and responsive instructor	1	2	3	4
Project plan execution	1	2	3	4
Time allocated to project	1	2	3	4
Number of students allocated to project	1	2	3	4
Communication with students	1	2	3	4
Communication with instructor or staff person	1	2	3	4

Comments:

Summative evaluation:

Goal attainment	1	2	3	4
We will adopt/use the project deliverable.	Y	N	NA	
We will adopt/use project deliverable with some modification.	Y	N	NA	

We would participate as a partner again in the future because
of this experience.   Y   N
Comments:

Top 10 Things for Community Partners to Discuss With Faculty or Staff Members

1. Clarify the engaged activity.

   Is this a course? Practicum or student teaching? Capstone course? Are these students required to do this work, or are they volunteers?

2. Share your organization's mission, history, and objectives.

   Provide an overview of your organization's mission, history, and constituencies served.

3. Discuss possible projects.

   Share your OPERA planning worksheet if you've completed one. If not, ask the campus center for one to complete with your staff before you go any further. Discuss what you have on the back burner that you've always wanted to pursue. See if your goals and aspirations are a match.

4. Determine student skill level.

   Ask if these are undergraduate or graduate students. Clarify if they are majors or if they are taking this class as an elective. Determine if they are at an introductory level or an advanced capstone level of learning.

5. Explain the time line.

   Discuss the duration of the project. There will be ramp-up time as well as winding-down time toward final exams. Discuss start and end dates. Explore number of hours per week students will be working at the site. Ask when any semester/holiday breaks occur.

6. Consider capacity.

   Explore how many students your agency can supervise and support.

7. Clarify roles.

   What are the roles and responsibilities of the instructor, partner, site supervisor, and students?

8.   Outline orientation process.

Establish when, where, and how students will be oriented to the community partner site, mission, history, population served, and project. Include policies and protocols students must know and follow.

9.   Identify and determine communication channels.

Clarify who will be the primary contact person and provide contact information and best times and mechanisms for communication. Determine if a student assistant will be serving as a liaison, and if so, provide his or her name and contact information.

10.   Create and sign a course agreement form.

The course agreement form articulates who does what, where, and when. It includes the instructional objectives and the partner objectives, describing the deliverables for the project.

REFERENCES

American Commonwealth Project.(2011). *The American commonwealth project: Colleges and universities as agents and architects of democracy.* Retrieved from http://cmapspublic3.ihmc.us/rid=1JKM5R4SP-M0Z56X-R1K/American%20 Commonwealth%20Project%20Description%20Final.pdf

Adler, R. P., & Goggin, J. (2005). What do we mean by "civic engagement"? *Journal of Transformative Education, 3*, 236–253.

American Association of State Colleges and Universities. (2002). *Stepping forward as stewards of place: A guide for leading public engagement at state colleges and universities.* Washington DC: Author.

American Psychological Association. (2016). Doctoral internships. Retrieved from http://www.apa.org/education/grad/internship.aspx

Arbnor, I., & Bjerke, B. (2009). *Methodology for creating business knowledge.* Thousand Oaks, CA: Sage Publishing.

Association of American Colleges and Universities. (2010). *Civic engagement value rubric.* Washington DC: Author.

Astin, A. W. (1998). Liberal education and democracy: The case for pragmatism. In R. Orrill (Ed.), *Education and democracy* (pp. 111–130). New York: College Board.

Axelroth Hodges, R., & Dubb, S. (2010, December). *The road half traveled: University engagement at a crossroads.* College Park, MD: Democracy Collaborative at the University of Maryland.

Axtell, S. (2012). *Creating a community-engaged scholarship (CES) faculty development program: Phase One: Program and skill mapping.* Retrieved from http://www .engagement.umn.edu/sites/default/files/CES_Faculty_Development_Report_ FINAL_000.pdf

Baer, D. M., & Schwartz, I. S. (1991). If reliance on epidemiology were to become epidemic, we would need to assess its social validity. *Journal of Applied Behavioral Analysis, 24*, 231–234.

Bandy, J. (2012, October). *Empowering community by assessing and developing service learning partnerships.* Paper presented at the annual Professional and Organizational Development Network Conference, Seattle, WA.

Barajas, H., Smalkoski, K., Kaplan, M., & Yang, Y. (2012). Hmong families and education: Partnership as essential link to discovery. *Cura Reporter, 42*(3), 3–9.

Barajas, H., Smalkoski, K., Yang, Y., Yang, L., & Yang, P. (2010, June). *Engaging research design: Reflections and ethics in working with newly arrived immigrants.* Paper presented at the Ethnics and Politics of Research with Immigrant Populations Conference, Minneapolis, MN.

Barefoot, B. O. (2008). Institutional structures and strategies for embedding civic engagement in the first college year. In M. J. LaBare (Ed.), *First-year civic engagement: Sound foundations for college, citizenship, and democracy* (pp. 23–25). New York, NY: New York Times Knowledge Network.

Barefoot, B. O., Fidler, D. S., Gardner, J. N., Moore, P. S., & Roberts, M. R. (1999). A natural linkage: The first year seminar and the learning community. In J. H. Levine (Ed.), *Learning communities: New structures, new partnerships for learning* (Monograph No. 26). Columbia, SC: University of South Carolina, National Resource Center for the First Year Experience & Students in Transition.

Barker, D. (2011). Eleven sticking points: Priorities for the future of civic engagement in higher education. In J. Saltmarsh & M. Hartley (Eds.), *To serve a larger purpose: Engagement for democracy and the transformation of higher education* (pp. 7–8). Philadelphia, PA: Temple University Press.

Battistoni, R. M. (1998). Making a major commitment: Public and community service at Providence College. In E. Zlotkowski (Ed.), *Successful service-learning programs: New models of excellence in higher education* (pp. 169–188). Bolton, MA: Anker Press.

Battistoni, R. M. (2002). *Civic engagement across the curriculum: A resource book for service-learning faculty in all disciplines.* Providence, RI: Campus Compact.

Beal, V. (2015). Program. In *Webopedia.* Retrieved from http://www.webopedia.com/TERM/P/program.html

Beere, C. (2009). Understanding and enhancing the opportunities of community-campus partnerships. In L. R. Sandmann, C. H. Thornton, & A. J. Jaeger (Eds.), *Institutionalizing community engagement in higher education: The first wave of Carnegie classified institutions* (pp. 55–64). San Francisco, CA: Jossey-Bass.

Beere, C. A., Votruba, J. C., & Wells, G. W. (2011). *Becoming an engaged campus: A practical guide for institutionalizing public engagement.* San Francisco, CA: Jossey-Bass.

Benson, L., Harkavy, I., & Hartley, M. (2005). Integrating a commitment to the public good into the institutional fabric. In J. Burkhardt, T. Chambers, & A. Kezar (Eds.), *Higher education for the public good: Emerging voices from a national movement* (pp. 185–216). San Francisco, CA: Jossey-Bass.

Benson, L., Harkavy, I., & Puckett, J. (2011). Democratic transformation through university-assisted community schools. In J. Saltmarsh & M. Hartley (Eds.), *To serve a larger purpose: Engagement for democracy and the transformation of higher education* (pp. 49–81). Philadelphia, PA: Temple University Press.

Binbasaran Tuysuzoglu, B., & Greene, J. A. (2015). An investigation of the role of contingent metacognitive behavior in self-regulated learning. *Metacognition and Learning, 10*(1), 77–98.

Blanchard, L., Hanssmann, C., Strauss, R., Belliard, J. C., Krichbaum, K., Waters, E., & Seifer, S. (2009). Models for faculty development: What it takes to be a community-engaged scholar. *Metropolitan Universities Journal, 20*(2), 47–65.

Blanton, J. (2007). Engagement as a brand position in the higher education marketplace. *International Journal of Educational Advancement, 7,* 143–154.

Blouin, D., & Perry, E. M. (2009). Whom does service-learning really serve? Community-based organizations' perceptions on service-learning. *Teaching Sociology, 37*(2), 120–135.

Boland, J. (2012). Strategies for enhancing sustainability of civic engagement: Opportunities, risks, and untapped potential. In L. McIlrath, A. Lyons, & R. Munck (Eds.), *Higher education and civic engagement: Comparative perspectives* (pp. 41–60). Dordrecht, Netherlands: Springer Science+Business Media.

Bowman, N. A., Brandenberger, J. W., Snyder, C., & Smedley, C. T. (2010). Sustained immersion courses and student orientation to equality, justice, and social responsibility: The role of short-term service-learning. *Michigan Journal of Community Service Learning, 17*(1), 20–31.

Boyer, E. L. (1990). *Scholarship reconsidered: Priorities of the professoriate.* Princeton, NJ: Carnegie Foundation for the Advancement of Teaching.

Boyer, E. L. (1996). The scholarship of engagement. *Journal of Public Service and Outreach, 1*(1), 11–21.

Boyer, E. L. (1997). *Selected speeches: 1979–1995.* Princeton, NJ: Carnegie Foundation for the Advancement of Teaching.

Boyte, H. (2004). *Everyday politics: Reconnecting citizens and public life.* Philadelphia, PA: University of Pennsylvania Press.

Boyte, H., & Fretz, E. (2011). Civic professionalism. In J. Saltmarsh & M. Hartley (Eds.), *To a larger purpose: Engagement for democracy and the transformation of higher education* (pp. 82–101). Philadelphia, PA: Temple University Press.

Boyte, H., & Hollander, E. (1999). *Wingspread declaration on the civic responsibilities of research universities.* Boston, MA: Campus Compact.

Bringle, R. G., Games, R., & Malloy, E. A. (1999). *Colleges and universities as citizens: Issues and perspectives.* Boston, MA: Allyn and Bacon.

Bringle, R. G., & Hatcher, J. A. (1996). Implementing service-learning in higher education. *Journal of Higher Education, 67*(2), 221–239.

Bringle, R. G., & Hatcher, J. A. (2011). Student engagement trends over time. In H. E. Fitzgerald, C. Burack, & S. D. Seifer (Eds.), *Handbook of engaged scholarship: Contemporary landscapes, future directions: Vol. 2. Community-campus partnerships* (pp. 411–430). East Lansing, MI: Michigan State University Press.

Brower, A. M., & Inkeles, K. K. (2010). Living-learning programs: One high-impact educational practice we now know a lot about. *Liberal Education, 96*(2), 36–43.

Bucco, D. A., & Busch, J. A. (1996). Starting a service-learning program. In B. Jacoby (Ed.), *Service-learning in higher education: Concepts and practices* (pp. 231–245). San Francisco, CA: Jossey-Bass.

Bush, V. (1945) *Science, the endless frontier.* Washington DC: United States Government Printing Office. Retrieved from https://www.nsf.gov/about/history/nsf50/vbush1945.jsp

Butin, D., & Seider, S. (2012). *The engaged campus: Certificates, minors, and majors as the new community engagement.* New York, NY: Palgrave Macmillan.

Cahill, C., & Fine, M. (2014). Living the civic: Brooklyn's public scholars. In J. N. Reich (Ed.), *Civic engagement, civic development, and higher education: New perspectives on transformative learning* (pp. 67–71). Washington DC: Bringing Theory to Practice.

Campus Compact. (2014). *2014 Campus Compact member survey.* Retrieved from http://compact.org/wp-content/uploads/2015/05/2014ALLPublicInstitutionsR eport.pdf

Cantor, N. (2010). *Academic excellence and civic engagement: Constructing a third space for higher education.* Keynote address delivered at the Association of American Colleges and Universities Conference on Faculty Roles in High-Impact Practices, Philadelphia, PA. Retrieved from http://surface.syr.edu/chancellor/1

Cantor, N., & Englot, P. (2013). Beyond the ivory tower: Restoring the balance of private and public purpose of general education. *Journal of General Education, 62*(2–3), 120–128.

Cantor, N., & Englot, P. (2014). Civic renewal of higher education through renewed commitment to the public good. In J. N. Reich (Ed.), *Civic engagement, civic development, and higher education: New perspectives on transformative learning* (pp. 3–12).Washington DC: Bringing Theory to Practice.

Carnegie Foundation for the Advancement of Teaching. (2008). *Carnegie Community Engagement Classification.* Boston, MA: New England Resource Center for Higher Education.

Carnegie Foundation for the Advancement of Teaching. (2012). *Community engaged elective classification.* Retrieved from http://carnegieclassifications.iu.edu

Carnevale, A. P., Cheah, B., & Hanson, A. R. (2015). *The economic value of college majors.* Retrieved from Georgetown University Center on Education and the Workforce website: https://cew.georgetown.edu/wp-content/uploads/The-Eco nomic-Value-of-College-Majors-Full-Report-Web.compressed.pdf

Center for Economic and Social Justice. (2015). *Defining social justice.* Retrieved from http://www.cesj.org/learn/definitions/defining-economic-justice-and-social -justice/

Center for Engaged Democracy Core Competency Committee. (2012). *Core competencies in civic engagement: A working paper in the Center for Engaged Democracy's Policy Paper Series.* Andover, MA: Merrimack College.

Checkoway, B. (2001). Renewing the civic mission of the American research university. *Journal of Higher Education, 72*(2), 125–147.

Clayton, P. H., Bringle, R. G., & Hatcher, J. A. (2012a). *Research on service learning: Conceptual frameworks and assessments: Vol. 2A. Students and faculty.* Sterling, VA: Stylus Publishing

Clayton, P. H., Bringle, R. G., & Hatcher, J. A. (2012b). *Research on service learning: Conceptual frameworks and assessments: Vol. 2B. Communities, institutions, and partnerships.* Sterling, VA: Stylus Publishing.

Cochran, T. C. (1972). *Business in American life: A history.* New York, NY: McGraw-Hill.

Colby, A., Beaumont, E., Ehrlich, T., & Corngold, J. (2008). *Educating for democracy: Preparing undergraduates for responsible political engagement.* San Francisco, CA: Jossey-Bass.

Colby, A., Ehrlich, T., Beaumont, E., & Stephens, J. (2003). *Educating citizens: Preparing America's undergraduates for lives of moral and civic responsibility.* San Francisco, CA: Jossey-Bass.

Cole, H. (1997). Interviews: Seamus Heaney: The art of poetry, no. 75. *The Paris Review, 75.* Retrieved from http://www.theparisreview.org/interviews/1217/the-art -of-poetry-no-75-seamus-heaney

Commission on Collegiate Nursing Education. (2013). *Standards for accreditation of baccalaureate and graduate nursing program.* Retrieved from http://www.aacn .nche.edu/ccne-accreditation/Standards-Amended-2013.pdf

Committee on Institutional Cooperation. (2005). *Engaged scholarship: A resource guide.* Retrieved from http://www.cic.net/docs/default-source/technology/engaged_ scholarship.pdf

Council for the Advancement of Standards in Higher Education. (2015). *CAS professional standards for higher education* (9th ed.). Washington DC: Author. Retrieved from http://standards.cas.edu/getpdf.cfm?PDF=E86EC8E7-9B94- 5F5C-9AD22B4FEF375B64

Council on Social Work Education. (2016). *Council on Field Education.* Retrieved from http://www.cswe.org/cms/15538.aspx

Covaleskie, J. F. (2014). What good is college? The economics of college attendance. *Philosophical Studies in Education, 45,* 93–101.

Cox, D. (2010). History of the scholarship of engagement movement. In H. E. Fitzgerald, C. Burack, & S. D. Seifer (Eds.), *Handbook of engaged scholarship: Contemporary landscapes, future directions* (pp. 25–37). East Lansing, MI: Michigan State University Press.

Crabtree, R. (2008). Theoretical foundations for international service-learning. *Michigan Journal of Community Service Learning, 15*(1), 18–36.

Cuban, L. (1988). A fundamental puzzle of school reform. *Phi Delta Kappan, 69*(5), 341–344.

Curley, M., & Stanton, T. (2012). The history of TRUCEN. *Journal of Higher Education Outreach and Engagement, 16*(4), 3–9.

DeBerri, E., & Hug, J. E. (2003). *Catholic social teaching: Our best kept secret.* Maryknoll, NY: Orbis Books.

Delgado, R. (2012). *Critical race theory: An introduction.* New York, NY: New York University Press.

Dempsey, S. B. (2015, November). *Understanding the impact of faculty development for service-learning courses.* Paper presentation at the annual conference of the International Association of Research on Service-Learning and Community Engagement, Boston, MA.

Dewey, J. (1933). *How we think: A restatement of the relation of reflective thinking to the education process.* Lexington, MA: Heath.

Diamond, R., & Adam, A. (1993). *Recognizing faculty work: Reward systems for the year 2000.* San Francisco, CA: Jossey-Bass.

Diener, M. L., & Liese, H. (2009). *Finding meaning in civically engaged scholarship: Personal journeys, professional experiences.* Charlotte, NC: Information Age Publishing.

Doberneck, D. M., Brown, R. E., & Allen, A. D. (2010). Professional development for emerging engaged scholars. In H. E. Fitzgerald, C. Burack, & S. D. Seifer (Eds.), *Handbook of engaged scholarship: Contemporary landscapes, future directions* (pp. 391–409). East Lansing, MI: Michigan State University Press.

Dorn, C. (2011). From "liberal professions" to "lucrative professions": Bowdoin College, Stanford University, and the civic functions of higher education. *Teachers College Record, 113*(7), 1566–1596.

Dostilio, L. D. (in press). The professionalization of community engagement: Association and professional staff. In C. Dolgon, T. Eatman, & T. Mitchell (Eds.), *The Cambridge handbook of service-learning and community engagement.* Cambridge, UK: Cambridge University Press.

Dostilio, L., Edwards, K., Harrison, B., Kliewer, B., & Clayton, P. (2011). Reciprocity in community engagement: Implications of a concept analysis for research. Presentation at the International Association for Research in Service-Learning and Community Engagement, Chicago, IL.

Dostilio, L. D., & Perry, L. G. (in press). An explanation of community engagement professionals as professionals and leaders. In L. D. Dostilio (Ed.), *The community engagement professional: Attributes and explanations.* Boston, MA: Campus Compact.

Driscoll, A. (2009). Carnegie's new community engagement classification: Affirming higher education's role in community. In L. R. Sandmann, C. H. Thornton, & A. J. Jaeger (Eds.), *Institutionalizing community engagement in higher education: The first wave of Carnegie classified institutions* (pp. 2–12). San Francisco, CA: Jossey-Bass.

Dubinsky, J. M., Welch, M., & Wurr, A. J. (2012). Composing cognition: The role of written reflection in service-learning. In I. Baca (Ed.), *Paving the way for literacy: Writing and learning through community engagement* (pp. 155–180). New York, NY: Emerald Publishing.

Dumlao, R., & Janke, E. (2012). Using relational dialectics to address differences in community-campus partnerships. *Journal of Higher Education Outreach and Engagement, 16*(2), 151–175.

Dunlap, M. R., & Webster, N. (2009). Enhancing intercultural competence through civic engagement. In B. Jacoby (Ed.), *Civic engagement in higher education: Concepts and practices* (pp. 140–153). San Francisco, CA: Jossey-Bass.

Eagan, M. K., Stolzenberg, E. B., Berdan Lozano, J., Aragon, M. C., Suchard, M. R., & Hurtado, S. (2014). *Undergraduate teaching faculty: The 2013–2014 faculty survey.* Los Angeles, CA: Higher Education Research Institute, University of California, Los Angeles.

Eatman, T. K., & Peters, S. J. (2015). Cultivating growth at the leading edges: Public engagement in higher education. *Diversity and Democracy, 18*(1), 4–7.

Eby, J. W. (1998). *Why service-learning is bad.* Retrieved from http://www.messiah .edu/documents/Agape/wrongsvc.pdf

Eby, J. W. (2010). Civic engagement at faith-based institutions. In H. E. Fitzgerald, C. Burack, & S. D. Seifer (Eds.), *Handbook of engaged scholarship: Contemporary landscapes, future directions* (pp. 165–180). East Lansing, MI: Michigan State University Press.

Ehrlich, T. (Ed.). (2000). *Civic responsibility and higher education.* Phoenix, AZ: Oryx Press.

Elder, L., Seligsohn, A., & Hofrenning, D. (2007). Experiencing New Hampshire: The effects of an experiential service-learning course on civic engagement. *Journal of Political Science Education, 3*(2), 191–216.

Ellison, J., & Eatman, T. (2008). *Scholarship in public: Knowledge creation and tenure policy in the engaged university: A resource on promotion and tenure in the arts, humanities, and design.* Retrieved from http://community-wealth.org/sites/clone.community-wealth.org/files/downloads/paper-ellison-eastman.pdf

Eraut, M. (1994). *Developing professional knowledge and competence.* London, UK: Routledge.

Etienne, H. F. (2012). *Pushing back the gates: Neighborhood perspectives on university-driven revitalization in West Philadelphia.* Philadelphia, PA: Temple University Press.

Eyler, J. S., & Giles, D. E. (1999). *Where's the learning in service-learning?* San Francisco, CA: Jossey-Bass.

Fisher, I. A. (1998). We make the road by walking: Building service-learning in and out of the curriculum at the University of Utah. In E. Slotkowski (Ed.), *Successful service-learning programs: New models of excellence in higher education* (pp. 210–230). Bolton, MA: Anker Press.

Fitzgerald, H. E., Bruns, K., Sonka, S. T., Furco, A., & Swanson, L. (2012). The centrality of engagement in higher education. *Journal of Higher Education Outreach and Engagement, 16*(3), 7–27.

Fogelman, E. (2002). Civic engagement at the University of Minnesota. *Journal of Public Affairs, 6,* 103–118.

Franco, R. W. (2010). Faculty engagement in the community colleges: Constructing a new ecology of learning. In H. E. Fitzgerald, C. Burack, & S. D. Seifer (Eds.), *Handbook of engaged scholarship: Contemporary landscapes, future directions* (pp. 149–163). East Lansing, MI: Michigan State University Press.

Freire, P. (1970). *Pedagogy of the oppressed.* New York, NY: Continuum.

Fretz, E. J., & Longo, N. V. (2010). Students co-creating an engaged academy. In H. E. Fitzgerald, C. Burack, & S. D. Seifer (Eds.), *Handbook of engaged scholarship: Contemporary landscapes, future directions* (pp. 313–330). East Lansing, MI: Michigan State University Press.

Fry, D., & Kolb, D. (1979). Experiential learning theory and learning experience in liberal arts education. *New Directions for Experiential Education, 6,* 79–92.

Furco, A. (1996). Service-learning: A balanced approach to experiential education. In Corporation for National Service (Ed.), *Expanding boundaries: Serving and learning* (pp. 2–6). Columbia, MD: Cooperative Education Association.

Furco, A. (1999). *Self-assessment rubric for the institutionalization of service-learning in higher education.* Berkeley, CA: Service-Learning Research and Development Center, University of California, Berkeley.

Furco, A. (2002a). Institutionalizing service-learning in higher education. *Journal of Public Affairs, 6,* 39–68.

Furco, A. (2002b). *Self-assessment rubric for the institutionalization of service-learning in higher education* (Rev. ed.). Berkeley, CA: Service-Learning Research and Development Center, University of California, Berkeley.

Furco, A. (2005). *Promoting civic engagement at the University of California.* Berkeley, CA: Center for Studies in Higher Education, University of California, Berkeley.

Gardner, J. N. (2008). Action steps to move the first-year civic engagement movement forward. In M. J. LaBare (Ed.), *First-year civic engagement: Sound foundations for college, citizenship, and democracy* (pp. 26–28). New York, NY: New York Times Knowledge Network.

Gelmon, S., & Agre-Kippenhan, S. (2002). Promotion, tenure, and the engaged scholar: Keeping the scholarship of engagement in the review process. *AAHE Bulletin, 54*(5), 7–11.

Gelmon, S. B., Holland, B. A., Driscoll, A., Spring, A., & Kerrigan, S. (2001). *Assessing service-learning and civic engagement: Principles and techniques.* Providence, RI: Campus Compact.

Glass, C. R., & Fitzgerald, H. E. (2010). Engaged scholarship: Historical roots, contemporary challenges. In H. E. Fitzgerald, C. Burack, & S. D. Seifer (Eds.), *Handbook of engaged scholarship: Contemporary landscapes, future directions: Vol. 1. Institutional change* (pp. 9–24). East Lansing, MI: Michigan State University Press.

Glassick, C. E. E., Huber, M. T., & Maeroff, G. I. (1997). *Scholarship assessed: Evaluation of the professoriate.* San Francisco, CA: Jossey-Bass.

Grace, K. S., & Wendroff, A. L. (2001). *High impact philanthropy: How donors, boards, and nonprofit organizations can transform communities.* Hoboken, NJ: Wiley.

Graham, N., & Crawford, P. (2012). Instructor-led engagement and immersion programs: Transformative experiences of study abroad. *Journal of Higher Education Outreach and Engagement, 16*(3), 107–110.

Grant, C., & Agosto, V. (2008). Teacher capacity and social justice in teacher education. In M. Cochran-Smith, S. Feinman-Nemser, J. McIntyre, & K. Demers (Eds.), *Handbook of research on teacher education: Enduring questions in changing contexts.* Mahwah, NJ: Lawrence Erlbaum Publishers.

Guarasci, R. (2006). On the challenge of becoming the good college. *Liberal Education, 92*(1), 14–21.

Guarasci, R., & Cornwell, G. H. (1997). *Democratic education in an age of difference: Redefining citizenship in higher education.* San Francisco, CA: Jossey-Bass.

Haas Center for Public Service. (2015). *Public service pathways.* Palo Alto, CA: Stanford University.

Hackensmith, T. S., & Barker, M. (2015). *Creating an impact report: How to effectively tell your community engagement story.* Paper presented at the 18th Annual Continuums of Service Conference, Long Beach, CA.

Hall, M. (2010). Community engagement in South African Higher Education. In *Community Engagement in South African Higher Education, Kagisano Series No. 6* (pp. 1–52). Pretoria, SA: Council on Higher Education.

Harkavy, I. (2004). Service-learning and the development of democratic universities, democratic schools, and democratic good societies in the 21st century. In M. Welch & S. H. Billig (Eds.), *New perspectives in service-learning: Research to advance the field* (pp. 3–22). Greenwich, CT: Information Age Publishing.

Harkavy, I. (2006). The role of universities in advancing citizenship and social justice in the 21st century. *Education Citizenship and Social Justice, 1*(1), 5–37.

Harkavy, I., Cantor, N., & Burnett, M. (2015). *Realizing STEM equity and diversity through higher education community engagement.* Philadelphia, PA: University of Pennsylvania, Netter Center for Community Partnerships.

Harkavy, I., & Hartley, J. M. (2012). Integrating a commitment to the public good into the institutional fabric: Further lessons from the field. *Journal of Higher Education Outreach and Engagement, 16*(4), 17–36.

Hartley, M. (2011). Idealism and compromise and the civic engagement movement. In J. Saltmarsh & M. Hartley (Eds.), *To serve a larger purpose: Engagement for democracy and the transformation of higher education* (pp. 27–48). Philadelphia, PA: Temple University Press.

Hartman, E., & Kiely, R. (2014). A critical global citizenship. In M. Johnson & P. M. Green (Eds.), *Crossing boundaries: Tension and transformation in international service-learning.* Sterling, VA: Stylus Publishing.

Hartman, E., Kiely, R., Friedrichs, J., & Boettcher, C. (2014). *Building a better world: The pedagogy and practice of global service-learning.* Sterling, VA: Stylus Publishing.

Hatcher, J. A., & Bringle, R. G. (1997). Reflections: Bridging the gap between service and learning. *Journal of College Teaching, 45,* 153–158.

Hatcher, J. A., & Bringle, R. G. (2010). Developing your assessment plan: A key component of reflective practice. In B. Jacoby & P. Matuscio (Eds.), *Looking in/reaching out: A reflective guide for community service-learning professionals* (pp. 211–230). Boston, MA: Campus Compact.

Henry, R. K. (1998). Community college and service-learning: A natural at Brevard Community College. In E. Zlotkowski (Ed.), *Successful service-learning programs: New models of excellence in higher education* (pp. 81–108). Bolton, MA: Anker Publishing.

Holland, B. (1997). Analyzing institutional commitment to service: A model of key organizational factors. *Michigan Journal of Community Service Learning, 4*(1), 30–41.

Holland, B. (1999). From murky to meaningful: The role of mission in institutional change. In R. G. Bringle, R. Games, & E. A. Malloy (Eds.), *Colleges and universities as citizens* (pp. 48–72). Boston, MA: Allyn & Bacon.

Holland, B. (2005a, April). *Every perspective counts: Understanding the true meaning of reciprocity in partnerships.* Keynote address to the Western Regional Campus Compact Conference, Portland, OR.

Holland, B. (2005b). *Scholarship and mission in the 21st century university: The role of engagement.* Paper presented at the Australian Universities Quality Forum, Sydney.

Holland, B. (2009). Will it last? Evidence of institutionalization at Carnegie classified community engagement institutions. In L. R. Sandmann, C. H. Thornton, & A. J. Jaeger (Eds.), *Institutionalizing community engagement in higher education: The first wave of Carnegie classified institutions.* (pp. 85–98). San Francisco, CA: Jossey-Bass.

Holland, B., & Langseth, M. N. (2010). Leveraging financial support for service-learning: Relevance, relationships, results, resources. In B. Jacoby & P. Mutascio

(Eds.), *Looking in/reaching out: A reflective guide for community service-learning professionals* (pp. 185–210). Boston, MA: Campus Compact.

Hollander, E., Saltmarsh, J., & Zlotkowski, E. (2001). Indicators of engagement. In L. A. Simon, M. Kenny, K. Brabeck, & R. M. Lerner (Eds.), *Learning to serve: Promoting civil society through service-learning.* Norwell, MA: Kluwer Academic Publishers.

Hollister, R. M. (2014). Building a university-wide college of citizenship and public service. In J. N. Reich (Ed.), *Civic engagement, civic development, and higher education: New perspectives on transformative learning* (pp. 51–54). Washington DC: Bringing Theory to Practice.

Hollister, R., Pollock, J., Gearan, M., Stroud, S., Reid, J., & Babcock, E. (2012). The talloires network: A global coalition of engaged universities. *Journal of Higher Education Outreach and Engagement, 16*(4), 81–101.

Hondagneu-Sotelo, P., & Raskoff, S. (1994). Community service-learning: Promises and problems. *Teaching Sociology, 22,* 248–254.

Honnet, E. P., & Poulson, S. J. (1989). *Principles of good practice for combining service and learning* (Wingspread Special Report). Racine, WI: Johnson Foundation.

hooks, b. (2000). *Feminist theory: From margin to center.* Cambridge, MA: South End Press.

Howard, J. (2001). *Service-learning course design workbook.* Ann Arbor, MI: University of Michigan, Edward Ginsberg Center.

Hoy, A., & Johnson, M. (2013). *Deepening community engagement in higher education: Forging new pathways.* New York: Palgrave Macmillan.

Hoy, A., & Meisel, W. (2008). *Civic engagement at the center: Building democracy through integrated co-curricular and curricular experiences.* Washington DC: Association of American Colleges and Universities.

Hoyt, L. (2011). Sustained city-campus engagement: Developing an epistemology for our time. In J. Saltmarsh & M. Hartley (Eds.), *To serve a larger purpose: Engagement for democracy and the transformation of higher education* (pp. 265–288). Philadelphia, PA: Temple University Press.

Hunter, M. S., & Moody, B. L. (2009). Civic engagement in the first college year. In B. Jacoby (Ed.), *Civic engagement in higher education: Concepts and practice* (pp. 69–84). San Francisco, CA: Jossey-Bass.

Jacoby, B. (Ed.). (1996). *Service-learning in higher education: Concepts and practices.* San Francisco, CA: Jossey-Bass.

Jacoby, B. (2003). *Building partnerships for service-learning.* San Francisco, CA: Jossey-Bass.

Jacoby, B. (2009). *Civic engagement in higher education: Concepts and practices.* San Francisco, CA: Jossey-Bass.

Jacoby, B. (2015). *Service-learning essentials: Questions, answers, and lessons learned.* San Francisco, CA: Jossey-Bass.

Jacoby, B., & Hollander, E. (2009). Securing the future of civic engagement in higher education. In B. Jacoby (Ed.), *Civic engagement in higher education: Concepts and practices* (pp. 227–248). San Francisco, CA: Jossey-Bass.

Jacoby, B., & Mutascio, P. (Eds.). (2010). *Looking in, reaching out: A reflective guide for community service-learning professionals.* Boston, MA: Campus Compact.

Johnson, B. T., & O'Grady, C. R. (Eds.). (2006). *The spirit of service: Exploring faith, service, and social justice in higher education.* Bolton, MA: Anker Publishing.

Jones, S. R. (2003). Principles and profiles of exemplary partnerships with community agencies. In B. Jacoby (Ed.), *Building partnerships for service-learning* (pp. 151–173). San Francisco, CA: Jossey-Bass.

Jordan, C., Jones-Webb, R., Cook, N., Dubrow, G., Mendenhall, T. J., & Doherty, W. J. (2014). Competency-based faculty development in community-based scholarship: A diffusion of innovations approach. *Journal of Higher Education Outreach and Engagement, 16*(1), 65–95.

Kaufman, J. (2009). Teaching English, reading poetry, living in the world. In M. L. Diener & H. Liese (Eds.), *Finding meaning in civically engaged scholarship: Personal journeys, professional experiences* (pp. 59–68). Charlotte, NC: Information Age Publishing.

Kecskes, K. (2006). *Engaging departments: Moving faculty culture from private to public, individual to collective focus for the common good.* San Francisco, CA: Jossey-Bass.

Kecskes, K., & Kerrigan, S. (2009). Capstone experiences. In B. Jacoby (Ed.), *Civic engagement in higher education: Concepts and practices* (pp. 117–139). San Francisco, CA: Jossey-Bass.

Kellogg Commission. (1999). *Returning to our roots: The engaged institution.* Washington DC: National Association of State Universities and Land-Grant Colleges.

Kellogg Commission. (2001). *Returning to our roots: Executive summaries of the reports of the Kellogg Commission on the Future of State and Land-Grant Universities.* Washington DC: National Association of State Universities and Land-Grant Colleges.

Kendall, J. C. (1990). *Combining service and learning: A resource book for community and public service* (Vols. 1 & 2). Raleigh, NC: National Society for Internships and Experiential Education.

Kerlinger, F. N. (1979). *Behavioral research: A conceptual approach.* New York, NY: Holt, Rinehart & Winston.

Kezar, A. J., Chambers, T. C., Burkhardt, J. C., & Associates (2005). *Higher education for the public good.* San Francisco, CA: Jossey-Bass.

Kiely, R. (2005). A transformative learning model for service-learning: A longitudinal case study. *Michigan Journal of Community Service Learning, 12*(1), 5–22.

Kimball, E. (2011, Winter). College admission in a contested marketplace: The 20th century and a new logic for access. *Journal of College Admissions, 210,* 20–30.

Kolb, D. (1984). *Experiential learning: Experience as the source of learning and development.* Upper Saddle River, NJ: Prentice-Hall.

Kowaleski, B. M. (2004). Service-learning taken to a new level through community-based research: A win-win for campus and community. In M. Welch & S. H. Billig (Eds.), *New perspectives in service-learning: Research to advance the field* (pp. 127–147). Greenwich, CT: Information Age Publishing.

Krier Mich, M. L. (2011). *The challenge and spirituality of Catholic social teaching.* Mary Knoll, NY: Orbis Books.

Kuh, G. D. (2008). *High impact educational practices: What they are, who has access to them, and why they matter.* Washington DC: Association of American Colleges and Universities.

Lake Snell Perry & Associates & the Tarrance Group Inc. (2002, March). *Short term impacts, long term opportunities: The political and civic engagement of young adults in America.* College Park, MD: Center for Information and Research on Civic Learning and Engagement.

Lang, E. M. (1999, Winter). Distinctly American: The liberal arts college. *Daedalus,* 133–150.

Lawler, P. (2003). Teachers as adult learners: A new perspective. In K. P. King & P. A. Lawler (Eds.), *New directions for adult and continuing education* (No. 98, pp. 15–22). New York, NY: Wiley.

Lawry, S., Laurison, D., & Van Antwerpen, J. (2006). *Liberal education and civic engagement: A project of Ford Foundation's Knowledge, Creativity and Freedom Program.* New York, NY: Ford Foundation.

Leisey, M., Holton, V., & Davey, T. L. (2012). Community engagement grants: Assessing the impact of university funding and engagements. *Journal of Community Engagement and Scholarship, 5*(2), 41–47.

Levine, P. (2007). *The future of democracy: Developing the next generation of American citizens.* Medford, MA: Tufts University Press.

Levine, P., & Lopez, M. (2002). *Youth voter turnout has declined, by any measure.* Retrieved from http://ncfy.acf.hhs.gov/library/2002/youth-voter-turnout-has-declined-any-measure

Lewin, K. (1946). Action research and minority problems. *Journal of Social Issues 2*(4), 34–46.

Littlepage, L., & Gazley, B. (2013). Examining service-learning from the perspective community organization capacity. In P. H. Clayton, R. G. Bringle, & J. A. Hatcher (Eds.), *Research on service-learning: Conceptual frameworks and assessment: Vol. 2B. Communities, institutions, and partnerships* (pp. 419–437). Sterling, VA: Stylus Publishing.

Littrell-Baez, M. K., Friend, A., Caccamise, D., & Okochi, C. (2015). Using retrieval practice and metacognitive skills to improve content learning. *Journal of Adolescent & Adult Literacy, 58*(8), 682–689.

Long, S. E. (2002). *The new student politics: The Wingspread statement on student civic engagement.* Providence, RI: Campus Compact.

Maher, C., & Bennett, R. E. (1984). *Planning and evaluating special education services.* Englewood Cliffs, NJ: Prentice-Hall.

Marullo, S., Cooke, D., Willis, J., Rollins, A., Burke, J., Bonilla, P., & Waldref, V. (2003). Community-based research assessments: Some principles and practices. *Michigan Journal of Community Service Learning, 9*(3), 57–68.

Mattar, S. (2011). Educating and training the next generations of traumatologists: Development of cultural competencies. *Psychological Trauma: Theory, Research, Practice, and Policy, 3*(3), 258–265.

Mattar, S. (2014). *Waiting to be invited: Developing cultural competencies* (Professional development workshop). Moraga, CA: Saint Mary's College of California.

Maurrasse, D. (2007). *City anchors: Leveraging anchor institutions for urban success.* Chicago, IL: CEOs for Cities.

McKee, C. W., & Tew, W. M. (2013, Spring). Setting the stage for teaching and learning in American higher education: Making the case for faculty development. *New Directions for Teaching and Learning, 133,* 3–14.

McRae, H. (2015). Situating engagement in Canadian higher education. In O. Delano-Oriarian, M. Penick-Parks, & S. Fondrie (Eds.), *The Sage sourcebook of service-learning and community engagement* (pp. 401–408). Thousand Oaks, CA: Sage Publishing.

McReynolds, M., & Shields, E. (2015). *Diving deep in community engagement: A model for professional development.* Boston, MA: Campus Compact.

McTighe Musil, C. (2003). Educating for citizenship. *Peer Review, 5*(3), 4–8.

McTighe Musil, C. (2015). *Civic prompts: Making civic learning routine across the disciplines.* Washington DC: Association of American Colleges and Universities.

Merriam-Webster. Platforms [Def. 5]. (2016). *Merriam-Webster Online.* Retrieved from http://www.merriam-webster.com/dictionary/platform

Merriam-Webster. Program [Def. 3]. (2016). *Merriam-Webster Online.* Retrieved from http://www.merriam-webster.com/dictionary/program

Merriam-Webster. Purpose [Def. 1 & 2]. (2016). *Merriam-Webster Online.* Retrieved from http://www.merriam-webster.com/dictionary/purpose

Mezirow, J. (1999). *Transformative dimensions of adult learning.* San Francisco, CA: Jossey-Bass.

Mitchell, T. (2008). Traditional vs. critical service-learning: Engaging the literature to differentiate two models. *Michigan Journal of Community Service Learning, 14*(2), 50–65.

Mitchell, T. (2013). Critical service-learning as a philosophy for deepening community engagement. In A. Hoy & J. Johnson (Eds.), *Deepening community engagement in higher education: Forging new pathways* (pp. 264–269). New York, NY: Palgrave Macmillan.

Morton, K. (1995). The irony of service: Charity, project and social change in service-learning. *Michigan Journal of Community Service Learning, 2*(1), 19–32.

Mundy, M. E. (2004). Faculty engagement in service-learning: Individual and organizational factors at distinct institutional types. In M. Welch & S. Billig (Eds.), *New perspectives in service-learning: Research to advance the field* (pp. 169–193). Charlotte, NC: Information Age Publishing.

Murphy, B. (2014). Civic learning in community colleges. In J. N. Reich (Ed.), *Civic engagement, civic development, and higher education: New perspectives on transformative learning* (pp. 19–30). Washington DC: Bringing Theory to Practice.

Murphy, D., Sahakyan, N., Yong-Yi, D., & Magnan, S. S. (2014). The impact of study abroad on the global engagement of university graduates. *Frontiers: The Interdisciplinary Journal of Study Abroad, 24,* 1–24.

Nanna, E., Skillman, L., & Zgela, A. (2011, October). *Living-learning communities best practice: A collaboration between academic and student affairs.* Paper presented at the conference of the Florida chapter of the NASPA, Tampa, FL.

National Association of Colleges and Employers. (2015). *Position statement: U.S. internships.* Retrieved from http://www.naceweb.org/advocacy/position-statements/united-states-internships.aspx

National Center for Education Statistics. (2012, December). *Table 5: Number of educational institutions, by level and control of institution: Selected years, 1980–81 through 2010–11.* Washington DC: U.S. Department of Education.

National Commission on Civic Renewal. (1998). *A nation of spectators: How civic disengagement weakens America and what we can do about it.* College Park, MD: University of Maryland.

National Commission on Service Learning. (2002). *The power of service learning for American schools.* Retrieved from http://www.wkkf.org/resource-directory/resource/2002/10/learning-in-deed-the-power-of-service-learning-for-american-schools-full-report

National Council for Accreditation of Teacher Education. (2016). *NCATE glossary.* Retrieved from http://www.ncate.org/Standards/UnitStandards/Glossary/tabid/477/Default.aspx#T

National Society for Experiential Education. (2014). *Vision and mission.* Retrieved from http://www.nsee.org/vision-mission-and-goals

National Task Force on Civic Learning and Democratic Engagement. (2012). *A crucible moment: College learning and democracy's future.* Washington DC: Association of American Colleges and Universities.

Ness, M. K., George, M. A., Turner, K. H., & Bolgatz, J. (2010). The growth of higher educators for social justice: Collaborative professional development in higher education. *Insight: A Journal of Scholarly Teaching, 5,* 88–105.

Netter Center for Community Partnerships. (2008). *Anchor institutions toolkit: A guide for neighborhood revitalization.* Philadelphia, PA: University of Pennsylvania.

Netter Center for Community Partnerships. (2012). *Our mission.* Retrieved from https://www.nettercenter.upenn.edu/about-us/our-mission

Newman, F. (1985). *Higher education and the American resurgence.* Princeton, NJ: Carnegie Foundation for the Advancement of Teaching.

Niehaus, E., & Kavaliauskas Crain, L. (2013). Act local or global? Comparing student experiences in domestic and international service-learning programs. *Michigan Journal of Community Service Learning, 20*(1), 31–40.

Norvell, K. H. (2010). *Examining community-engaged scholarship in public administration programs* (Unpublished doctoral dissertation). Portland State University, Portland, OR.

O'Meara, K. (2010). Rewarding multiple forms of scholarship and tenure. In H. E. Fitzgerald, C. Burack, & S. D. Seifer (Eds.), *Handbook of engaged scholarship: Contemporary landscapes, future directions: Vol. 1. Institutional change* (pp. 271–293). East Lansing, MI: Michigan State University Press.

O'Meara, K. A. (2011). Faculty civic engagement: New training, assumptions, and markets needed for the Engaged American Scholar. In J. Saltmarsh & M. Hartley

(Eds.), *To serve a larger purpose: Engagement for democracy and the transformation of higher education* (pp. 177–198). Philadelphia, PA: Temple University Press.

O'Neill, N. (2010). Internships as a high-impact practice: Some reflections on quality. *Peer Review, 12*(4), 4–8.

Paige, R. M., Fry, G. W., Stallman, E. M., Josic, J., & Jon, J. (2009). Study abroad for global engagement: The long-term impact of mobility experiences. *Intercultural Education, 20*(S1–2), S29–S44. doi: 10.1080/14675980903370847

Palmer, P. (2000). *Let your life speak: Listening for the voice of vocation.* San Francisco, CA: Jossey-Bass.

Paul, E. L. (2009). Community-based research: Collaborative inquiry for the public good. In B. Jacoby (Ed.), *Civic engagement in higher education: Concepts and practices* (pp. 196–212). San Francisco, CA: Jossey-Bass.

Pearson, N. (2002). Moving from placement to community partner. *Journal of Public Affairs, 7*, 183–202.

Pew Foundation. (1993). *University + community research partnerships: A new approach.* Charlottesville, VA: Pew Partnership for Civic Change.

Pigza, J. M., & Troppe, M. L. (2003). Developing an infrastructure for service-learning and community engagement. In B. Jacoby (Ed.), *Building partnerships for service-learning* (pp. 106–130). San Francisco, CA: Jossey-Bass.

Plater, W. M. (2011). Collective leadership for engagement: Reclaiming the public purpose of higher education. In J. Saltmarsh & M. Hartley (Eds.), *To serve a larger purpose: Engagement for democracy and the transformation of higher education* (pp. 102–129). Philadelphia, PA: Temple University Press.

Post, M., Ward, E., Longo, N., & Saltmarsh, J. (in press). *Voices of next generation engagement: Toward a more collaborative, publicly engaged future in higher education.* Sterling, VA: Stylus Publishing.

President's Commission on Higher Education. (1947). *Higher education for American democracy: A report.* Retrieved from http://catalog.hathitrust.org/Record/001117586

Presidents' declaration on the civic responsibility of higher education. (1999). Providence, RI: Campus Compact.

Presley, J. W. (2011). Chief academic offices and community-engaged faculty work. In J. Saltmarsh & M. Hartley (Eds.), *To serve a larger purpose: Engagement for democracy and the transformation of higher education* (pp. 120–153). Philadelphia, PA: Temple University Press.

Pribbenow, P. (2012, Spring). Hospitality is not enough: Claims of justice in the work of colleges and universities. *Intersections*, 23–30.

Purce, T. L. (2014). The habit of civic engagement. In J. N. Reich (Ed.), *Civic engagement, civic development, and higher education: New perspectives on transformative learning* (pp. 13–17). Washington DC: Bringing Theory to Practice.

Ramaley, J. A. (2000). The perspective of a comprehensive university. In T. Ehrlich (Ed.), *Civic responsibility and higher education* (pp. 227–248). Phoenix: Oryx Press.

Ramaley, J. A. (2010). Students as scholars: Integrating research, education, and professional practice. In H. E. Fitzgerald, C. Burack, & S. D. Seifer (Eds.), *Handbook of engaged scholarship: Contemporary landscapes, future directions* (pp. 353–368). East Lansing, MI: Michigan State University Press.

Ray, D. K. (2014). Civic diffusion: Moving the center to the center. In J. N Reich (Ed.), *Civic engagement, civic development, and higher education: New perspectives on transformative learning* (pp. 55–58). Washington DC: Bringing Theory to Practice.

Rice, E. (2003). Re-thinking scholarship and engagement: The struggle for new meanings. *Campus Compact Reader, 4*(1), 1–9.

Rimmerman, C. A. (2006). *The new citizenship: Unconventional politics, activism, and service* (3rd ed.). Boulder, CO: Westview Press.

Ronning, E. A., Keeney, B. E., & Sanford, T. (2008). *Advocating for the public good: A student of presidential communication.* Paper presented at the annual conference of the American Education Research Association, New York, NY.

Roper, C. D., & Hirth, M. A. (2005). A history of change in the third mission of higher education: The evolution of one-way service to interactive engagement. *Journal of Higher Education Outreach and Engagement, 10*(3) 3–21.

Ross, L. (2010). Notes from the field: Learning cultural humility through critical incidents and central challenges in community-based participatory research. *Journal of Community Practice, 18,* 315–335.

Rubin, S. (1996). Institutionalizing service-learning. In B. Jacoby (Ed.), *Service-learning in higher education: Concepts and practices* (pp. 297–316). San Francisco, CA: Jossey-Bass.

Rue, P. (1996). Administering successful service-learning programs. In B. Jacoby (Ed.), *Service-learning in higher education: Concepts and practices* (pp. 246–275). San Francisco, CA: Jossey-Bass.

Saltmarsh, J. A. (1996). Education for critical citizenship: John Dewey's contribution to the pedagogy of service-learning. *Michigan Journal of Service Learning, 3*(1), 13–21.

Saltmarsh, J. (2005). The civic promise of service-learning. *Liberal Education, 91*(2), 50–55.

Saltmarsh, J. (2010). Changing pedagogies. In H. E. Fitzgerald, C. Burack, & S. D. Seifer (Eds.), *Handbook of engaged scholarship: Contemporary landscapes, future directions* (pp. 331–352). East Lansing, MI: Michigan State University Press.

Saltmarsh, J., Giles, D. E., Ward, E., & Buglione, S. M. (2009). Rewarding community-engaged scholarship. In L. R. Sandmann, C. H. Thornton, & A. J. Jaeger (Eds.), *Institutionalizing community engagement in higher education: The first wave of Carnegie classified institutions* (pp. 25–36). San Francisco, CA: Jossey-Bass.

Saltmarsh, J., & Hartley, M. (2011). *To a larger purpose: Engagement for democracy and the transformation of higher education.* Philadelphia, PA: Temple University Press.

Saltmarsh, J., & Hartley, M. (2016). The inheritance of next generation engagement scholars. In M. Post, E. Ward, N. Longo, & J. Saltmarsh (Eds.), *Publicly engaged scholars: Next-generation engagement and the future of higher education.* Sterling, VA: Stylus.

Saltmarsh, J., Hartley, M., & Clayton, P. (2009). *Democratic engagement white paper.* Boston, MA: New England Resource Center for Higher Education.

Saltmarsh, J., Warren, M. R., Krueger-Henney, P., Rivera, L., Fleming, R. K., Friedman, D. H., & Uriarte, M. (2015). Creating an academic culture that supports community-engaged scholarship. *Diversity & Democracy, 18*(1), 1–9.

Saltmarsh, J., & Welch, M. (2014, October). *Research into practice: Creating an assessment tool for strategically advancing centers for community engagement.* Paper presented at the 14th annual conference of the International Association for Research on Service-Learning and Community Engagement, New Orleans, LA.

Sanchez, D., & Rivera-Mills, S. (2014). *Engaged scholarship: A promising road-less-traveled for STEM science cultures.* Retrieved from http://sacnas.org/about/stories/sacnas-news/summer-2014/engaged-scholarship

Sandmann, L. R., & Plater, W. M. (2009). Leading the engaged institution. In L. R. Sandmann, C. H. Thornton, & A. J. Jaeger (Eds.), *Institutionalizing community engagement in higher education: The first wave of Carnegie classified institutions* (pp. 13–24). San Francisco, CA: Jossey-Bass.

Sandmann, S. (2006). Building a higher education network for community engagement. *Journal of Higher Education Outreach and Engagement, 11*, 41–54.

Sandy, M. (2007). *Community voices: A California Campus Compact study on partnerships.* San Francisco, CA: California Campus Compact.

Savicki, V. (2008). *Developing intercultural competence and transformation: Theory, research and application in international education.* Sterling, VA: Stylus Publishing.

Scheuermann, C. D. (1996). Ongoing co-curricular service-learning. In B. Jacoby (Ed.), *Service-learning in higher education* (pp. 135–155). San Francisco, CA: Jossey-Bass.

Schmidt, A., & Robby, M. A. (2002). What's the value of service-learning to the community? *Michigan Journal of Community Service Learning, 9*(1), 27–33.

Schnaubelt, T., Welch, M., Lobo, K., & Robinson, G. (2015, April). *Pathways of public service: A comprehensive framework for social change and diagnostic tool.* Paper presented at the 18th annual Continuums of Service Conference, Western Region Campus Compact, Long Beach, CA.

Schön, D. (1983). *The reflective practitioner: How professionals think in action.* London, UK: Temple Smith.

Schwartz, I. S., & Baer, D. M. (1991). Social validity assessments: Is current practice state of the art? *Journal of Applied Behavioral Analysis, 24*, 189–204.

Seattle University. (2014). *University-led place-based initiatives project descriptions and report.* Seattle, WA: Center for Service and Community Engagement.

Senge, P. (1990). *The fifth discipline: The art and practice of the learning organization.* New York, NY: Doubleday.

Shiarella, A. H., McCarthy, A. M., & Tucker, M. L. (2000). Development and construct validity scores on the Community Service Attitude Scales. *Educational and Psychological Measurement, 60*(2), 286–300.

Sigmon, R. L. (1979). Service-learning: Three principles. *Synergist, 8*(1), 9–11.

Simon, L. A. K. (2011). Engaged scholarship in land-grant and research universities. In H. E. Fitzgerald, C. Burack, & S. D. Seifer (Eds.), *Handbook of engaged scholarship: Contemporary landscapes, future directions: Vol. 1. Institutional change* (pp. 99–118). East Lansing, MI: Michigan State University Press.

Simpson, J. B. (1998). *Contemporary Quotations 66.* New York, NY: William Morrow.

Singleton, S., Hirsh, D., & Burack, C. (1999). Organizational structures for community engagement. In R. G. Bringle, R. Games, & E. A. Malloy (Eds.), *Colleges and universities as citizens* (pp. 121–140). Boston, MA: Allyn & Bacon.

Sobel, D. (2004). *Place-based education: Connecting classrooms and community.* Barrington, MA: Orion Society.

South Salt Lake City. (2015). *Promise South Salt Lake.* Retrieved from http://www.southsaltlakecity.com/department-listings/promise-ssl

Sponsler, L. E., & Hartley, M. (2013). *Five things student affairs professionals can do to institutionalize civic engagement.* Washington DC: NASPA Research and Policy Institute.

Stanford University. (2015). Fellowships and other stipend supports. In *Graduate Academic Policies and Procedures.* Retrieved from http://gap.stanford.edu/7-2.html

Stanton, T. K. (Ed.). (2007). *New times demand new scholarship: Research universities and civic engagement—Opportunities and challenges.* Los Angeles, CA: University of California.

Stanton, T. K., Giles, D. E., & Cruz, N. I. (1999). *Service-learning: A movement's pioneers reflect on its origins, practice, and future.* San Francisco, CA: Jossey-Bass.

Stark, J. (1995/1996). *The Wisconsin idea: The university's service to the state* (Wisconsin Blue Book). Madison, WI: Legislative Reference Bureau.

Steup, M. (2005). Epistemology. In E. N. Zalta (Ed.), *Stanford encyclopedia of philosophy.* Retrieved from http://plato.stanford.edu/entries/epistemology/

Strand, K., Marullo, S., Cutforth, N., Stoecker, R., & Donohue, P. (2003). *Community-based research and higher education: Principles and practice.* San Francisco, CA: Jossey-Bass.

Strickland, S. (2007). Partners in writing and rewriting history: Philanthropy and higher education. *International Journal of Educational Advancement, 7,* 104–116.

Study Group on Civic Learning and Engagement. (2014). *Preparing citizens: Report on civic learning and engagement.* Retrieved from www.mass.edu/preparingcitizensreport

Sturm, S., Eatman, T., Saltmarsh, J., & Bush, A. (2011). *Full participation: Building the architecture for diversity and public engagement in higher education* (White paper). New York, NY: Center for Institutional and Social Change, Columbia University Law School.

Tisch College of Citizenship and Public Service. (2005). *Civic engagement: A global movement.* Retrieved from http://activecitizen.tufts.edu/about/dean-rob-hollister/publications-and-presentations/civic-engagement-a-global-movement/

Torney-Purta, J. (2002). The schools' role in developing civic engagement: A study of adolescents in twenty-eight countries. *Applied Developmental Science, 6*(4), 202–211.

University of Delaware. (2014). Commitment to community engagement. *University of Delaware Messenger, 21*(4). Retrieved from http://www.udel.edu/udmessenger/vol21no4/stories/otg-community-engagement.html

University of Minnesota Office of Public Engagement. (2012a). *Public engagement definition*. Retrieved from http://www.engagement.umn.edu/about-engagement/about-office/mission

University of Minnesota Office of Public Engagement. (2012b). *A ten point plan for advancing and institutionalizing public engagement at the University of Minnesota*. Retrieved from http://engagement.umn.edu/sites/default/files/10points_web.pdf

University Neighborhood Partnership. (2015). *UNP's partnership principles*. Retrieved from http://partners.utah.edu/how-we-work-in-partnership/

U.S. Department of Housing and Urban Development. (2013a, December). Nancy Cantor: A scholar in action. *Partners in Progress E-Newsletter, 1*(3). Retrieved from http://www.huduser.org/portal/oup/newsletter_121313_3.html

U.S. Department of Housing and Urban Development. (2013b, December). Wagner College concentrates civic efforts in Port Richmond community. *Partners in Progress E-Newsletter, 1*(3). Retrieved from https://www.huduser.gov/portal/oup/newsletter_121313_2.html#1

U.S. Department of Labor. (2010, April). *U.S. Department of Labor wage and hour division, fact sheet #71: Internships under the Fair Labor Standards Act*. Washington DC: Author.

Van Note Chism, N., Palmer, M. M., & Price, M. F. (2013). Investigating faculty development for service-learning. In P. H. Clayton, R. G. Bringle, & J. A. Hatcher (Eds.), *Research on service-learning: Conceptual frameworks and assessment: Vol. 2A. Students and faculty* (pp. 187–214). Sterling, VA: Stylus Publishing.

Versey, L. R. (1965). *The emergence of the American university*. Chicago, IL: University of Chicago Press.

Vogel, A. L., Fichtenberg, C., & Levin, M. B. (2010). Students as change agents in the engagement movement. In H. E. Fitzgerald, C. Burack, & S. D. Seifer (Eds.), *Handbook of engaged scholarship: Contemporary landscapes, future directions* (pp. 369–389). East Lansing, MI: Michigan State University Press.

Votruba, J. C. (1996). Strengthening the university's alignment with society: Challenges and strategies. *Journal of Public Service and Outreach, 1*(1), 29–36.

Votruba, J. C. (2004). *Leading the engaged institution*. President-to-presidents lecture at the annual meeting of the American Association of State Colleges and Universities, Charleston, SC.

Vygotsky, L. S. (1978). *Mind in society: The development of higher psychological processes*. Cambridge, MA: Harvard University Press.

Wagner College. (2014a). *Dr. Richard Guarasci, President*. Retrieved from http://wagner.edu/about/leadership/

Wagner College. (2014b). *Student learning assessment*. Retrieved from http://wagner.edu/academics/provost/assessment/

Walshok, M. L. (1999). Strategies for building the infrastructure that supports the engaged campus. In R. G. Bringle, R. Games, & E. A. Malloy (Eds.), *Colleges and universities as citizens* (pp. 74–93). Boston, MA: Allyn & Bacon.

Ward, E., Buglione, S., Giles, D. E., Jr., & Saltmarsh, J. (2013). The Carnegie classification for community engagement: Helping create the "new normal" in American higher education? In P. Benneworth (Ed.), *University engagement with socially excluded communities* (pp. 285–308). Dordrecht, Netherlands: Springer Science+Business Media.

Ward, K., & Moore, T. L. (2010). Defining the engagement in the scholarship of engagement. In H. E. Fitzgerald, C. Burack, & S. D. Seifer (Eds.), *Handbook of engaged scholarship: Contemporary landscapes, future directions* (pp. 39–54). East Lansing, MI: Michigan State University Press.

Ward, K., & Wolf-Wendel, L. (2000). Community-centered service-learning: Moving from doing for to doing with. *American Behavioral Scientist, 43*(5), 769–780.

Waters, S., & Anderson-Lain, K. (2014). Assessing the student, faculty, and community partner in academic service-learning: A categorization of surveys posted online at Campus Compact member institutions. *Journal of Higher Education Outreach and Engagement, 18*(1), 89–122.

Weerts, D., & Hudson, E. (2009). Engagement and institutional advancement. In L. R. Sandmann, C. H. Thornton, & A. J. Jaeger (Eds.), *Institutionalizing community engagement in higher education: The first wave of Carnegie classified institutions* (pp. 65–74). San Francisco, CA: Jossey-Bass.

Weerts, D. J., & Ronca, J. M. (2006). Examining differences in state support for higher education: A comparative study of state appropriations for research universities. *Journal of Higher Education, 77*(6), 935–965.

Weerts, D. J., & Sandmann, L. R. (2008). Building a two-way street: Challenges and opportunities for community engagement at research universities. *Review of Higher Education, 32*(1), 73–106.

Weisbuch, R. (2015). Imagining community engagement in American higher education. *Diversity and Democracy, 18*(1), 8–11.

Welch, M. (1999). The ABCs of reflection: A template for students and instructors to implement written reflection in service-learning. *National Society of Experiential Education Quarterly, 25*(2), 1, 23–25.

Welch, M. (2009). Moving from service-learning to civic engagement. In B. Jacoby (Ed.), *Civic engagement in higher education: Concepts and practice* (pp. 174–195). San Francisco, CA: Jossey-Bass.

Welch, M. (2010a). O.P.E.R.A.: A first letter mnemonic and rubric for conceptualizing and implementing service-learning courses. *Australian Journal of Educational Research, 20*(1), 76–82.

Welch, M. (2010b). Shedding light on the shadow-side of reflection in service-learning. *Journal of College and Character, 11*(3), 1–4.

Welch, M. (2014). *A professional development tool kit for community engagement.* Moraga, CA: Catholic Institute for Lasallian Social Action, Saint Mary's College of California.

Welch, M., & James, R. C. (2007). An investigation on the impact of a guided reflection technique in service-learning courses to prepare special educators. *Teacher Education and Special Education, 30*(4), 276–285.

Welch, M., Liese, L. H., Bergerson, A., & Stephenson, M. (2004). A qualitative assessment project comparing and contrasting faculty and administrators' perspectives on service-learning. *Journal of Higher Education Outreach and Engagement, 9*(2), 23–42.

Welch, M., & Saltmarsh, J. (2013a, July). *Best practice and infrastructure for centers of community engagement.* Paper presented at the 4th annual Summer Research Institute on the Future of Community Engagement in Higher Education, Tufts University, Boston, MA.

Welch, M., & Saltmarsh, J. (2013b). Current practice and infrastructure for campus centers of community engagement. *Journal of Higher Education Outreach and Engagement, 17*(4), 25–55.

Welch, M., & Saltmarsh, J. (2015). *Institutional community engagement readiness inventory.* Boston, MA: New England Resource Center for Higher Education.

Westminster College. (2015). Promise South Salt Lake Partnership. Retrieved from https://www.westminstercollege.edu/civic_engagement/?parent=6462&detail=16052

Whitchurch, C. (2008). Shifting identities and blurring boundaries: The emergence of *third space* professionals in UK higher education. *Higher Education Quarterly, 62*(4), 377–396.

Whitchurch, C. (2013). *Reconstructing identities in higher education: The rise of the third space professionals.* New York, NY: Routledge.

White, B. P. (2016). Building an organizational structure that fosters blended engagement. In M. Post, E. Ward, N. Longo, & J. Saltmarsh (Eds.), *Publicly engaged scholars: Next generation engagement and the future of higher education.* Sterling, VA: Stylus Publishing.

Yamamura, E. K. (2015). *Developing the next generation of university-community engagement initiatives: Promising practices and lessons learned from the Seattle University Youth Initiative.* Seattle, WA: Seattle University.

Youniss, J., & Yates, M. (1997). *Community service and social responsibility in youth.* Chicago, IL: University of Chicago Press.

Zlotkowski, E. (Ed.). (1998). *Successful service-learning programs: New models of excellence in higher education.* Bolton, MA: Anker Publishing.

Zlotkowski, E., Longo, N. V., & Williams, J. R. (2006). *Students as colleagues: Expanding the circle of service-learning leadership.* Providence, RI: Campus Compact.

ABOUT THE AUTHOR

Marshall Welch served as the assistant vice provost for engagement at Saint Mary's College of California. Before he took this role, he was the director of the Catholic Institute for Lasallian Social Action (CILSA), which coordinates service-learning, community-based research, and social justice courses at Saint Mary's College. Welch began his career as a professor at the University of Utah in 1987. He was the coordinator of a teacher education program in the Department of Special Education (designed to prepare teachers to serve students with mild disabilities) and later served as chair of his department. He was introduced to service-learning when he advised a student who was completing a service-learning project. As a result, he began teaching service-learning courses and served as a faculty fellow and member of the advisory board for the Lowell Bennion Community Service Center. In 2001 Welch became the director of the center, which is an internationally recognized leader in service-learning, coordinating over 150 service-learning courses. He also hosted the third annual conference on service-learning research in 2003 and currently serves on the board of the International Association of Research on Service-Learning and Community Engagement (IARSLCE). Welch played an instrumental role in conceptualizing the Campus Compact Professional Development Institute and hosted the first institute at the University of Utah in 2004. Welch has taught numerous service-learning courses and has several publications, presentations, and workshops on service-learning, civic engagement, and spiritual development in education. He has over 100 refereed journal publications and conference presentations, has published a textbook, and has produced a number of videos and national teleconferences. He is the coeditor of a new refereed online journal, *Engaging Pedagogy in Catholic Higher Education*. He earned his doctorate in special education from Southern Illinois University in 1987 and completed his undergraduate work in education and sociology at Concordia College in Moorhead, Minnesota.

Welch now lives in the Portland, Oregon, area with his wife and works as an independent scholar and consultant

collaborations, it demystifies the often confusing terminology of education; explains how to locate the right individuals on campus; and addresses issues of mission, expectations for roles, tasks, training, supervision, and evaluation that can be fraught with miscommunication and misunderstanding.

Most importantly it provides a model for achieving full reciprocity in what can be an unbalanced relationship between community and campus partners so that all stakeholders can derive the maximum benefit from their collaboration.

Learning through Serving
A Student Guidebook for Service-Learning and Civic Engagement across Academic Disciplines and Cultural Communities
Second Edition
Christine M. Cress , Peter J. Collier, and Vicki L. Reitenauer

Review of the first edition: "[This] is a self-directed guide for college students engaged in service-learning. The purpose of the book is to walk the reader through elements of learning and serving by focusing on how students can 'best provide meaningful service to a community agency or organization while simultaneously gaining new skills, knowledge, and understanding as an integrated aspect of the [student's] academic program.' [The authors] bring their expertise to the pages of this helpful and practical guide for college students engaged in service-learning. Intended as a textbook, this work reads like a conversation between the authors and the college student learner. The publication is student-friendly, comprehensive, easy to follow, and full of helpful activities."—*Journal of College Student Development*

22883 Quicksilver Drive
Sterling, VA 20166-2102

Subscribe to our e-mail alerts: www.Styluspub.com

Also available from Stylus

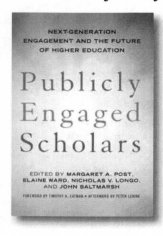

Publicly Engaged Scholars
Next-Generation Engagement and the Future of Higher Education
Edited by Margaret A. Post, Elaine Ward, Nicholas V. Longo, and John Saltmarsh
Foreword by Timothy K. Eatman
Afterword by Peter Levine

"*Publicly Engaged Scholars* is a much-needed look at the future of higher education as more of the public, increasingly diverse in every way, pushes for more of the academy to engage in high-impact scholarship, collaborate broadly, and be a locus of democratic practice and educator of democratic citizens. Its authenticity comes from the powerful voices of our students, who have emerged as the new generation of publicly engaged scholars looking to make a difference in the world. This is an exciting time, and this volume pulls us enthusiastically into that future."—**Nancy Cantor, Chancellor**, *Rutgers University–Newark*

The concern that the democratic purposes of higher education—and its foundation as a public good—is being undermined, together with the realizations that existing structures are unsuited to addressing today's complex societal problems and that our institutions are failing an increasingly diverse population, is giving rise to questioning the current model of the university.

This book presents the voices of a new generation of scholars, educators, and practitioners who are committed to civic renewal and the public purposes of higher education. They question existing policies, structures, and practices and put forward new forms of engagement that can help shape and transform higher education to align it with societal needs.

Community Partner Guide to Campus Collaborations
Enhance Your Community by Becoming a Co-Educator With Colleges and Universities
Christine M. Cress, Stephanie T. Stokamer, and Joyce P. Kaufman

"Interacting with colleges can be confusing and frustrating. We learned the hard way through trial and error over the years. This guide has great strategies for developing effective collaborations from the outset so that resources are leveraged for education and improvement."—**Sheila**, *Boys and Girls Club*

This guide offers insights and strategies to leverage student learning and community empowerment for the benefit of both community partners and higher education institutions. Recognizing both the possibilities and the pitfalls of community-campus

(Continues on previous page)